A Wealth Manager's Guide to Structured Products

A Wealth Manager's Guide to Structured Products

Introduced by Robert Benson

Published by Risk Books, a Division of Incisive Financial Publishing Ltd

Haymarket House
28–29 Haymarket
London SW1Y 4RX
Tel: +44 (0)20 7484 9700
Fax: +44 (0)20 7484 9800
E-mail: books@riskwaters.com
Sites: www.riskbooks.com
       www.riskwaters.com

Every effort has been made to secure the permission of individual copyright
holders for inclusion.

© Incisive Media Investments Limited 2004

ISBN 978 1 904 339 32 8

British Library Cataloguing in Publication Data
A catalogue record for this book is available from the British Library

Managing Editor: Sarah Jenkins
Copy Editor: Andrew John
Editorial Assistant: Stephen Fairman

Typeset by Mizpah Publishing Services, Chennai, India

Printed and bound in Spain by Espacegrafic, Pamplona, Navarra

Contents

List of Contributors

Robert Addison has 14 years of experience in the investment banking sector, 11 of which have involved the use of equity and other derivatives to structure and create innovative investment and hedging products for institutional and retail investors. This experience was gained at UBS Investment Bank and NatWest Markets. Robert is currently a partner in Bespoke Financial Consulting, which designs and delivers structured products to the retail and institutional market using a tax efficient regulated UK mutual fund wrapper. He also runs an educational and advisory consultancy on the use of derivatives for structured products and is an independent director of Assured. Robert holds a BSc in economics.

Giovanni A. Adragna completed a PhD in solid state physics within the department of physics at the University of Rome "Tor Vergata". After this he began work at TradingLab Banca SpA as a quantitative analyst. His research interests are equity and interest rates derivatives models in a stochastic volatility environment, with a particular focus on hedging strategies.

Urs Alder is a vice president at Glenwood Capital Investments, a key fund of funds manager of the Man Group, based in Chicago and he represents the Glenwood Investment Committee in Europe and the Middle East. Urs joined RMF Investment Management in 2001 as a financial structurer, developing and implementing structured fund of funds products, moving to Glenwood after Man Group acquired RMF in 2002. Prior to that Urs spent three years on the strategy team of the UBS Group, with focus on strategic projects related to UBS' investment banking division, UBS Warburg. Urs received his masters degree in business administration from the University of Zurich, specialising in finance and banking.

Catherine Barker is a member of Investment Solutions, part of the Global Index and Markets Group in BGI Europe, which designs optimal investment and transactional solutions for BGI's strategic clients. Before joining Investment Solutions, Catherine was product manager for the European cash management team in London and was responsible for the development of new products and product strategy. Prior to joining Barclays Global Investors in 1999, Catherine was part of the fixed income sales team at Morgan Stanley Asia in Singapore. Catherine has a BSc in economics from Bristol University.

Vladimiro Ceci is senior vice president at TradingLab Banca SpA (Unicredito Group), where he has been head of financial modelling (financial engineering, risk analytics and model implementation) since May 2002. His previous working experience was mainly in the risk management area, and includes positions as head of development and research at IntesaBci and head of the econometric unit at Banca Intesa. He holds a PhD in econometrics and a degree in monetary economics, both from Bocconi University.

Andrea C. Cosentini is head of financial engineering and a vice president at TradingLab Banca SpA, the retail investment bank of Unicredito Group. He joined TradingLab in 2002, having previously worked as a quantitative analyst in Caboto, Banca Intesa. He holds a BS in physics and he has worked for three years as physicist researcher in Rome's University La Sapienza. Andrea's current responsibilities include the development of models for both equity and fixed income desks.

Hans Duquet is head of Fixed Income at KBC Asset Management. In 1998, he joined the company as a fixed income manager. In 2001 he became department head. His responsibilities are for the coordination, monitoring and structuring of the investment process on the fixed income side. Hans studied at the Katholieke Universiteit Leuven (KUL) where he gained a Master in law and Master in economics 1986). He joined KBC Bank in 1988, where he first worked in the credit department and the accounting department. In 1994 he moved to the research department (macro economics), from where he went to KBC AM.

Eleanor de Freitas joined BGI Europe's Index Strategy team in March 2003. Before returning to the UK she was a portfolio manager in the Developed International Equity Management Group in BGI's San Francisco office. Prior to joining BGI in June 2001, she spent over five years as a quantitative analyst at ING Barings where she played an instrumental role in developing their global quantitative equity research product. Eleanor graduated from St. Anne's College, Oxford University with a BA Hons in mathematics and has subsequently been awarded an MA Oxon.

Gian Carlo Frugoli was born in 1969 in Sondrio, Italy. He obtained a BA (1996) from Politecnico di Milano and a PhD (2000) from the University of

Parma in engineering. He joined UBM in April 2000, where he is currently in charge of risk technologies and product development. He has published papers in the field of industrial engineering and robotics.

Peter Gardner is the head of product development at SG Hambros Bank & Trust Limited where his primary responsibilities are the development and distribution of structured products and alternative investments. Prior to joining SG Hambros, Peter worked for Schroders Salomon Smith Barney in London where he was part of the team establishing a European private client business. He studied at the University of Edinburgh and Université Montesquieu Bordeaux IV and has an honours degree in business studies and the IMC.

Andreas Homberger works for UBS Wealth Management and Business Banking in the department of Investment Solutions. His responsibilities include the product management for discretionary portfolio solutions and the development of such solutions and suitable instruments. In addition, he is a regular participant in various investment committee meetings of UBS Wealth Management and Business Banking. Andreas studied economics at the Universities of Basel and St. Gall. He received a doctorate on a dissertation entitled "Equilibrium Risk Premia for Equities, Bonds and Currencies" from the University of St. Gall.

David Lake is head of UK listed products within SG Equity Derivatives. He set up and has run the UK Covered Warrants desk for SG since the market launched in 2002. Prior to this he spent five years as a derivative analyst for a US$3 bn global macro hedge fund.

Allan Lane has worked as a quantitative analyst in the financial markets since 1992, for institutions such as Banque Paribas and JP Morgan. Until quite recently, Allan was head of quantitative research at The Royal Bank of Scotland. Allan graduated from the University of Washington in 1987, with a PhD in physics.

Michael Lewis joined Deutsche Bank in 1990 and is now the global head of commodities research. Michael's group analyses the macro fundamental forces driving commodity markets with the ultimate aim of delivering directional, curve and volatility trading strategies with particular focus on the global energy, industrial metals, precious metals and European power, freight and coal markets. Before joining commodities research last year, Michael was the deputy head of foreign exchange research where he had worked for the previous seven years. Michael holds a BSc in economics from the University of Bristol and an MSc in economics from the London School of Economics.

Luca Lotti is currently a senior quantitative analyst at the financial modelling department of TradingLab Banca SpA, part of the UniCredito Italiano Group. He is currently involved in market risk measurement and in the design of dynamic allocation products based on constant proportion portfolio insurance. Before joining TradingLab Banca in 2002, he worked as a quantitative analyst at the risk management and research department at Banca Intesa, focusing on applications of GARCH models and extreme value theory to market risk measurement. Luca has a degree in economic and social sciences from Bocconi University of Milan.

Kristien Meykens joined KBC Asset Management, Belgium, in 2001. She is a senior product development manager, responsible for generating creative product ideas and designing and developing structured products. Prior to her position at KBC Asset Management, she worked as a research fellow at the Institute for Materials Research. Kristien received her PhD in experimental physics in 2000 from the Limburgs Universitair Centrum in Belgium and her masters degree in physics from Katholieke Universiteit Leuven in Belgium in 1994.

Anthony Morris has been based in London since November 1997 and is part of the global credit derivatives team at UBS, where he focuses on new product development. Before moving to London, he worked for Swiss Bank Corporation's sovereign risk analysis group in Basel, where he developed models to infer expected default probabilities, recovery rates and default correlations from the prices of traded credit exposures. He also contributed to the formation of sovereign risk policy. Anthony majored in economics and English literature at Dartmouth College, graduating *Phi Beta Kappa*. Later, he earned a doctorate in finance at New York University's Stern School of Business. His dissertation applied contingent claim models to emerging market sovereign credit risk, shedding light on empirical puzzles in the finance and international macroeconomics literature.

Stanley Myint is currently a director of rates structuring at The Royal Bank of Scotland, where he has been since 2002. Prior to this he was a consultant at McKinsey after a five-year spell as an associate-executive director at the Canadian Imperial Bank of Commerce. Stanley graduated in 1994 from Boston University with a PhD in physics.

Andrew Popper is the chief investment officer of SG Hambros Group. He has overall responsibility for investment policy and originating and implementing alternative investments and structured products for clients. In 1994, Andrew joined ED&F Man as executive vice president and director with responsibilities for marketing and product development in their subsidiary MINT Investment Management Co. In 1996 he then moved to the private bank of what was then Bankers Trust (which subsequently merged with Deutsche Bank) becoming regional product head for Deutsche Bank Private Banking in London prior to working for SG Hambros. Andrew holds a degree in economics from the Institute of Economic Studies in Bucharest and did PhD work in economics at the New York University.

Ferdinando Samaria has a BA (1991), MA (1994) and PhD (1994) in engineering from Trinity College, Cambridge University. After spending two years researching in the field of image processing with Olivetti Research Laboratories in Cambridge, he joined Credit Suisse Financial Products, London, in 1996 where he worked on the development of mathematical models for derivatives. In August 1998 he moved to UniCredito Italiano as a founding member of UBM, the investment-banking subsidiary of the UniCredito Group, where he is a managing director in the area of risk management and chief financial officer. He has published numerous scientific works in the fields of artificial intelligence, image processing and risk management.

Lode Roose is senior product development manager at KBC Asset Management, Belgium. His responsibilities include generating creative product ideas and designing and developing structured products. Lode started his career at KBC Bank in 1994 as a trader of eurobonds and interest rate swaps. Later, he headed KBC Bank's corporate risk management department and after that, the Financial Institution risk management department. Lode received an MBA in 1994 at the Katholieke Universiteit Leuven (KUL), Belgium. In 1992 he obtained a masters degree in civil engineering at the KUL and in 1993 was awarded an additional university degree in technical economics.

Introduction

Robert Benson

The rapid growth in the financial services world has been one of the major by-products of the globalisation of the world economy. Both at wholesale and retail levels, financial markets have increased in their size and complexity with billions of dollars trading daily in the major financial centres and a plethora of financial products available to corporate, institutional and retail clients.

Within these expanding markets, increasing competition has led to a spiral of innovation as providers of financial services have produced ever more sophisticated products to meet their clients' needs.

This in turn has been facilitated by the rapid deployment of information technology, increasing computing power and, perhaps most importantly, the brain drain of highly numerate and quantitative skills from the academic to the financial sector.

Probably the most impressive example of this phenomenon can be seen in the explosive growth over the last twenty years in the financial derivatives markets. The numbers speak for themselves with close to US$200 trillion dollars in notional over-the-counter (OTC) derivatives contracts outstanding at the end of 2003, according to the Bank for International Settlements.

While derivatives have been criticised by some as "weapons of financial mass destruction", there is no doubt that their role in the global financial system has become increasingly significant. Indeed, the benefits that they have brought to a wide range of corporate and individual clients cannot be understated, as they have become the essential building blocks for a host of commonly used financial products, from fixed-rate mortgages to guaranteed-equity bonds.

This book is focused on perhaps the leading edge of the derivatives market, so-called *structured products*. It covers a wide range of underlying markets with chapters covering a variety of issues from the complexity of the underlying derivatives to the way in which products are packaged or "wrapped" for the end user.

The breadth of the structured products market is so wide that it would be impossible to cover all aspects of them in a single book. In addition, the pace of product development means that new structures are being developed all the time.

What this book does provide is a sample of some of the key products from the range that are currently available and highlights some of the most important issues that practitioners and end users need to be aware of. In this sense it will be a useful reference both for those coming into the market and for product developers and clients who are already involved.

To begin with it is perhaps important to provide some form of definition for what we mean by a structured product.

WHAT ARE STRUCTURED PRODUCTS?

Although the term is widely used in the financial community, there is no single established definition for a structured product. In fact the term often means different things to different people.
One suggested definition is:

> A financial product that provides a pre-defined return at one or more future dates linked to one or more underlying financial prices, rates or indexes. A key feature of such products is that they can be broken down into a number of separate financial instruments, one of which is typically a derivative product.

The most important feature of these products, therefore, is that they are made up of other financial products that are "bolted together" to form the unique structured product created for the individual end user.

In this sense, creating a structured product is like playing with a Lego set, using standard shapes to create an infinite number of new products from a set of basic building blocks. In fact, however, structured products are even more flexible that the Lego analogy implies, since new building blocks, in terms of new forms of derivatives, can be created at the same time so that the range of possibilities is endless.

It is this flexibility and the opportunity for innovation that have attracted both banks and end users to the market. On the one hand, the product developers see opportunities to gain competitive advantage through new and innovative structures; on the other hand, consumers gain from the ability to have a product tailored to fit their individual needs more precisely.

This brings us on to the question of who uses structured products and why.

WHO USES STRUCTURED PRODUCTS?

Structured products are used by both investors (individual and institutional) and corporations to provide exposure to specific underlying financial markets in ways that are not available with conventional financial products.

It is this bespoke nature that is one of the key characteristics of these products, with, in many cases, a new product being created for just a single client. Indeed, the ability to customise the product return to fit an individual investor's need is one of the main drivers behind the growth of the market.

That is not to say that structured products are available only to large corporate or institutional investors. For many years high-net-worth investors have been active users of structured products, typically high-yield notes or more recently capital-protected products, with all of the major private banks now having active product development capabilities.

In the retail markets, too, the use of structured products has been growing significantly. The rise of structured retail products over the last 10 to 15 years has been dramatic with equity-linked capital-protected products for example being available in nearly every major economy, in many cases via retail channels such as the local post office.

HOW BIG IS THE MARKET?

Due to the nature of OTC, as well as private placement business, the size of the institutional structured products market is virtually impossible to estimate. It is clear, however, that structured Euro Medium Term Notes (EMTN) business alone has risen significantly over the last few years. *Capital Markets Daily* conservatively estimates that issuance of international structured Medium Term Notes (MTN) in 2003 was US$195 billion, with between 50 and 100 new issues every day.

Large markets exist for structured retail products, too. The European market was estimated by Morgan Stanley and Boston Consulting Group at over US$400 billion in 2002 with a projected growth rate of 8% per annum.

Some of the individual markets in Europe are significant, with BNP Paribas stating that the largest markets, such as Italy and France, each exceeded €20 billion in annual sales in 2003.[1]

Large markets have also developed in recent years in Asia. In HK there were US$7 billion in capital-guaranteed funds at the end of 2003 (from virtually none in 2000) according to the Investment Funds Association, although other estimates put the actual market size at more than double this figure. Deutsche Bank, for example, estimates that the Singapore market for capital-protected funds is more than US$5 billion and the Korean market for structured products in 2003/04 is estimated at US$25 billion in new issuance.

In the US the structured products market is also growing but from a much lower base, as investors have tended to manage their investment more actively rather than buy packaged products. Nevertheless, the combined issuance of Equity Linked Notes on the American Stock Exchange and Nasdaq grew from US$2.7 billion in 2002 to US$5.6 billion in 2003.

MARKET DYNAMICS

The structured products market is driven by innovation. New product ideas are continually being developed both by investment banks and their retail and institutional clients with ever more sophisticated and complex payoffs.

In fact the development of new products takes place in two key dimensions simultaneously. First, innovation in the product payoff involves the creation of new payoff formulas whereby the product return is calculated by reference to a specific outcome in the evolution of the underlying price, rate or index.

At this level, product development typically involves the creation of new forms of derivatives with ever more complex payoffs. Typical examples involve the use of such features as:

❑ averaging;
❑ barriers;
❑ binary or digital payoff;
❑ cliquet or reset conditions; and
❑ callable and puttable features.

The list is endless with each new innovation often coming with a new name so that the level of jargon in the structured products market is almost impossible to keep up with.

In the other dimension, product innovation is present in the nature of the underlying or reference price, rate or index that determines the product payoff. Today products can be linked – among others – to:

❑ individual shares or share baskets;
❑ equity indexes;
❑ interest rates;
❑ exchange rates;
❑ commodity prices;
❑ inflation;
❑ credit events; and
❑ mutual funds and even hedge funds.

In fact, many structured products are hybrid products in that they provide exposure to more than one of these underlyings at the same time. So, for example, a structure may provide a link to a basket of indexes made up of an equity index, a bond index and a commodity index.

The combination of continuing developments in both product payoff and the range of available underlying links leads to an almost infinite set of possibilities to satisfy almost any investor's requirement. The competitive nature of the market, and the resources now being applied in this area by the major investment banks, will undoubtedly drive the pace of innovation even further.

Finally it might be argued that a third dimension to the product development process is in how the product is packaged or "wrapped" for the end investor. That is, in what form does the product need to be provided so that it meets the user's individual requirements, such as regulatory or tax efficiency, or liquidity.

Once again, developments in this area have provided end users with a wide variety of wrappers to choose from. Typical examples include:

❑ OTC swaps or options;
❑ warrants;
❑ MTNs;
❑ special-purpose vehicles;
❑ funds;
❑ deposits; and
❑ life assurance bonds.

The choice of wrapper will be driven by the needs of the individual investor but will often be a key element in determining the way in which the product is actually delivered.

The chapters that follow deal with all of these dimensions of structured products with many examples of actual structured products that have been sold in the market. They are organised by underlying, with the first five chapters dealing primarily with equity-linked products, the next two looking at FX-linked products, the following two interest rate and inflation products and the final three chapters looking at some of the more recently developed markets in commodity, credit-linked and hedge-fund-linked structured products.

EQUITY LINKED PRODUCTS

The first chapter from Barclays Global Investors provides an overview of exchange-traded funds and looks at how they compare to futures in tracking indexes. ETFs have been used as the underlying in structured products, in particular constant proportion portfolio insurance (CPPI) based products, for example, in the UK retail market.

Following on from this, SG provides a useful introduction to covered warrants and how they are priced and used. Warrants are essentially securitised options and, as such, in their basic form, a relatively straightforward form of structured product. More complex warrants and certificates, however, have also been issued and the chapter goes on to examine some of these examples, too.

The next chapter, from TradingLab, leads on from this to a more technical subject, which is the pricing and hedging of a common form of option used in structured equity products, the Cliquet.

Although popular with investors, this type of option has some very interesting features from a pricing perspective, which can easily lead to mispricing if not properly understood. The chapter sets out very clearly the reasons why, for example, a simple Black–Scholes option-pricing model is inadequate to price (and hedge) this type of instrument.

One of the particularly useful features of the article is the way quantitative examples are combined with intuitive explanations to point out the weaknesses of the Black–Scholes model.

The Cliquet product is typically used when offering a capital-protected equity-linked investment. In the following chapter, UBM look at another way of providing capital protection using a technique called Portfolio Insurance. This is a technique that has been used for many years but recently has been adapted in a number of new ways that have resulted in a significant growth in the number of products that have utilised these techniques.

The most common new development has been so-called Constant Proportion Portfolio Insurance or CPPI. However, in this chapter UBM go on to explain two more recent developments in this area namely Variable Proportion Portfolio Insurance (VPPI) and Multi-Level Portfolio Insurance (MLPI). These techniques allow a certain degree of flexibility to be factored into the rules-based trading strategy that is typically used with a CPPI product and may offer some advantages to certain end investors.

The final chapter in this section is a review of product wrappers, with a focus on the UK retail market. Bespoke Financial Consultants take us on a tour of the wide variety of different wrappers that are used in this market and examine some of the key tax and regulatory issues that affect the choice of the most appropriate one.

FX-RATE-LINKED PRODUCTS

The foreign exchange, or FX, market is the largest single financial market, and movements in exchange rates will impact on any investment or exposure outside one's home country.

The two chapters on FX-linked products look at the ways in which FX hedging is relevant to individual private clients and some of the typical structured notes that are offered in this market.

The first chapter, by UBS, deals with FX hedging for private clients and examines how currency certificates can be used to take or manage FX exposure.

The following chapter, from SG Private Bank, focuses more on the different forms of FX-linked structured products, providing a comprehensive analysis of the most common forms of structured products in this market.

INTEREST-RATE- AND INFLATION-LINKED PRODUCTS

Interest-rate-linked structured products are a large and growing part of the structured products market. In their chapter KBC, who are one of the largest and most active providers of structured products to retail investors in Europe, provide a background to interest rate derivatives and how they are used to create structured products.

This chapter provides a very thorough analysis of these products from both a pricing and hedging perspective and goes on to examine in detail one of the most popular retail interest-rate-linked products, the KBC Maxisafe product, which sold more than €2 billion.

The next chapter examines the growing market in inflation-linked derivatives. The authors, from RBS, look at the issuers of inflation-linked debt and the range of derivative products that have been created. Although inflation has been low for many years there has been a growing interest in inflation-linked products recently as global economic uncertainty has risen.

The final three chapters look at some of the newer underlyings that have appeared in the structured products market in the last few years.

COMMODITY-LINKED PRODUCTS

In this chapter, Deutsche Bank present research on why commodities, especially energy, should be part of a diversified portfolio. The author sets out clearly how commodity indexes work and introduces the concepts of backwardation, contango, convenience yield and so forth in a very easy-to-understand way.

An example of a commodity-linked structured note is also provided.

CREDIT-LINKED PRODUCTS

Credit derivatives have been the most rapidly growing sector of the derivatives market in the last five years.

In this chapter UBS provide a fairly non-technical look at credit derivatives from the perspective of private client portfolios. The reason why credit derivatives can provide added value to these investors is presented, along with an example of the type of credit-linked note that is typically structured.

HEDGE-FUND-LINKED PRODUCTS

Probably the most widely discussed and fastest-growing investment market at the moment is the hedge fund market.

In this final chapter, Man Glenwood provide an overview of hedge funds and in particular funds of funds, with some examples of typical hedge-fund-linked structured products. Capital-protected hedge fund products have been particularly popular in Asia recently and it will be interesting to see how this market develops in Europe over the next few years.

---

1 The website http://www.StructuredRetailProducts.com lists more than 2,000 individual products that have been launched in the UK and France alone since 1997.

Exchange Traded Funds – Tactical Asset Allocation Tools

Eleanor De Freitas, Catherine Barker

Barclays Global Investors

Exchange traded funds (ETFs), combine the advantages of both index funds and stocks. They are liquid, easy to use and can be traded in any quantity, just like stocks. At the same time an ETF provides the diversification, market tracking and low expense of an index fund. These characteristics combine to create an investment tool that provides investors with the broad exposure they require, at the level they want, at the moment they need it. As such they have been promoted and branded as an innovative investment opportunity – a claim greatly supported by the accelerated growth in ETFs, as will be discussed later, which clearly illustrates the appetite for such a product.

The major participants in the ETF market have historically been institutional investors. Some common institutional applications of ETFs include:

- cashflow equitisation;
- transition management;
- core holdings – for smaller segregated accounts;
- hedging key exposures; and
- asset allocation – global and tactical.

TACTICAL ASSET ALLOCATION

Institutional investors will make a strategic asset allocation, broadly between bonds and equities, based on long-term views of market opportunities and risks – this is sometimes called the "policy

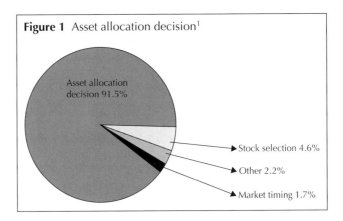

Figure 1 Asset allocation decision[1]

Asset allocation decision 91.5%

Stock selection 4.6%

Other 2.2%

Market timing 1.7%

mix". The decision on how a fund's investments are allocated between stocks, bonds and cash has considerable impact on the performance and risk profile of the portfolio. In fact, the asset allocation decision has been shown to explain over 90% of the return variability of a multi-asset fund, as demonstrated in Figure 1.

Tactical asset allocation (TAA) is a quantitatively based investment strategy that maximises the "risk-adjusted return" by identifying and exploiting relative mispricings across asset classes. Although many strategies focus on finding the right mix between domestic stocks, bonds and cash, they can also extend to other asset classes such as real estate and international equities.

TAA complements the strategic asset allocation chosen by constantly reallocating around the portfolio's policy mix. The process assesses the expected return and risk of each asset class and rebalances the portfolio to optimally trade off total portfolio risk and total return. The source of the added return through TAA is attained exclusively through active shifts among the asset classes. The process is dynamic and will respond to changes in expectations and opportunities, adjusting the allocations within a portfolio to take advantage where these deviate from the expectations and opportunities of the strategic mix chosen.

A TAA strategy often implements the desired tilt towards each of the broad asset classes by gaining exposure to highly diversified index portfolios representing the asset class. This is typically achieved by direct investment in the underlying assets, through futures contracts or mutual funds and, over recent years, using ETFs.

THE BENEFITS OF INDEXING

It is widely acknowledged that indexation is an extremely efficient and cost-effective method of gaining diversified exposure to "the market". An index fund offers consistency and reliability in long-term returns, removing surprise factor and "manager risk" from an investment strategy.

> "… the return on the average actively managed dollar will equal the return on the average passively managed dollar …"
>
> – William Sharpe[2]

In terms of costs, index tracking is certainly the more desirable investment option. An index fund will generally have lower turnover than an actively managed portfolio and, therefore, spends less on trading. An active portfolio manager must also pay for research and other analysis tools. In addition to having lower investment costs, index funds generally come with lower management fees than their more active counterparts. For example, while the average actively managed US equity fund has management fees in excess of 1%, index funds have a median fee of just 0.44%.[3]

The broad exposure gained from an investment in an index fund can be achieved through direct investment in the underlying assets or by holding a single entity that provides equivalent exposure. Since direct investment requires the ability to trade, settle and monitor numerous assets and involves daily maintenance, a "one-stop" solution presents a more desirable alternative. Investment tools such as mutual funds, futures contracts and ETFs enable investors to gain exposure to multiple assets with a single investment. In particular, ETFs allow investors to implement asset allocation decisions at every level from the bond/equity mix to sector rotation.

WHERE THERE'S AN INDEX …

One of the key strengths of the ETF as an investment tool is the wide range of products available and the sheer breadth of equity and fixed-income benchmarks they track. Since the mid-nineties, the ETF market has witnessed dramatic growth in every respect. In 1996 there were just 21 listed ETFs but, by the end of September 2003, there were more than 260 different ETFs trading on 28 exchanges around the world. The relatively low level of product overlap between fund advisers means that the variety of ETFs available is quite staggering.

In contrast, futures present limited options in terms of asset or specific index exposure and some investors may be restricted from utilising certain derivative products. For a particular asset class, the tracking risk of using an index other than the one to which you are benchmarked can be high. With some applications such as equitising accruals or small cashflows, the impact of this tracking error may be tolerable. However, for other applications highlighted earlier, the effect of using a product that deviates noticeably from the desired benchmark can be significant.

One such function is asset allocation. The decision to tilt towards a particular asset class or country is, most likely, based upon the risk-and-return profile of the fund's benchmark. If this choice has to be implemented through an instrument that does not track that benchmark, then the fund takes on additional security-specific risk – a risk not accounted for in the model that can be exceptionally high and is potentially uncontrollable. The ETFs available cover a far broader range of indices than futures, giving investors more opportunity to action allocation tilts without this risk. In addition, they allow investors to easily gain exposure to a far deeper variety of asset class – fixed-income, sectors and additional countries and regions.

Table 1 European listed ETFs

Asset	Available?
Equity exposure	
European regional	✓
European countries	✓
European sectors	✓
US sector	✓
Japanese equity	✓
Global	✓
Fixed income	
European corporate	✓
German treasury	✓
UK corporate	✓
US corporate	✓

Source: Barclays Global Investors Limited

PANEL 1 EFFICIENT IMPLEMENTATION FOR FIXED-INCOME EXPOSURE

Fixed-income ETFs offer institutional investors a way to implement clean, efficient asset allocation strategies that was previously unavailable. Historically, gaining diversified exposure to fixed-income markets required the use of mutual funds. The lack of transparency of these instruments meant that an allocation could be skewed away from the intended tilt, due to the fund's manager taking a different view to that of the end investor.

A large investor might be in a position to purchase individual issues, as long as they had the necessary credit and trading resource. However, for many investors the transaction costs could be prohibitive, especially when trading smaller amounts.

Fixed-income ETFs solve these problems in one trade. Real-time intraday trading allows immediate implementation of a tilt or allocation at spreads that are considerably tighter than those on mutual funds. The size of a trade is not an issue and transaction and administrative costs are limited to one trade. Diversification is immediate and completely transparent – the investor knows exactly what exposure they achieve and the ongoing management of components to match the index is outsourced to the manager of the ETF.

WHICH INSTRUMENT? ETFs VERSUS FUTURES

In the numerous current and potential applications of ETFs, they most frequently come up against the index future as an alternative investment tool. The decision to use one instrument over the other typically depends upon:

- ❏ investment time horizon;
- ❏ relative richness/cheapness of instrument;
- ❏ desired benchmark;
- ❏ required position size; and
- ❏ ability to deliver cash for settlement;

The first two attributes in combination drive the actual costs of holding or transacting in each product to achieve a particular investment objective. For asset allocation purposes it is this assessment of cost, the desired benchmark and, perhaps to a lesser extent, the required position size that are of great importance. In fact, the need to gain exposure to a certain asset class, country or sector through a particular benchmark can far outweigh the additional

Table 2 Key attributes of futures and ETFs

Future	ETF
❑ Low explicit costs ❑ Require quarterly rolls with associated costs ❑ Need special documentation and accounts ❑ Daily margin requirements ❑ Track a limited number of benchmarks ❑ Many with limited liquidity ❑ Often traded in larger size	❑ High explicit costs ❑ No rolls or special documentation ❑ No margin requirements or accounts ❑ A single security – not a derivative ❑ Track a wide variety of benchmarks ❑ Pool liquidity from underlying securities ❑ Can be traded in relatively small size

Source: Barclays Global Investors Limited

costs associated with an instrument. Table 2 summarises some of the key attributes of ETFs and futures that might influence a decision to use each device.

FUTURES VERSUS ETFs: THE COSTS

An evaluation of futures and ETFs would not be complete without considering the key issues and relative expense involved in holding and trading the two devices. The costs can be broken down into explicit costs that have a definite direction and implicit costs that may impact performance positively or negatively. These implicit costs can be driven by numerous factors and have undesirable performance consequences that far outweigh any explicit transaction or holding costs (See Figure 2).

For both methods of investment, the explicit costs include those incurred upon entry and exit of each position such as commissions, bid–ask spreads and taxes. A future will also incur such costs during the quarterly contract rolls. ETFs have an additional explicit cost in the form of the management fee, which varies between products and regions. There are implicit costs associated with a futures investment as they are subject to contract and calendar roll mispricing and may trade rich or cheap relative to fair value. An ETF carries no such costs, but may experience a degree of mistracking due to investment constraints.

In the US, there are much lower overall costs connected with holding ETFs versus the equivalent future. This is partly a consequence of

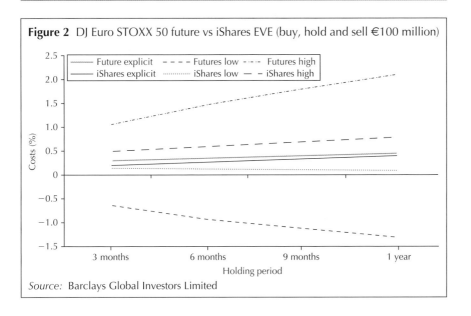

Figure 2 DJ Euro STOXX 50 future vs iShares EVE (buy, hold and sell €100 million)

Source: Barclays Global Investors Limited

PANEL 2 IMPROVED ACCESS TO INTERNATIONAL EXPOSURE

Some markets impose limits on the access available to foreign investors. For example, in Taiwan, investors must comply with qualifying foreign institutional investor rules, which can be onerous to achieve and maintain. Even those that qualify to invest must be resourced to research and trade the stocks in that specific market. An ETF, such as the MSCI Taiwan iShare, offers a simple solution to institutional investors – listed on the American Stock Exchange, one trade in the ETF provides indexed exposure to the Taiwanese market without administrative complications or requiring special licences.

---

the small management fees of US equity ETFs, but also a result of the comparatively higher cost of holding/trading US futures. The annual roll costs of an S&P 500 contract have risen remarkably in recent years, with the contracts currently rolling at a consistent premium to fair value. The picture is slightly different in Europe, where some (but not all) index futures have witnessed a steady decrease in the annual cost of rolls. This, coupled with the larger management fees due on European-listed ETFs, often makes futures the cheaper option.

It is, however, worth pointing out that some of the conclusions surrounding costs referred to above do not hold in the short term. Some studies would suggest that, even in Europe, ETFs have a more desirable cost structure in the short term. This is mainly a result of the proportionally lower impact of management fees, which are drawn on a daily basis.

THE "RIGHT" INDEX

The heightened interest in index investing over the past 10 years has seen an explosion of benchmark choice across many asset classes. For example, an investor desiring pan-European equity exposure is presented with more than 15 index options. As mentioned earlier, when implementing an asset allocation strategy, using the "right" index for a particular asset class is important. An allocation decision is based on the risk-and-return profile of a certain benchmark and so executing that strategy by gaining exposure to a different index brings additional tracking risk – this can be high.

When it comes to asset allocation strategies the impact on performance of any benchmark mismatch can be noticeable. In the past, investors looking to gain broad asset exposure through a single entity have been limited to a few asset classes and very specific

Table 3 Historic tracking error of local equity indices[4]

Country/ region	Local index	Tracking versus MSCI Standard index series	Tracking versus FTSE All-world index series
Eurobloc	DJ EuroSTOXX 50	2.91	2.48
UK	FTSE 100	1.41	1.67
France	CAC 40	2.99	2.15
Germany	DAX	2.99	2.49
Switzerland	SMI	1.16	1.58
Netherlands	AEX	4.13	5.03
Italy	MIB 30	2.51	3.79
Spain	IBEX 35	4.23	4.70
US	S&P 500	0.73	1.01
Canada	S&P/TSE 60	2.79	1.92
Japan	Topix	2.60	3.62
Australia	S&P/ASX 200	3.43	2.42
Hong Kong	Hang Seng	5.99	9.89

Source: Barclays Global Investors Limited analysis of Datastream data

PANEL 3 NOT ALL ETFs TRACK PERFECTLY

It is important to note that not all ETFs are based on full replication and so will not necessarily track their benchmark perfectly. For the ETF to maintain many of its desirable qualities it may have to compromise on tracking error to some degree. For example, to ensure tax efficiency the funds must often adhere to certain concentration constraints dictated by legislation ie, '40 Act (US) or UCITS (UK). If a benchmark is heavily concentrated and does not satisfy such rules (often the case for many single-country indices) it becomes difficult for an ETF to track perfectly. In most cases even those ETFs that hold an optimised basket of securities offer a superior option in terms of tracking to many of the futures.

indices. The wider range of asset classes and indices for which an ETF product is available has gone a long way to reduce this issue. For example, where equity index futures are limited to local market indices, there are ETFs tracking global benchmarks such as MSCI and FTSE. It can be far easier to track fully global benchmarks such as these with a basket of ETFs than with a basket of futures.

THE COMPLETE SOLUTION?

The pace of innovation and expansion in the ETF marketplace has clearly opened up new and unique alternatives for fund management. ETFs can present opportunities for cost savings, improved tracking, efficiency and simplicity. For investors attempting to implement asset allocation tilts, this improvement in tracking is essential, particularly for investors benchmarked to a global series such as MSCI or FTSE. The breadth of indices covered by ETFs allows investors to easily and simply gain exposure to a whole host of additional "asset classes" from fixed-income to specific equity market sectors, industries, size segments and styles. Either in isolation, or in combination with futures, ETFs can be used in numerous ways to improve and enhance the investment management process.

1 *Financial Analysts Journal*, May–June 1993.
2 "The Arithmetic of Active Management", *Financial Analysts Journal*, January–February 1991.
3 May 1989 to May 1999. Source: Barclays Global Investors Limited analysis of Morningstar data.
4 Annualised standard deviation of the difference in monthly price returns (local currency) from January 2000 to September 2003.

2

Introduction to Covered Warrants and Certificates

David Lake

SG Equity Derivatives

Traded on a stock exchange in the same manner as shares, warrants are powerful and transparent investment tools for investors. They can enable investors to maximise financial returns. Put warrants also give investors the opportunity to make money even when markets are falling.

Warrants have been traded in the main European financial markets for more than a decade. The three largest European warrant markets of Germany, Switzerland and Italy witnessed more than £30 billion of warrant trading volume in 2002. Many investors now regard warrants as an essential part of their investment portfolio.

Warrant basics

Warrants are part of the derivatives family as their value depends on the value of an underlying security. This can be a share, a basket of shares, a commodity, an exchange rate or a price index. Warrants are geared instruments. This means that a warrant investor can gain economic exposure to an underlying security with less capital invested than an equivalent investment in the security itself.

Covered warrants are long-dated options. That is, a warrant is a financial instrument that gives the holder the right, but not the obligation, to buy (for calls) or sell (for puts) a defined quantity of a specified underlying security at a predetermined price (the *strike* or *exercise* price of the warrant) on a certain date in the future (the *expiry*).

Covered warrants can either be physically settled (ie, the holder takes physical delivery of shares at expiry), or, more commonly, cash-settled. In this case, if held to expiry, a cash payout made is based on the difference between the price of the underlying security at expiry and the exercise price of the warrant, ie:

For a call warrant

$$\text{Payout formula} = \frac{\left(\begin{array}{c}\text{Price of underlying security}\\ -\text{Exercise price of warrant}\end{array}\right)}{\text{Parity}}$$

For a put warrant

$$\text{Payout formula} = \frac{\left(\begin{array}{c}\text{Exercise price of warrant}\\ -\text{Price of underlying security}\end{array}\right)}{\text{Parity}}$$

The minimum payout in each case is zero – ie, the maximum loss on a warrant trade is the initial amount invested. The parity is a fixed number such as 1, 10, 100 or 1,000 depending on the type of underlying.

For a call warrant, the more the price of the underlying security exceeds the exercise price of the warrant, the larger the cash payout will be. This makes call warrants attractive to investors who believe that markets will rise.

For a put warrant, the further the price of the underlying security falls below the exercise price of the warrant, the larger the cash payout will be. This makes put warrants attractive to investors who believe that markets will fall.

It is important to note that, to benefit from a positive move in the underlying security, you do not need to hold a warrant until expiry. Throughout its life, the price of a warrant moves in line with the underlying security on which it is based on a second-by-second basis (assuming that the other pricing parameters do not change). This means that profits can be taken or losses can be cut at any time. As a geared instrument, the warrant price magnifies the movements in the underlying, meaning that far higher returns are available by trading the warrant than trading the underlying security itself.

Warrant definitions

As the terms of each warrant are unique, it is important to be aware of a warrant's characteristics before you trade. These terms are fixed at issue (although in some cases they can change, eg, as a result of a corporate action such as a share split). The definitions of these terms are given below.

The underlying security

The underlying security is the share, index, commodity or currency on which the warrant is issued. The performance of this security is one of the key elements in determining the value of the warrant. The price of the underlying security is often referred to as the Spot price.

The expiry date

The expiry date is the day on which the expiry level of the underlying security is fixed. No trading in the warrant may take place after the expiry date.

The strike or exercise price

The strike or exercise price is the price level that the underlying security needs to be above (in the case of a call warrant) or below (in the case of a put warrant) for the warrant to pay out with positive value at expiry. In response to market trends, SG continually updates its product range to provide investors with a choice of warrants across a range of strikes and expiries. The exercise price is fixed in the initial terms and conditions of the issue but can be adjusted following a corporate action by the underlying company, eg, as a result of a share split.

Parity

A warrant's parity (sometimes called conversion ratio) is a number, generally 1, 10, 100 or 1,000, applied to a warrant's payout formula as a divisor. This reduces the payout amount and consequently allows the price of the warrant to be traded in pence rather than in units of, in some instances, hundreds of pounds. Parity has no impact on the relative cheapness of a warrant, nor does it affect the gearing.

A warrant's parity may be adjusted following a corporate action by the underlying company, eg, as a result of a capital reconstruction.

Exercise

To exercise a warrant means to exercise the right to receive a cash pay-out based on the difference between the exercise price of the warrant and the current market price of the underlying security. Exercising a warrant prior to expiry is not generally in the interest of the warrant holder as they should receive a higher price by selling the warrant in the market. Warrants have automatic exercise at expiry, meaning any positive value is automatically paid to the warrant holder.

European- and American-style warrants

Warrants are classified as either European or American in style, meaning that they can be exercised at any time during the life of the warrant (American style) or only on the expiry date (European style).

HOW WARRANTS ARE PRICED

The price of a warrant before expiry is determined by the issuer using a standard options calculator. Although the calculation itself is complicated (based on a pricing model such as Black–Scholes), the principle is straightforward.

There are five key variables that affect the warrant's price: the price of the underlying security, the time to expiry, the dividend

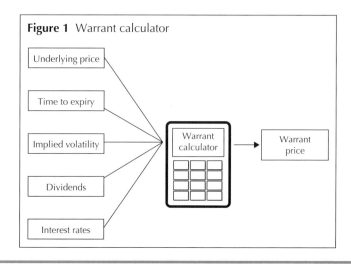

Figure 1 Warrant calculator

Table 1 How a change in underlying price impacts the warrant price

	Call price	Put price
Underlying price increases	↑	↓
Underlying price decreases	↓	↑

yield, implied volatility (a measure of the market's expectation of future levels of volatility in the underlying) and the level of interest rates.[1] It is important to note, however, that a warrant price is calculated *automatically* by an options calculator based on known variables. As such, unlike share prices, warrant prices are not affected by day-to-day changes in supply and demand.

Underlying price

As discussed earlier, the impact of movements in the price of the underlying security (the spot price) on the warrant price is straight-forward and summarised in Table 1.

Hence, call warrants are attractive to bulls (who believe markets will rise) and put warrants attractive to bears (who believe markets will fall). However, investors need to be aware of other factors that can affect a warrants price prior to expiry.

Time value

The price of a warrant is theoretically made up of two components, known as the *intrinsic value* and the *time value*. The intrinsic value of a call warrant is equal to the difference between the price of the underlying security and the exercise (strike) price of the warrant, if this is positive, or zero, if not.

So, for example, a call warrant on Barclays with a strike price of 400p and a current share price of 450p would have an intrinsic value of 50p. If the price of Barclays fell to 390p, the warrant would have zero intrinsic value.

Conversely, the intrinsic value of a put warrant is positive only if the price of the underlying is *below* the strike price of the warrant, in which case intrinsic value is equal to the difference between the strike price and the spot price. Otherwise the put warrant has no intrinsic value.

So, a put warrant on Vodafone with a strike price of 150p and a current share price of 130p would have an intrinsic value of 20p. If Vodafone increased to 160p, the warrant would have zero intrinsic value.

Time decay

A warrant that has no intrinsic value will still be worth something in the market prior to expiry. This component is called the time value of the warrant. This represents the price paid for the possibility that the warrant will finish either in-the-money or more deeply so.

The price of a warrant before expiry is thus composed of the sum of the two components:

$$\text{Warrant price} = \text{Intrinsic value} + \text{Time value}$$

It is now clear why it is not in the interest of a warrant holder to exercise an American-style warrant early, as all they will receive is the intrinsic value of the warrant. Only by selling the warrant in the market will they receive the full value of the warrant.

The probability that any particular warrant will expire with a higher positive value decreases with the passage of time, as the underlying security has less opportunity to move in a favourable direction.

Similarly, the time value of a warrant is eroded as expiry approaches, and is zero at expiry itself. This phenomenon is known as *time decay*. Time decay for a warrant does not reduce in a straight line. Instead it accelerates rapidly as the warrant nears expiry.

Figure 2 shows the theoretical price of a two-year out-of-the-money call warrant (ie, where the price of the underlying security is below the strike price). The price of the underlying remains unchanged throughout the life of the warrant, so the warrant expires with zero value.

The price of the warrant falls rapidly as it approaches expiry, with the largest fall occurring in the last month. To reduce the impact of this time decay, one strategy is to buy warrants that have at least six months to expiry and to sell them at least one month before expiry.

In summary, the choice of expiry is an important element in the investment decision-making process for warrants. Contrary to a classic long position in the underlying security, where returns are made

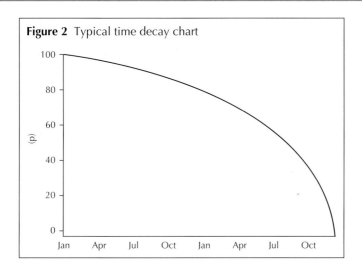

Figure 2 Typical time decay chart

when the security moves in the anticipated direction, profitable warrant investment involves being right on two counts: the *direction* of movement in the value of the underlying security and the *timing* of this move.

Volatility

Volatility is one of the most influential factors on a warrant's price, and one of the hardest to understand. Defined simply, volatility is a measure of the frequency and amplitude of price movements in the underlying security. Yahoo!, for example, tends to be a volatile stock, whereas the Dow Jones Index, say, tends to be less so.

Historical volatility gives an indication of the way an underlying security has behaved in the past. However, when pricing a warrant, one must take into consideration the volatility anticipated for the underlying security for the remaining life of the warrant. This anticipated level is used when pricing warrants and is referred to as "implied volatility".

Generally, for both calls and puts, the higher the implied volatility level, the more expensive the warrant. Bearing in mind the fact that the price of a warrant is a reflection of the probability that the warrant will expire in-the-money (or more deeply so), this makes intuitive sense.

It is possible that the market's view on the future volatility of a particular security – the implied volatility – will change during the warrant's lifetime: if a company announces a change of business focus, for example. If this happens then the price of the warrant may change *even if there is no movement in the underlying security itself.*

The movement in the warrant price may be positive or negative depending on whether the impact of the event is expected to increase or decrease future volatility in the stock price.

Dividends and interest rates

Changes in dividends and interest rates have a relatively minor impact on the value of warrants compared with the other variables detailed above. However, there are some important points worth noting for the investor.

First, a holder of a warrant (either call or put) is not entitled to any dividends paid out by the underlying security.

Second, it is important to note that the price of a warrant discounts any dividends expected to be paid out by the underlying security over the warrant's life. For instance, if a share, priced at 100p, will pay out a 3p dividend during the year, then a one-year warrant (either a put or call) will be valued as if the share were actually priced at 97p. This means that, on the day the share price falls as the share goes ex-dividend, there will be no impact on the price of the put or call warrant.

If the company announces that it will increase or decrease its dividend yield, however, there will be a change in the warrant price. In general, the higher the dividend yield expected, the lower the price of calls and the higher the price of puts.

From a financial point of view, buying a warrant is comparable to buying (call warrant) or selling (put warrant) the underlying security on margin. As a result, a rise in Bank of England interest rates will generally bring about a rise in the price of a call warrant and a drop in the price of a put warrant.

In order to make informed investment decisions, investors must have a good understanding of how each variable affects the price of the warrant on the secondary market. It should be borne in mind that warrants are liquid securities that can be easily bought and sold throughout the life of the warrant under normal market conditions. As a result, profits can be locked in prior to expiry by reselling the warrant.

Table 2 How a change in a pricing parameter
impacts the warrant price

	Call price	Put price
Underlying price decreases	↑	↓
Time to expiry decreases	↑	↑
Implied volatility decreases	↑	↑
Dividend yield decreases	↓	↑
Interest rates decreases	↑	↓

Table 2 summarises the impact of a *decrease* in a given pricing
parameter on a warrant's price.

Finally, it should be noted that, for warrants on non-domestic
underlyings (such as Nasdaq 100 or the Bombay Stock Exchange
Index), a further variable affecting the warrant price is the exchange
rate that converts the price of the warrant into local currency. This
may have a net positive or negative effect.

HEDGING A PORTFOLIO WITH INDEX PUT WARRANTS

Put warrants can act as an insurance policy as they effectively guarantee a minimum value for a portfolio or underlying security. This
is equal to the exercise price of the warrant. Should the market fall,
the value of the portfolio will decrease. However, this loss can be
either partially or fully offset by the appreciation in value of the put
warrants.

Hedging formulae

The number of warrants needed to insure an individual holding
with a put warrant at maturity is calculated as follows:

Warrants to buy = Number of units of underlying held
× warrant parity

The parity of a warrant (also called the *conversion ratio* or just
ratio) is the theoretical number of warrants that give the right to one
unit of the underlying security. Parity is generally equal to 1, 10,
100 or 1,000. Parity has no effect on gearing or the relative cheapness or expensiveness of a warrant.

Therefore, to hedge 100,000 shares in Nokia with a warrant that
has a parity of 10, for example, requires the purchase of 1,000,000
Nokia put warrants.

When hedging a portfolio with an index warrant, you first need to calculate the equivalent number of units of the underlying index held. For FTSE 100 warrants, one index point is attributed the value of one pound, therefore the equivalent number of units held is calculated by dividing the value of the portfolio by the exercise price of the warrant.

ie, equivalent units of

$$\text{FTSE 100 held} = \frac{\text{Value of portfolio}}{\text{Exercise price of the warrant}}$$

The calculation for the number of warrants to buy to insure the portfolio below a certain level in the FTSE 100 with an at-the-money warrant becomes:

$$\text{Warrants to buy} = \frac{\text{Value of portfolio} \times \text{warrant parity}}{\text{Exercise price of the warrant}}$$

Consideration must be given to how closely a given index will act as a suitable hedge for the portfolio. The poorer the correlation, the less exactly the warrant will offset losses in the portfolio at expiry. If a portfolio is dominated by large individual holdings, it may prove more effective to hedge these positions with individual put warrants.

Example
With the FTSE at 4,500, an investor holds a portfolio of UK blue-chip shares worth £1 million. On a 12-month view, they are fairly bullish, but wish to make a one-off payment to protect their portfolio against a fall below 4,500. If the FTSE rallies, they are happy to write off the investment in the put warrant as they will benefit from an increase in value in their portfolio. As such they decide to invest in the following SG warrant:

Underlying	Type	Strike	Expiry	Parity	Price
FTSE 100	Put	4,500	one year	1,000	40p

The number of warrants required to insure the portfolio is calculated as follows:

$$\text{Warrants to buy} = \frac{\text{Value of portfolio} \times \text{warrant parity}}{\text{Exercise price of the warrant}}$$

So, to hedge her £1 million portfolio, the investor needs to buy:

$$\text{Number of warrants} = \frac{\text{£1m}}{4{,}500} \times 1{,}000$$
$$= 222{,}222$$

With the FTSE 100 at 4,500, assume the price of the warrant is 40p. The investor therefore needs to pay 222,222 × 40p = £88,889 (before broker costs). This effectively means they are paying an insurance premium of 8.8% to protect the value of her portfolio below a FTSE 100 level of 4,500 for 12 months.

At expiry, if the level of the FTSE 100 had fallen back to 3,300 (−27%) and their portfolio had performed exactly in line, the values of their portfolio and warrant holdings would be as follows:

$$\text{Value of portfolio} = £733{,}333 \ (-27\%)$$

$$\text{Value of warrants} = \frac{\left(\begin{array}{c} \text{exercise price of warrant} \\ - \text{expiry price of index} \end{array} \right)}{\text{warrant parity}}$$
$$= \frac{(4{,}500 \ - \ 3{,}300)}{1{,}000} = £1.20$$

$$\text{Warrant holding} = £1.20 \times 222{,}222$$

$$= £266{,}666$$

Warrant + portfolio value = £1m

Therefore, the value of the warrant holding plus the portfolio value remains at the previous level (although the investor has incurred the cost of purchasing the warrant).

Alternatively, consider the scenario where the FTSE 100 has *increased* to 5,500 at expiry (up 22.2%). In this instance, the warrant expires with zero value. However, the value of their portfolio (assuming it increased in line with the FTSE 100) is now £1.2 million, which more than compensates for the £88,889 loss incurred on the warrant trade.

In either of these cases, if the investor wished to hedge their portfolio for another year, they would simply repeat the exercise with another FTSE 100 put warrant.

Remember also that there is no obligation to hold the warrant through to expiry. In the case above, had the FTSE risen to 5,000 in three months and the investor decided they no longer required protection at the 4,500 level, they could have sold the put warrant for 18p (assuming all other factors remained constant).

In summary, the advantage of hedging in the manner above is that only a one-off warrant purchase is required and, at expiry, any losses made in a share holding or portfolio below the exercise price of the warrant are compensated for by a corresponding increase in value in the warrant holding. It is also worth noting that losses on covered warrant investments are generally treated in the same manner as warrants on equity investments. This means that losses arising from put warrants used as insurance – when the insurance is not needed – can often be written off against capital gains tax.

Pricing matrix

Table 3 shows an indicative pricing matrix for the cost of insuring a £1 million portfolio of UK shares with a FTSE 100 index put over a variety of time scales.

With 100% protection for one year, achieved by purchasing an at-the-money put warrant as in the example in Table 3, the portfolio would be hedged if 9% of the portfolio value were invested in a put warrant.

Table 3 Indicative pricing matrix for portfolio protection

% Protection	6m (%)	1y (%)	2y (%)
100	6	9	12
95	4.25	7	9.50
90	2.50	5	7
85	0.75	3	4

Alternatively an investor may prefer to be insured against a fall below 90% of the present level. In this case, at expiry, the investor would suffer a 10% fall in accordance with a decline in index level, but be protected thereafter. For one year's protection, this would involve the initial investment of approximately 5% of the portfolio value in a 90% out-of-the-money warrant (ie, with the FTSE 100 at 4,500, a warrant with a strike price of 4,050).

A further option would be the "crash protection" selection of a deep out-of-the-money put warrant (eg, a 3,825 strike if the FTSE 100 is at 4,500). This would only cost 3% of portfolio value a year, but would pay out only if the FTSE 100 fell by more than 25% in a calendar year (as was the case, in fact, in 2002).

CURRENCY WARRANTS

SG Currency Warrants open up both strategies – speculation and hedging – to retail and institutional investors, with the same ease of execution as buying a share. The transparency and high liquidity of the underlying FX market means that Currency Warrants have good bid–ask spreads (the difference between the buy price and sell price of the warrant) and track movements in the underlying exchange rate on a second-by-second basis.

Currency warrants use the same parameters as equity warrants (strike, maturity, call, put, effective gearing, etc). The major difference is the underlying, which is an exchange rate instead of a stock or index. If, for example, you believe the US dollar will strengthen against the euro (eg, the EUR/USD rate will fall from 1.20 to 1.10) within 12 months, then an appropriate instrument would be one of the SG EUR/USD put warrants.

Nominal and parity

The *nominal* value for a currency warrant represents how many units of the underlying currency are controlled by one warrant. GBP/USD and GBP/EUR each have a nominal value of £10, indicating that the warrant gives the holder the right to £10 worth of the underlying currency. This is a very similar concept to a warrant's *parity* for equity warrants.

As with equity warrants, the parity or nominal value is only strictly necessary if you are looking to hedge a certain amount of the underlying that you already hold, eg, a portfolio of US$500,000 in US stocks or a euro-denominated mortgage on a European property.

Payout formula

The payout formula for a currency warrant is as follows:

$$\text{Call warrant} = (\text{Exchange rate} - \text{Strike price}) \times \text{Nominal}$$

$$\text{Put warrant} = (\text{Strike Price} - \text{Exchange Rate}) \times \text{Nominal}$$

This amount will then be converted to local currency using the prevailing exchange rate. The price of the warrant moves on a second-by-second basis in line with movements in the underlying exchange rate, meaning that warrant positions can be initiated or cut at any time.

Currency Warrants can also be highly effective tools for hedging currency risk. A GBP-based investor who owns a non-GBP-denominated asset – eg, a portfolio of US shares or a European property – stands to lose money in sterling terms if the pound strengthens. This risk can be offset by using an GBP/USD or GBP/EUR call warrant.

Conversely, if an investor has a non-sterling liability – eg, they needs to pay for goods imported from the US or to buy a property in Europe – at a future date, then he has the risk that the pound may fall against the other currency, which would increase the liability in sterling terms. If so, they should consider hedging his risk with an GBP/USD or GBP/EUR put warrant.

TRACKER AND BONUS CERTIFICATES
Tracker certificates

Tracker certificates, sometimes called *benchmark certificates* or simply *certificates*, are the most basic form of index-based investments. The certificate directly tracks the price of a share, index or commodity on which it is based.

Certificates tend to be much longer dated when they are issued – typically three to five years. They can also be open-ended, with no fixed expiry date at issue. In this case, the issuer will have the right to stipulate an expiry date on a fixed day, once a year (eg, 1 December). At least two months notice would be given to the holders of a certificate that is to be wound up.

Traded through a stockbroker in exactly the same manner as shares, tracker certificates offer the ability to gain fast and transparent exposure to some of the world's most exciting invest-ment products. Tracker certificates differ significantly from war-rants in that they offer unleveraged exposure to an asset.

The advantages of trading tracker certificates are as follows:

Low cost

There are, most of the time, no annual management fees, very tight bid–ask spreads (the difference between the price at which you can buy the product and the price at which you can sell it) and there is nothing more than stockbroker commission to pay.

Flexibility

There is no minimum or maximum trading size; all tracker certifi-cates are priced and traded in local currency, meaning no foreign currency transactions are required; and there is no fixed expiry date for tracker certificates at issue.

Liquidity

Liquidity – the ability to buy or sell the product at any time – is a requirement of the exchange on which the product is listed. This means you will be able to find a price for and trade your invest-ment at any time.

Certificates

The main attraction of certificates is the very diverse range of underlyings in which to invest, from main international indices, such as the FTSE 100 and Dow Jones Industrial Average, to pre-cious metals such as gold, silver and platinum, to industry sectors and baskets of shares that share an investment theme.

As with all covered warrants, certificates do not pay dividends to the holder. For certificates with a fixed maturity, any dividends to be paid out will generally be reflected by the certificate price trading at a discount to the price of the underlying index.

As ungeared products, tracker certificates represent a lower-risk investment than an investment in a geared instrument such as a covered warrant. Prices of tracker certificates are not influenced by extra factors such as time decay and changes in implied volatility, which affect covered warrant prices.

A WEALTH MANAGER'S GUIDE TO STRUCTURED PRODUCTS

As they are priced and traded in local currency, tracker certificates are far more accessible to investors. Holders should be aware, however, that the value of the certificate could fluctuate with currency changes if the currency of the underlying security is not the same as the local currency. This may have a net positive or negative effect.

Despite their name, no physical document is received upon purchase of an SG certificate. Entitlements are stored electronically by your broker.

An example list of underlying on which SG and other companies currently offer tracker certificates is as follows:

Commodities
❑ Gold;
❑ Silver; and
❑ Platinum.

Indices
❑ FTSE 100
❑ FTSE 250
❑ Dow Jones Industrial Average
❑ Dow Jones EuroStoxx50
❑ Nikkei 225
❑ Hang Seng
❑ Hang Seng China Enterprises Index
❑ Latibex Index

Example trade
A UK investor wishes to gain long-term exposure to the FTSE 250 mid-cap index. She has £100,000 to invest. The price of the FTSE 250 is currently trading at 6,320 and the FTSE 250 tracker certificate is trading at £6.32. The investor therefore buys 15,822 FTSE 250 tracker certificates, costing £99,995, plus brokerage commission.

One year later, assume the FTSE 250 had risen to 7,000 (up 11%). With a parity of 1,000, the FTSE 250 tracker certificate in this case would be worth £7.00 (£7,000/1,000). The investor is therefore able to sell their 15,822 tracker certificates for £110,754, making a profit of £10,759 (before broker commission).

Bonus certificates

Bonus certificates are innovative new ways for investors to gain exposure to the international indices. They are an example of a "semi-structured" product. They are designed for long-term investors looking for the same low-investment risks as are available through an index investment, but with the possibility of higher returns.

We will consider an example of a bonus certificate recently issued on the FTSE 100 in the UK. The new bonus certificate offers the same benefits of a FTSE 100 tracker, in that it offers direct, unleveraged exposure to the FTSE 100 index, with the bonus feature of an index redemption level of 6,000 – or the prevailing level of the FTSE 100 – at expiry in December 2008, whichever is the greater. This bonus level is available provided that the FTSE 100 does not trade below a barrier level of 3,000.

In other words, provided the FTSE 100 never trades at or below 3,000 (a 10-year low) at any point before December 2008, the holder will receive a return of at least 35% (on the prevailing FTSE 100 level of 4,400 at issue in April 2004), even if the FTSE 100 gives a negative return over the same time period.

The details of an example certificate are as follows:

Code	Underlying	Bonus level	Barrier level	Expiry
S598	FTSE 100	6,000	3,000	19 Dec 08

At issue, the price of the bonus certificate is obtained by dividing the price of the FTSE 100 by a fixed divisor, called the *parity*. This is 1,000 for the FTSE 100 bonus certificate.

At issue, the FTSE 100 was trading at 4,520, so the mid-price of the bonus certificate was 452p. If the FTSE 100 is 7,500 at expiry, the value of one bonus certificate will be £750. Or, if the FTSE 100 collapses to 2,500 at expiry the value of one bonus certificate will be 250p.

There is no minimum trading size in the Bonus Certificate. An investor could buy one certificate for 452p or invest £4.5 million by buying 1 million. There is no stamp duty to pay on a trade, no annual management fees to pay and the product can be traded at any time during London Stock Exchange trading hours. If the

Table 4 Payout value of bonus certificate if barrier level not hit

FTSE 100 start level	3,000 level hit	FTSE 100 level at expiry	Return on FTSE 100 (%)	Payout value of bonus certificate	Return on bonus certificate (%)
4,500	No	7,000	+56	700 p	+56
4,500	No	5,000	+11	600 p	+33
4,500	No	3,500	−22	600 p	+33

Table 5 Payout value of bonus certificate if barrier hit

FTSE 100 start level	3,000 level hit	FTSE 100 level at expiry	Return on FTSE 100 (%)	Payout value of bonus certificate	Return on bonus certificate (%)
4,500	Yes	7,000	+56	700 p	+56
4,500	Yes	5,000	+11	500 p	+11
4,500	Yes	3,500	−22	350 p	−22

bonus certificate is held to expiry, the investor will automatically receive the cash value of the product.

The typical profile of an investor in a bonus certificate is someone who feels neutral to bullish on the market, but who does not expect a sharp fall. As can be see from Tables 4 and 5, if the FTSE 100 climbs sharply by December 2008, the investor receives the same return as the market.

Where the bonus certificate is most effective is in the scenario highlighted. In this case, the FTSE 100 falls by expiry, but never breaches the 3,000 barrier level. In these circumstances, far higher returns are available from the bonus certificate than from an investment in a FTSE 100 tracker.

Note that a bonus certificate is not a capital-guarantee product. At expiry, if the FTSE 100 has breached the 3,000 ("barrier") level, the return on the bonus certificate is the same as a return on an ordinary index tracker. ie, if the FTSE 100 breaches 3,000 and returns –5% to December 2008, the return on the bonus certificate is −5%.

Even if the 3,000 level is hit, the investor will still benefit from any strong recovery in the market, as the bonus certificate is now simply a tracker certificate, as shown in Table 5.

In summary, a bonus certificate offers 100% of the upside in the FTSE 100, whatever the outcome, and offers a redemption value of at least 600p (equivalent to a FTSE 100 index level of 6,000) at expiry provided the 3,000 barrier level is never breached during the certificate's lifetime.

What are the risks involved?

The bonus certificate offers direct, unleveraged exposure to the FTSE 100 share index, so has the same risk profile as an investment in a tracker fund or exchange-traded fund. The bonus element means that your return could be positive, even though the return on the FTSE 100 may be negative.

At expiry, the cash value of the bonus certificate is automatically paid out to the holder. The payout formula for the bonus certificate depends on whether the bonus level has been hit or not and is defined as follows:

$$\frac{\text{Payout at expiry}}{\text{(bonus level not hit)}} = \frac{6,000 \text{ or level of FTSE 100 if higher}}{1,000 \text{ (parity)}}$$

$$\text{Payout at expiry (bonus level hit)} = \frac{\text{Level of FTSE 100}}{1,000 \text{ (parity)}}$$

For example, if the FTSE 100 is at 5,000 at expiry and the barrier level has not been hit, the payout level is equal to the bonus level of 6,000 and the payout is 6,000/1,000 = 600p per certificate. Had an investor bought 2,000 certificates at 450p and held to expiry, they would automatically receive a cash payout in this case of 2,000 × 600p = £12,000. A profit of £3,000, or 33% (before broker commission).

If, on the other hand, the FTSE 100 is 7,500 at expiry, the payout is 7,500/1,000 = 750p irrespective of whether the barrier has been hit or not (in this case the return on the FTSE 100 is higher than the return on the bonus).

Again, as with all warrants and certificates, the FTSE 100 bonus certificate does not pay dividends to the holder. These are retained by the company and used to create the bonus payout structure. With a relatively high-yielding index like the FTSE 100, the bonus levels can be attractively high. In essence, the investor in the bonus certificate is choosing to forgo dividend income in exchange for the possibility of higher returns provided the barrier level is not hit.

COVERED WARRANT RISKS

While Covered Warrants offer tremendous benefits to investors through their qualities of gearing, transparency and ease of trade, it is important to be aware of the higher risk involved. Warrants are not suitable for all investors. As they magnify movements of the underlying security on which they are based, they can be highly volatile instruments. Under certain circumstances, warrants may expire worthless, therefore investors should not buy a warrant unless they are prepared to lose all the money invested plus any commission charges incurred. Investors should not deal in warrants unless they understand their nature and the risk involved.

---

1   Warrant calculators are easily accessible on the Internet – one is available at our website, http://www.warrants.com, for instance.

3

Cliquet Products as Investment Opportunities and Source of Hidden Risks

G. A. Adragna, V. Ceci, A. C. Cosentini, L. Lotti

TradingLab

A number of reasons lie behind the interest in exotic equity products. Leaving aside considerations relating to investment guidelines, regulation and taxation (see Kat, 2001), a structured product may fit a portfolio manager's strategy either because it seconds their market views or because it fits their overall portfolio management strategy as an attractive risk hedge. Moreover, both investment bankers and distributors enjoy the benefits of structured products in terms of business revenues. Sometimes, however, portfolio managers and distributors struggle with an increasing complexity of products which prevents them from appreciating the appropriateness of the products, shaded by the doubt of being the "dumping" of risks that dealers do not want to keep in their books. Distributors, in particular, need to understand the risks and to discern whether the product has been structured correctly; in other words, they have to be aware of what they sell. In Italy the insurance market regulator, ISVAP, has stated this concept explicitly in a circular (451/D, July 24, 2001) requiring a full pricing capability.

INTRODUCTION

For large deals to be effectively managed by structurers, exotic options are usually "drowned" in large books where they find

---

*In this chapter we use the Heston (1993) approach to accent some aspects of the model risk arising from the use of the Black–Scholes model for exotic options of cliquet type.

natural hedges and risks are diluted by an insurance-type mechanism, ie, by means of diversification along the relevant risk dimensions. A distributor might wonder, though, if the dealer is accounting properly for the risks embedded in the products they structure, and if they are concentrating hidden risks in his book. In this case, they would be exchanging market risk for counterparty risk. This is another compelling reason why distributors might want to know about these products: a few hints may offer the coordinates to detect the wrong structuring counterparty.

The reason why we centre our analysis on the cliquet options is that they have become, in a sense, "sadly" famous across dealers, thanks to their elusive forward skew sensitivity. A superficial reading of this feature can lead to a sharp mispricing, as put forward by the recent practitioners and academic debate. In this chapter, we will try to highlight some non-obvious aspects relevant for risk and allocation analysis.

Structures with embedded cliquet options are traded OTC; it is difficult to mark prices to market, and this practice is replaced by marking to model.[1] Moreover, a static hedge not being possible for the skew risk factor, pricing and hedging are strictly dependent on the model selected. For the concurrent complexity of valuation and lack of liquid markets, prices turn out to be often heavily inconsistent among traders. For all of these reasons we deem it proper to use of a range of alternative models and of extensive simulation and scenario analyses in order to fully appreciate the features of the products and to quantify the model risk. An and Suo (2003) show that Black–Scholes, as used by traders (ie, continuously recalibrated) still performs worthily in relative terms when competing with alternative models (continuously recalibrated as well) on the grounds of hedging performance of barrier options (path-dependent without restrike feature). This finding is consistent with a set of continuity theorems (see Corielli, 2003) warranting that the use of implied volatilities instead of a finer model (say stochastic volatility) leads to a small pricing error if the distance between the "true" volatility and the value plugged in the model is not "big": a small change in parameters does not go along with an exploding error. What matters is to assign upper bounds to the margins of error and, only when these are unacceptable, to agree on a change of model, bearing in mind that a simple model (probably perceived also as fast and stable) makes it also easier to measure the margins of error. In this direction moves the worst-case-analysis approach developed by Avellaneda, Levy and Paras (1995) for a class of stochastic volatility models, which provides a safe margin for the option price, given a min–max range for the volatility.

For a strongly path-dependent payout we have a complex dependence on the joint probability distribution of the asset price at several times. The smile implied by the European options prices contains information about the eventual departure of the distribution of the asset value from the Black and Scholes lognormality at option maturity, but does not provide any indication about the cause of this discrepancy. Many different processes may be postulated, all of them compatible with the volatility smile, but leading to different prices of path-dependent options. The specification of a stochastic process for the volatility is a possible answer to the problem at hand. Heston (1993) is our modelling choice, as it is suited both to overcome the Black–Scholes limit of deterministic volatility and to take into account the return–volatility correlation. It is also a somewhat fashionable choice, representing a balance between the flexibility of more general models and the challenges that they pose in terms of hedging complexity and parameters reasonableness valuation. Moreover, the mean-reversion of the volatility process allows it to capture a stylised fact of the returns distribution: volatility clustering. Another feature of the empirical distribution receives an adequate representation, excess kurtosis.[2] In the following paragraphs we analyse the relevance of this model for cliquet options.

The remainder of the chapter is organised as follows. The next section reviews shortly a selection of cliquets and focuses on the two most common payouts, the *Standard* and the *Reverse* Cliquet. In particular, we try to highlight the payout dependence on volatility. The following section analyses the products in a Black–Scholes setup, marking an analogous link between option price and volatility. In this section the reader has the opportunity to place these findings in an asset-allocation perspective: as a matter of fact, the Black–Scholes framework turns out to be particularly useful for exemplification purposes. Finally, the section following unfolds the weaknesses of the Black–Scholes pricing approach, emphasising the mispricing with respect to the Heston (1993) model and discussing the sources of the discrepancy.

HISTORICAL PERSPECTIVE AND GENERAL PROPERTIES OF CLIQUET OPTIONS

Cliquet options are commonly used exotic options, often part of well-known retail structured products such as Accumulator and Predator.

The characteristic feature of the cliquet family is that the payouts are expressed in terms of the percentage change in the value of the underlying over a stated time period. At the beginning of each period, the strike is reset to the current value of the underlying. Cliquet options are equivalent to a series of forward-starting, at-the-money (ATM) options, but with a single premium determined upfront.

We focus on the two most common types of cliquets, the *Standard* and *Reverse* Cliquet.

The payout for the Standard Cliquet can be written as:

$$\text{Notional} \times \text{Min}\left\{ M, G + \sum_{j=1}^{N} \text{Max}\left[F, \text{Min}\left(C, \frac{S_j - S_{j-1}}{S_{j-1}} \right) \right] \right\}$$

while for the Reverse Cliquet we have:

$$\text{Notional} \times \text{Max}\left\{ G, M + \sum_{j=1}^{N} \text{Min}\left[C, \text{Max}\left(F, \frac{S_j - S_{j-1}}{S_{j-1}} \right) \right] \right\}$$

In the above expressions G is the *Guaranteed*, the minimum percentage of notional that is redeemed to the investor at expiry, in the common case of $F = 0$ and $M > G$. The parameter M is called the *MaxCoupon* and caps the investor's income, in the common case of $C = 0$.

The index j of the summation runs over the entire set of fixing dates specified by the contract.

The parameters C (*Cap*) and F (*Floor*) locally reduce the variance of the terms

$$P_j = \frac{S_j - S_{j-1}}{S_{j-1}}$$

which is what the investor ultimately wishes to obtain.

These contracts are appealing to investors since they offer an insurance against the risk of a market downside, while at the same time offering appreciable profit opportunities from a market upside.

Reverse Cliquet options offer a high maximum coupon eroded by periodic negative performances eventually scored by the underlying stock.

The success of cliquets did not come without opposition. Many institutions have ascribed competitors overly aggressive pricing of products at auctions, bringing to light the issue of a possible systematic mispricing. The consequent quest for transparency has led to the birth of pricing services that allow dealers to position themselves relative to market average.

The correct valuation of cliquets can present difficulties since it requires the correct modelling of forward volatility skew.[3]

Notwithstanding embedded risks and pricing problems, cliquets remain appealing, and cliquet-type structures are involved in an innovation process that has recently led to products such as Napoleon and Swing, launched over the past two years. The Napoleon is contingent on an underlying equity index and allows investors to sell the volatility skew. At the end of each year it pays out the sum of a fixed central coupon plus the worst monthly performance of an index (eg, EuroStoxx 50) from the previous 12 months. Its maturity typically is between three and five years, and the payout is expressed in terms of the monthly performance of the underlying.

The Swing option is an option whose payout is proportional to the lowest monthly performance (in absolute value) of an index, as measured at the end of each year in relation to the previous 12 months. The fourth moment, the kurtosis, has in this case a substantial impact on the price.

In the rest of the chapter we focus on the issues raised by the Standard and Reverse Cliquet options. The understanding of these issues is the first step towards the analysis of more recent types of cliquet option.

In order to achieve a better understanding of the mechanics of Standard and Reverse Cliquet payouts, we need to take a closer look at the role of each parameter.

The parameters G and M fix large-scale limits on the option payout.

When the investor has the possibility to choose in a well-differentiated range of cliquet options, they should choose G and M in a way consistent with their views about long-term market behaviour. He faces the risk that the option loses its value before the market fulfils his expectations. Thus the choice of such parameters must reflect a trade-off between the cheapness of the option and the probability that the option effectively expires in-the-money.

The parameters C and F, on the contrary, act locally on the option payout: they limit each of the performances, not just the whole payout. For this reason they should be chosen consistently with investors' expectations on directional movements of the underlying in between the fixing dates specified by the contracts.

To make clear all of these considerations, we shall focus in what follows on two examples of cliquet options that we deem as representative of a large portion of the traded contracts, as already mentioned. The contract details of the cliquet options we shall consider are shown in Table 1.

Both contracts are characterised by yielding the same maximum payout to the investor at maturity (24%); both are directionally oriented towards the upside. The difference is in the underlying view about market movements.

First of all, an investor choosing to buy the Standard Cliquet is confident that on average the underlying will move up. If this circumstance fails to happen, the option payout will be negligible.

Investors choosing the Reverse Cliquet, instead, believe that on average the underlying will not move down. This is not significant if the underlying ultimately moves up or stays unchanged, they will be left with a substantial fraction of the MaxCoupon at expiry.

Table 1 Sample contract details

Cliquet	Standard	Reverse
Start date	1-1-2004	1-1-2004
Expiry date	1-1-2005	1-1-2005
Fixing	Monthly	Monthly
MaxCoupon	24%	24%
Guaranteed	0%	0%
Cap	2%	0%
Floor	0%	No floor

The second important difference between the contracts lies in the dependence of the two options payouts on volatility.

A first clue about such different behaviour is that while the Standard contract (locally floored by F) is well protected against extreme events (such as large downward market movements), the other doesn't contain any such crash-insurance feature except for the variant with the global floor set at -24%. If the global floor is hit on a fixing date preceding the option's expiry, the contract automatically becomes worthless.

Investors buying the Reverse Cliquet should be convinced that the probability of such an extreme event is negligible, and should be aware that a high-volatility scenario would likely bring no payout at expiry.

To get a closer feeling about the differences between the two contracts, we have summarised in Table 2 the payouts of the two options contingent on nine possible future scenarios. To obtain the scenarios, we have picked the monthly performance of the EuroStoxx 50 index from March 2003 to February 2004. We have called this scenario the medium volatility (MV) lateral trend (L) scenario.[4] We have then modified this scenario using different levels for the volatility and the average performance.

Therefore, the first three scenarios refer to a low-volatility (LV) underlying dynamics, characterised by a downward (D) overall trend, by a lateral trend (L) or by an upward trend (U) respectively; the last scenario refers to a high-volatility (HV) upward (U) trend; and so on for the other columns.

As we mentioned above, the more bullish the market, the higher the payout of both contracts. Indeed, whatever the assumption made about volatility, the scenario bringing the highest payout is always the one corresponding to an up-trending market (U) for both the cliquets. However, while the payout of the Standard Cliquet reacts positively to an increase in the underlying volatility, the opposite is true for the Reverse Cliquet.[5] In jargon, the buyer of a Standard Cliquet option is long *Vega*, while the owner of the Reverse Cliquet is short *Vega*.

Finally, as one may notice from the Table, in the case of the Reverse Cliquet option it is possible to get closer and closer to the maximum payout by progressively decreasing the volatility. This implies that the Reverse Cliquet price should be reasonably

Table 2 Payouts of cliquet options under alternative scenarios

Volatility	LV			MV			HV		
Trend	D (%)	L (%)	U (%)	D (%)	L (%)	U (%)	D (%)	L (%)	U (%)
P_1	−4.25	−3.25	−2.25	−5.85	−4.85	−3.85	−7.45	−6.45	−5.45
P_2	8.45	9.45	10.45	13.11	14.11	15.11	17.76	18.76	19.76
P_3	−0.83	0.17	1.17	−0.75	0.25	1.25	−0.67	0.33	1.33
P_4	1.57	2.57	3.57	2.84	3.84	4.84	4.11	5.11	6.11
P_5	1.78	2.78	3.78	3.14	4.14	5.14	4.51	5.51	6.51
P_6	−0.02	0.98	1.98	0.47	1.47	2.47	0.95	1.95	2.95
P_7	−5.21	−4.21	−3.21	−7.29	−6.29	−5.29	−9.37	−8.37	−7.37
P_8	4.01	5.01	6.01	6.48	7.48	8.48	8.95	9.95	10.95
P_9	0.44	1.44	2.44	1.15	2.15	3.15	1.86	2.86	3.86
P_{10}	2.32	3.32	4.32	3.95	4.95	5.95	5.58	6.58	7.58
P_{11}	0.90	1.90	2.90	1.84	2.84	3.84	2.78	3.78	4.78
P_{12}	0.28	1.28	2.28	0.90	1.90	2.90	1.53	2.53	3.53
Payout Standard	10.97	15.77	19.15	14.36	17.62	19.25	16.34	18.28	19.33
Payout Reverse	13.68	16.53	18.53	10.11	12.86	14.86	6.51	9.18	11.18

a monotonic function of volatility independently of the volatility level. The same cannot be said of the Standard Cliquet.

In Table 2 we notice that the volatility increase ceases to exercise significant effects on the Standard payout beyond a certain level. This happens because there is a cap.

Keeping in mind these considerations, one can: (1) understand OTC quoted cliquet prices; (2) detect a potential mispricing in the market and profit from it; and (3) allocate funds in an equity derivatives portfolio consistently with one's own market view.

In the following section we formalise these concepts within the framework of the Black–Scholes pricing model.

BLACK–SCHOLES PRICING OF CLIQUET OPTIONS

In a significant period people have tried to model mathematically the random character of the stock price dynamics. The Black–Scholes pricing model, developed in the early 1970s, is based on the assumption that a single number, the stock volatility, is needed to account for such randomness.

Volatility is a measure of the "speed" of market reactions. It can be viewed as the rate of change of the stock price in response to fresh news, market rumours or other sources of noise.

Denoting with S_0 and S_1 the values of an asset, say the price of a stock, at two instants of time t_0 and t_1, one defines the log-return of the stock for the period (t_0, t_1) as

$$\log \frac{S_1}{S_0}$$

If t_0 is the present time and t_1 an instant in the future, the quantity above is a random variable. The Black–Scholes model assumes that such a variable is distributed according to a Gaussian law with a standard deviation given by the product of the stock price volatility σ and the square root of the time distance between t_0 and t_1.

Under this and some other assumptions, which we are not discussing here, Black and Scholes were able to develop a coherent framework for the pricing of contingent claims, including the kind of exotic options we are considering here.

As already mentioned, the key feature of the Black–Scholes model is that the value of an option depends only on the current value of the stock and on the stock volatility.[6]

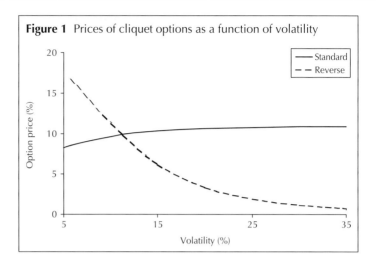

Figure 1 Prices of cliquet options as a function of volatility

Now, while the stock value is an observable quantity, volatility is an unknown parameter. In order to quote prices, exotic-options traders adopting the Black–Scholes pricing model must produce a sensible estimate for the future volatility.

The scenario analysis presented in the preceding section highlighted a clear dependence on the volatility of the payout corresponding to the two cliquet contracts. It is then quite unsurprising that such dependence is directly reflected in option prices.

In Figure 1 we show the behaviour of the prices of the two contracts as predicted by the Black–Scholes model for different volatility assumptions.

As you may notice from Figure 1, option prices dependence on volatility is similar to the payout dependence on volatility.

In particular, we notice that:

❑ The Standard Cliquet appreciates as the volatility increases, but beyond a certain level, it becomes rather insensitive to changes in volatility.[7]

❑ More precisely, the Standard Cliquet price reaches an asymptotic value (11%) which does not correspond to the maximum payout (24%) that characterises the contract.[8] Thus, at least for the range of volatility values that we have plotted, the Standard Cliquet shows a mild positive dependence upon volatility.

❑ Conversely, the Reverse Cliquet price appears strongly dependent on the volatility assumption. For example, as the volatility passes from 10% to 15% the option loses about five points in value. Furthermore, the Reverse Cliquet price spans the entire range of possible values (0–24%) as the volatility varies between 0% and, say, 40%.

It must be stressed that the highlighted features depend on the contract details that we have chosen for the cliquets under examination. The very fact, mentioned above, that the Reverse Cliquet does not have a local floor makes it much more sensitive to volatility than the Standard Cliquet. Indeed, if one considered the terms for a Standard Cliquet option shown in Table 3, one would rather obtain the marked volatility dependence shown in Figure 2 of the Standard Cliquet price.

Thus in the sequel, whenever we assert properties regarding the two kind of option, we refer to the contracts outlined in Table 1.

Table 3 Contract details for an uncapped standard cliquet option

Cliquet	Standard
Start date	1-1-2004
Expiry date	1-1-2005
Fixing	Monthly
MaxCoupon	24%
Guaranteed	0%
Cap	No cap
Floor	0%

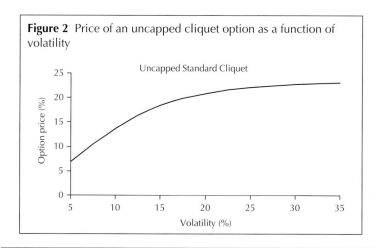

Figure 2 Price of an uncapped cliquet option as a function of volatility

ADVANCED APPROACH TO CLIQUET OPTIONS PRICING

From an investor's point of view it is essential to be able to assess the richness/cheapness of cliquet options that can be bought on the market. In this section we provide an overview of an advanced pricing approach. Hopefully, this will help the reader to understand why the prices of a cliquet contract are often very different from those obtained in the Black–Scholes framework.

Historically, exotic options on equity underlyings were first traded OTC in the 1980s, when a large number of equity options traders were already well acquainted with the Black–Scholes model.

With hindsight, we can say that the challenge of dealing with complex path-dependent options within such a model was undertaken somewhat thoughtlessly.

It is likely that, at that time, short-term revenues were preferred to investments on research projects that are known to bring profits only in the long run. The recognition of such a preference has played a major role in developing the modern approach to risk management, as highlighted in Crouhy, Galai and Mark (2001).

Traders and financial institutions in general were certainly aware that, simple as it is, the Black–Scholes model could not capture all the risk components embedded in the options they were selling.

However, while obvious drawbacks of the Black–Scholes model (such as the hypothesis of absence of market frictions) were taken into account, charging some rough estimate of transaction costs on option premia, some non-trivial biases of the Black–Scholes model were, at that time, largely overlooked. A systematic option price underestimation was brought to light, and this discovery induced financial institutions to heavily invest in internal research departments in order to quantify and offset what was recognised as a new form of risk, for which the name *model risk* was coined.

One important step beyond the Black–Scholes model has been that of recognising that stock price volatility is not, as postulated by the Black–Scholes model, a constant quantity.

Several empirical studies (see Bollerslev, Engel and Nelson, 1994) have: (1) concluded that volatility itself can be fruitfully modelled as a stochastic process; and (2) identified some regular patterns in the volatility time series such as mean reversion and the clustering of extreme observations.

Such findings are an important hint for those willing to build consistent pricing models addressing the issue of random volatility.[9]

As a consequence, during the 1990s a new generation of pricing models, the stochastic volatility models, entered the scene (see Heston, 1993; Hull and White, 1987; Stein and Stein, 1991). Most of these models hypothesised a mean reverting process for the volatility.

The impact of the new pricing models was soon recognised to be relevant. When calculating the new mark-to-market of exotic-options books, sometimes big losses appeared as a result of the switch from the deterministic volatility (Black–Scholes) setup to the stochastic volatility paradigm.

In this section we make comparisons between cliquet options prices as predicted by the Black–Scholes model as opposed to those derived from one of the most popular stochastic volatility mode, the Heston model.[10] The Heston model is fully described by a state variable and four parameters:

❑ the spot volatility σ, which has the same meaning of the Black–Scholes volatility but is now allowed to change randomly through time;
❑ the mean volatility $\bar{\sigma}$, which is the level at which the spot volatility reverts, and in this sense represents the long-run average volatility experienced by the underlying;
❑ the mean reversion speed k, the force that pushes volatility towards its mean value $\bar{\sigma}$;
❑ the volatility of volatility η, which specifies the degree of uncertainty about future volatility levels; it multiplies the shock, so that it contributes to the variance of σ^2;
❑ the correlation between the stock dynamics and the volatility dynamics (ρ), which takes into account the fact that, on average, changes in volatility are not independent from changes in the value of the underlying.[11]

In order to make sensible comparisons between the two kind of model, we shall suppose that the underlying of our contracts is the EuroStoxx 50 index (with spot value 3,000) and that two traders are quoting exotic-option prices simultaneously.

The first trader, the "BS-trader", adopts the Black–Scholes model and assumes that volatility is equal to the quoted implied volatility of ATM Call options on EuroStoxx 50 with expiry one year.[12]

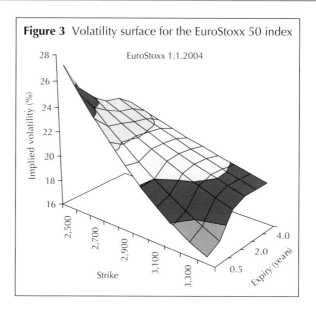

Figure 3 Volatility surface for the EuroStoxx 50 index

Table 4 Parameter of the Heston model calibrated on 1.1.2004 to EuroStoxx 50 index options

σ	σ̄	k	η	ρ
22%	23.7%	1.3	35%	−88%

The second, the "H-trader", instead uses the Heston model and estimates all the five parameters described above, calibrating them to the EuroStoxx 50-implied volatility surface.

In [Figure] 3 we show the EuroStoxx 50 surface as of January 1, 2004.[13] Implied volatilities are plotted in this figure as a function of strike and expiry. Reading the implied volatility for an expiry of one year and a strike of 3,000 (at-the-money), one gets a value of 20%, we shall assume that the BS-trader will use such a value to price the contracts.

Calibrating the Heston model to the surface one obtains the parameters shown in Table 4.

Table 5 reports the prices for the two cliquet contracts as quoted by the two traders.

Prices for the Standard Cliquet are different, while prices for the Reverse Cliquet are dramatically different. This is because the

Table 5 Prices of the cliquet options under the two different approaches

	BS-trader (%)	H-trader (%)
Standard	10.6	11.4
Reverse	3.3	5.7

Standard Cliquet is less sensitive to volatility. Let's see if there is a simple way to understand where such differences come from. It is a well-known fact that the concept of convexity plays a major role in determining the price of an option.[14]

By convexity we mean a curvature in the function that links the value of the option to one of its determinants. For example, the gamma expresses the convexity with respect to the value of the underlying. An option with higher convexity will have a higher value than an otherwise identical option with lower convexity. This happens because, when the underlying moves up, the value of the most convex option experiences a larger increase, while, when the underlying moves down, the value of the most convex option experiences a smaller drop. This is very similar to what happens for convex bonds when interest rates move.

What is perhaps less well known is that convexity with respect to the value of the underlying (gamma convexity) is not the only kind of nonlinearity embedded in an option. It turns out that there is also a volatility convexity, which is captured by Heston's model. This feature, in association with a substantial uncertainty regarding future volatility, has a significant impact on option prices. This is the case, for example, of deeply in-(out-)the-money plain vanilla options, which are known to be characterised by a marked volatility convexity (see Taleb, 1997).

In a regime of stochastic volatility the price of these options keeps increasing as one increases volatility uncertainty, which, in the Heston model, is proportional to the coefficient η, the volatility of volatility.

It must be stressed that in the Black–Scholes framework (volatility being a constant), the volatility convexity contribution to option prices is completely disregarded. This is the main reason why large differences may arise between Black–Scholes and Heston cliquet prices.

Let us focus, for example, on the Reverse Cliquet option. Recall that we have chosen a MaxCoupon parameter of 24%. At the first fixing date, if the performance

$$P_j = \frac{S_j}{S_{j-1}} - 1$$

is positive, then the investor still has the chance of gaining the whole MaxCoupon at expiry. If, by contrast, the performance is negative, the investor has lost automatically a fraction of the MaxCoupon.

Qualitatively, the situation for the investor is similar to being short an ATM put.

However, even being short a put, the investor is protected against extreme downside movements. Indeed, if the performance is lower than the threshold represented by the MaxCoupon (-4%), the investor enjoys a crash protection (and the option expires worthless).

Thus the investor is also long (at the first fixing date) an out-the-money (OTM) put option struck at

$$K = S_0 - 24\% \cdot S_0 = 76\% \cdot S_0$$

where S_0 is the underlying spot price at January 1, 2004.

As fixing dates pass by, the situation recurs. Every month the investor is short a put option ATM and long another put OTM stroke at

$$K = S_{i-1} - M' \cdot S_{i-1}$$

where S_{i-1} is the underlying spot price registered at the preceding fixing date and M' is the net difference between the MaxCoupon M and the (absolute value of the) partial sum of negative performances registered up to that month.

Now it should be clear why the Heston model predicts a higher price for the Reverse Cliquet option: the investor is short ATM put options, which are almost linear in volatility (which means no convexity at all), and long OTM put options, which are instead markedly convex in volatility. The investor has an overall convex position in volatility and, on average, will profit from movements in volatility. The consequence is that, renouncing to modelling volatility as a random quantity, the BS-trader is selling convexity for free to the investor.

It must be clear that the Black–Scholes model is contemplated as a particular case of the Heston model. Indeed, if we run price simulations in the Heston framework using the parameters in Table 6, we are in all respects obtaining Black–Scholes prices with a volatility assumption of 20%. This point helps us to visualise the impact of volatility convexity on the cliquet prices. In fact, if we start increasing the coefficient η, keeping fixed all the other parameters, on the basis of what was said above we expect to see the price of the Reverse Cliquet passing from the Black–Scholes value (3.3%) to higher and higher values as a result of an increase in volatility uncertainty. Figure 4 shows that this is indeed the case.

The price of the Reverse Cliquet, in fact, keeps increasing with the coefficient η, while, on the contrary, the Standard Cliquet price moves down.

Table 6 Parameters of the Heston model corresponding to the Black-Scholes special case

σ	σ̄	k	η	ρ
20%	20%	1	0%	0%

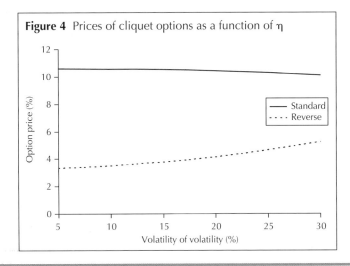

Figure 4 Prices of cliquet options as a function of η

Repeating the analysis done for the Reverse Cliquet contract, one realises that an investor buying the Standard Cliquet is long ATM Call options and short OTM Call options. This time the investor's position is overall concave with respect to volatility and loses value as uncertainty with respect to volatility increases.

The careful reader might object that this result is in contradiction with the results presented in Table 5, where the price 11.4% is reported for the Heston model as compared with the price 10.6% corresponding to the Black–Scholes model.

How can one justify the Standard Cliquet costing more in the Heston stochastic volatility model given that we have just pointed out that it should decrease as a result of its concavity with respect to volatility? The fact is that the price curves shown in Figure 4 are calculated under the hypothesis of a vanishing correlation coefficient ρ (Table 6), while prices in Table 5 have been derived using a correlation coefficient of -88% (Table 4). A negative correlation between stock price movements and volatility movements has been recognised as a possible mechanism (also referred to as the leverage effect) for reproducing what is commonly called the skew of volatility.

Precisely, plain vanilla options having a strike price greater than the spot price (for example OTM call options) are characterised by quoted implied volatilities systematically higher than those of ATM options. The opposite is true for options with strike smaller than the spot price. In Figure 5 we show the skew of volatility for plain vanilla options written on the EuroStoxx 50, expiry one year, as of January 1, 2004. For comparison we show in the figure the volatility assumption of the BS-trader. The volatility implied by the Heston model (with the calibrated parameters shown in Table 4), not shown in Figure 5, is nearly the same as that quoted by the market.

The negative slope of the market curve in Figure 5, the skew of volatility, has received since its appearance in the 1980s a great deal of attention, and the leverage effect is but one of the several mechanisms proposed to reproduce the skew. Returning to the Standard Cliquet, we are now able to explain why such a contract is worth more in the Heston model than in the Black–Scholes model.

As previously mentioned, an investor holding a Standard Cliquet is long ATM call options and short OTM call options. From

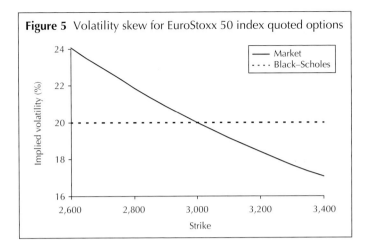

Figure 5 Volatility skew for EuroStoxx 50 index quoted options

Figure 5 it is clear that the latter are overpriced by the BS-trader as long as the trader is assuming 20% volatility for any kind of option expiring in one year.

The consequence is that the Black–Scholes model overestimates the liability side of the investor position and thus underestimates the investor's overall position, the option price.

One might wonder why the leverage effect prevails on the convexity effect in determining the Standard Cliquet price. Indeed, while the option price is supposed to increase owing to the former effect it is also supposed to decrease by reason of the latter.

It transpires that while the (positive) leverage effect correction to the Black–Scholes price is of the first order in η, that is, it is proportional to the first power of the η coefficient, the (negative) convexity correction is only of second order in η.[15]

This is easily seen in Figure 4, where the second-order dependence gives rise to a parabolic curve for both the option prices as a function of η. In this figure there is no trace of the leverage effect since the prices have been obtained imposing a zero correlation coefficient ρ.

In Figures 6 and 7 we plot again the curves shown in Figure 4, comparing them with those obtained varying the parameter η while keeping the correlation coefficient ρ fixed at the value -100% and all the other parameters at the values indicated in Table 6.

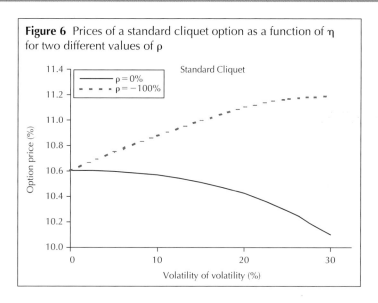

Figure 6 Prices of a standard cliquet option as a function of η for two different values of ρ

Figure 7 Prices of a reverse cliquet option as a function of η for two different values of ρ

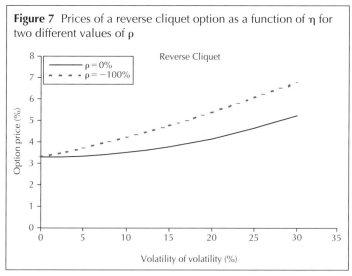

It is clear from the plots that, for small values of η, the linear correction corresponding to the leverage effect largely prevails on the convexity correction.

The latter, being of second order, emerges only for relatively large values of η, as can be noticed, for example, in Figure 6, where the Standard Cliquet prices curve starts to bend downwards only for η greater than 20%.

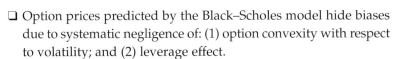

To conclude this section, we briefly summarise our findings:

❏ Option prices predicted by the Black–Scholes model hide biases due to systematic negligence of: (1) option convexity with respect to volatility; and (2) leverage effect.

❏ While, for the Standard Cliquet, the Heston model brings in a relatively small change in the price, for the Reverse Cliquet the change is dramatic.

❏ The Heston correction may be split into two contributions, one of the first order in η, the leverage effect, and one of the second order, the convexity adjustment.

❏ For the Standard Cliquet, the two effects tend to cancel out. This, together with the small Vega sensitivity of the Standard Cliquet structure, explains the small size of the stochastic volatility correction to the price predicted by the Black–Scholes model.

❏ By contrast, for the Reverse Cliquet the two effects sum up, resulting in an enormous difference between the Black–Scholes price and the Heston price.

The approach discussed in this section is – of course – one of many possible approaches that have gained some favour by practitioners and academics in the pricing of products with significant sensitivity to the dynamics of the volatility skew. Virtually all of the available approaches need to be implemented by calibrating the model of choice to the prices of vanilla options for different strikes and maturities. This practice triggers a potentially controversial issue: are we allowed to extract exotic option prices – which depend on forward volatilities – from parameters backed out from vanilla options? At the moment this is an open issue.

An interesting approach was proposed by Avellaneda, Levy and Paras (1995). Recently, Wilmott (2002) and Windcliff, Forsyth and Vetzal (2003) have discussed the applications of this approach to cliquet options. The key point of these works involves specifying a range for volatility, which is considered an "uncertain" parameter. One assumes that volatility can take any value within the chosen range, and gets an upper bound for the prices of exotic options by considering the worst possible volatility realisation in correspondence with each instant of time and of each value of the underlying.

The uncertain volatility approach turns out to be very conservative for Standard *Capped* Cliquets, in the sense that most of the time the resulting price is too high for a trader to be competitive on the market. Using the Heston model, as we have done in this section, leads to very different conclusions. This stems from the fact that the Heston model accounts for both adverse and favourable changes in volatility and for the correlation between the price of the underlying and volatility. If one believes that such a model represents a reasonable approximation to market behaviour, then stochastic volatility offers an acceptable compromise that takes into account the dynamics of the volatility skew without giving rise to extremely wide ranges of prices.

1 Typically capital guaranteed, which means that they guarantee a notional value to the investor, besides any fixed or variable coupons. Capital guaranteed and protected products have been a response to investors' quest for safety in the aftermath of the bear market. With structured products, distributors put cards on the table with clients, who are left without uncertainty about the investment policy. This transparent game can be complex, however, and strong communication skills are required for the outcome to be successful.

2 It is important to keep in mind that the deviations from normality of the empirical returns distribution do not necessarily entail a non-normal risk neutral distribution (see Rogers and Satchell (1999) for a demonstration). As a hint, consider for example that the empirical distribution can record a higher skewness because of a higher risk premium. If we represent the risk premium in the usual way, ie, $\lambda^*\sigma$, and if λ is a function of the underlying asset spot price S, $\lambda(S)$, a skew is generated under the objective measure but not under the risk neutral measure. Bakshi et al (2001) show instead how risk aversion introduces skewness in the risk-neutral density. The bottom line is: no matter the origin of stochastic volatility (for example, non-normality, transaction costs, parameters uncertainty), stochastic volatility is an appealing answer to the pricing and hedging challenge stated by path dependent exotic options.

3 Notice that this term is meaningful in a Black–Scholes setting.

4 For the definition of the volatility see next section.

5 For the range of volatilities considered.

6 For the sake of simplicity we are assuming zero interest rates and dividends.

7 If one enlarged enough the range of volatilities plotted in the figure, one would observe the Standard Cliquet becoming slightly short Vega.

8 The existence and the level of the asymptotic value is a consequence of the fact that the cliquet is capped.

9 See note 2 for a critical discussion on this issue.

10 The Heston dynamics in the risk-neutral measure is the following:

$$d\ln S_t = \left(r - q - \frac{\sigma_t^2}{2} \right) dt + \sqrt{\sigma_t^2} \, dW_1$$

$$d\sigma_t^2 = k(\bar{\sigma}^2 - \sigma_t^2) dt + \eta \sqrt{\sigma_t^2} \left(\rho dW_1 + \sqrt{1-\rho^2} dW_2 \right)$$

where S is the underlying, r is the risk free rate, q is the dividend rate and W_1 & W_2 are standard and independent Wiener processes. The other quantities are described in the main text.

11 To understand the need for modeling correlation between volatility and stock price, the reader should ask himself if it is more likely to see an increase or a decrease in volatility in the occurrence of a market crash.

12 Recall that the cliquet options we are considering expire in one year.

13 The surface has been obtained interpolating quoted vanilla options implied volatilities with a polynomial in the log-moneyness.

14 The argument we make here to give an intuition of the volatility convexity effect on the pricing of cliquets is largely heuristic. It is perhaps useful to underscore that there is a link between Heston volatility sensitivities (which are consistent with the model assumptions) and Black–Scholes volatility sensitivities (inconsistent with model assumptions), even if the latter are derivatives calculated with respect to a parameter. It can be easily shown that, if the volatility of volatility $\to 0$, Heston delta-vol $\to$ Black–Scholes Vega. The same is true for higher-order derivatives. We can devise stochastic volatility models for which this is not true: it is enough to assume a suitable relation between price and volatility. All in all, Heston offers a reason why Vega makes sense in practical use of the Black–Scholes model.

15 For the reasons behind this result see, for example, Lee (2001).

REFERENCES

An, Y., and W. Suo, 2003, "The Performance of Option Pricing Models on Hedging Exotic Options", Mimeo. Available at http://finance.business.queensu.ca/~wsuo/downloadable.html

Avellaneda, M., A. Levy, and A. Paras, 1995, "Pricing and Hedging Derivative Securities in Markets with Uncertain Volatilities", *Applied Mathematical Finance*, **2**, pp. 73–88.

Bakshi, G., N. Kapadia, and D. Madan, 2001, "Stock Return Characteristics, Skew Laws, and the Differential Pricing of Individual Equity Options", Mimeo.

Bollerslev, T., R. Engle, and D. B. Nelson, 1994, "ARCH Models", *Handbook of Econometrics*, **IV**, Chapter 49.

Corielli, F., 2003, "Hedging with Energy: Simple Error Bounds for Mis-Specified Diffusions", Mimeo.

Crouhy, M., D. Galai, and R. Mark, 2001, *Risk Management* (New York: McGraw-Hill).

Heston, S., 1993, "A Closed-Form Solution for Options with Stochastic Volatility with Application to Bond and Currency Options", *Review of Financial Studies*, **6**, pp. 327–43.

Hull, J., and A. White, 1987, "The Pricing of Options on Assets with Stochastic Volatilities", *Journal of Finance*, **42(2)**, pp. 281–300.

Kat, H. M., 2001, *Structured Equity Derivatives* (New York: John Wiley & Sons).

Lee, R. W., 2001, "Implied and Local Volatilities Under Stochastic Volatility", *International Journal of Theoretical and Applied Finance*, **4**, pp. 45–89.

Stein, E. M., and J. C. Stein, 1991, "Stock Price Distributions with Stochastic Volatility: An Analytic Approach", *Review of Financial Studies*, **4**, pp. 727–52.

Taleb, N., 1997, *Dynamic Hedging* (New York: John Wiley & Sons).

Wilmott, P., 2002, "Cliquet Options and Volatility Models", *Wilmott Magazine*, pp. 78–83, December.

Windcliff, H. A., P. A. Forsyth, and K. R. Vetzal, 2003, "Numerical Methods for Valuing Cliquet Options", Mimeo.

4

Seeking Capital Protection through Portfolio Insurance

Giancarlo Frugoli, Ferdinando Samaria

UniCredit Banca Mobiliare

Capital-guaranteed products have grown considerably in volumes over recent years. Following uncertainty in the equity markets, European retail banks have issued numerous products that offer their customers the opportunity of participating in some measure in the upside of the equity markets with limited or no risk to their capital. Three types of capital-guaranteed products have been commercialised:

❑ structured bonds;
❑ unit and index-linked life policies; and
❑ discretionary accounts.

This chapter analyses the rationale behind the design of these products, illustrating at first the two principal risk management techniques widely adopted in the market, ie, strategies based on acquiring options and those based on portfolio insurance theory. A detailed description of portfolio insurance techniques will follow with emphasis on multilevel methodologies, leading to the definition of risk management and pricing models in the context of managing a book of such products. This is followed by a case study and conclusions.

CAPITAL-GUARANTEED PRODUCTS
All risk management techniques that address the issue of protecting investments (which here will be assumed to be 100 units of capital

in whatever currency) are based in some way on the notion that markets express a price for the cost of returning 100 units to the investor at some future date. An investor with 100 units of capital wishing to preserve the value of the investments, say, over a period of five years, could consider investing initially in a so-called *zero-coupon bond*. These bonds do not pay any coupon during their life and return 100 at expiry. In a context of positive interest rates, it follows that the value of the bond is less than 100, giving the investor the opportunity to use the remaining cash to invest in riskier activities. Buying the bond exposes the investor to issuer's risk; here it is assumed that the investor will find an issuer with a suitably high rating to make this risk negligible. As an example, the value of the zero-coupon bond expiring in five years is assumed to be 80, allowing the investor to put the remaining 20, for example, in the equity markets. No matter what the performance of the equity markets will be, if no issuer default occurs the bond will be valued at 100 in five years, thus protecting the original investment.

This strategy presents a number of problems. First of all, the zero-coupon bond market does not offer sufficient liquidity and the investor might have difficulties in finding a suitable issuer and expiry. Furthermore, the level of participation in the equity markets is limited to 20%, which implies that the investor will benefit for only one-fifth of the market performance.

Structurers in investment banks have devised more sophisticated products based on derivatives, which increase the investor's leverage, while continuing to protect the initial capital. The two principal techniques behind these products are presented next.

Option plus bond

Derivatives are financial instruments that link their value to the value of some underlying market variable, such as shares, equity indices, currencies and interest rates. A simple derivative contract is a *call option*, which gives the holder the right to buy some financial asset at a specified price in the future. For example, an investor with a positive view on an equity index valued at 10,000 today purchases a call option to buy the index in five years' time at 10,000. If the index in five years from today is above 10,000, the holder will gain one unit of capital, say, for every point above 10,000. If the index is at 10,000 or below, the holder will lose the full premium paid for the option, as it will be more convenient to buy the index on the market at its current price, rather than exercise the option to buy it at the higher price of 10,000. The cost of the option premium is a fraction of the value of the index. This means that the holder will benefit from the full appreciation of the index despite paying only a fraction of it value. The ratio between the index value today and the value of the premium is the gearing that the investor obtains: if the value of the premium is 2,000 (or 20%), the gear is 5. Leverage is a basic concept that most people experience when buying a house through a mortgage.

Instead of investing the 20 units of capital remaining after buying the bond on the index, the investor can combine the bond with a call option on the same index, assuming that the cost of the option is 20. The difference between the two strategies in terms of performance of the portfolio at expiry is illustrated in Figure 1. Structured bonds and index-linked life policies are constructed following this strategy and are the combination of a bond element (normally not a simple zero-coupon bond, but a coupon bearing bond that includes the fees charged by the structurer, the distributor and the life company in the case of index-linked products) and an option, where this spans from the simple call option to exotic options.

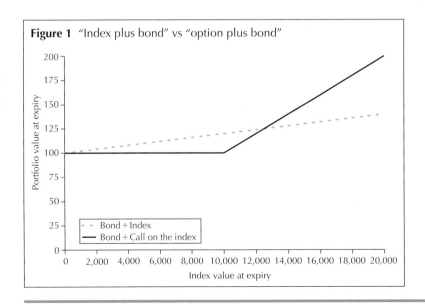

Figure 1 "Index plus bond" vs "option plus bond"

Portfolio value at expiry

Index value at expiry

- - Bond + Index
— Bond + Call on the index

Portfolio insurance techniques

The value of the zero-coupon bond represents the amount of money required to return 100 of capital at a given future date; in the example discussed the cost is 80 units of capital in order to have 100 in five years from today. Provided that the value of the portfolio stays above the zero-coupon level, the investor could, in principle, carry out any type of investment. If the portfolio devalues to a level "too close" in some way to the zero-coupon value, the investor should sell the portfolio and buy the zero-coupon bond. Portfolio insurance is a methodology that lays down the rules for monitoring the risk of the portfolio and deciding when to switch to zero-coupon investments. The portfolio gets fully invested in risky assets from the start and, based on the performance of the assets, further adjustments are made to keep the probability of the downside risk (defined as the probability that the portfolio loses enough to be worth less than the zero-coupon bond) within manageable levels. The final performance of the portfolio does not depend exclusively on the value of the assets at expiry, but also during the life of the product. Therefore the final payoff is said to be path-dependant.

The advantage of this technique is that, if markets have a positive trend, the investor will enjoy 100% participation in the upside. The principal limitation of this technique is that if markets have a sustained negative trend, the portfolio gets converted permanently into zero-coupon bonds, renouncing all future market upside. The recent combination of equity devaluation and interest rate decline (which implies higher zero-coupon levels) has made the possibility of permanent zero-coupon investments a reality for many products of this kind.

PORTFOLIO INSURANCE MODELS

The three main models currently traded on the market are presented, with particular emphasis on multilevel portfolio insurance. All three techniques can be used to design financial products that offer not only capital guarantee but also regular coupons, single coupons at expiry and look-back options.

Constant-proportion portfolio insurance (CPPI)

CPPI is a portfolio balancing technique that aims to maintain the level of risk in the portfolio constant throughout the life of the investment. The value of the portfolio is calculated on a daily basis and compared with the zero-coupon level. The difference between the two values is multiplied by the gear factor (normally between 3 and 4) to determine the amount of risky assets allowed in the portfolio. When the sale of risky assets is required, the risky assets are sold in the same proportion. From the point of view of the structurer selling protection, this is equivalent to selling volatility at a predefined level for the duration of the trade. The mechanism for translating assets from risky ones to zero-coupon bonds is simple and deterministic. The portfolio is always invested in risky assets in the maximum proportion allowed. Normally the product is designed to have a set of rules that include thresholds to avoid continuous rebalancing.

Variable-proportion portfolio insurance (VPPI)
VPPI works in a very similar way to CPPI. The gear value is not fixed for the duration of the trade but is linked to measurable market variables, such as implied volatilities, so as to adjust the levels of risk in case of market turbulence. In all other respects, this technique is analogous to CPPI.

Multilevel portfolio insurance (MLPI)
Both CPPI and VPPI remain invested with the maximum possible level of risky assets at all times, regardless of market conditions. These portfolio insurance techniques have been used primarily with mutual funds as underlying assets, yet no role is given to the money manager as all decisions are taken by simple, predefined rules. MLPI addresses the need to give the money manager room to manoeuvre and take independent asset allocation decisions. MLPI works on the same idea as other portfolio insurance techniques, but adds the possibility of managing money without a set of predetermined rules. It is a risk management tool for protecting investments in asset management products. In normal market conditions it does not interfere with the allocation activities of the manager. However, since the manager can allocate funds without following strict, predetermined rules, the structurer from the investment bank guaranteeing the product requires technology to collect and monitor data on a daily basis.

From the point of view of the investor there are a number of advantages:

❑ high initial leverage;
❑ the benefit of a dynamic investment strategy;
❑ the opportunity to capture the performance of the leading world bond and stock markets;
❑ the possibility of enjoying unlimited potential for profit; and
❑ 100% capital protection plus a minimum profit or look-back option.

From the point of view of the money manager the advantages are:

❑ 100% of the notional is initially invested in funds;
❑ in normal market conditions, unrestrained investment strategies can be traded;
❑ transparent integration with proprietary asset allocation techniques; and
❑ use of real-time calculators to continuously monitor the portfolio performance.

The dynamics of MLPI are based not only on the zero-coupon level, but also on multiple barriers that are influenced by the volatility of the portfolio. Three asset classes are initially identified:

❑ equity-like assets (normally the riskiest asset class);
❑ bond-like assets; and
❑ risk-free (or zero-coupon) assets.

The money manager can rebalance the portfolio between these asset classes freely for as long as no trading signal is generated by the monitoring system. The following quantities are defined:

N is the value of the portfolio;
T is the expiry of the guarantee;
Z is the zero-coupon value of a bond that at T pays 100;
e is the weight of the equity-like assets;
b is the weight of the bondlike assets;
m is the weight of the risk-free assets;
B_L is the low barrier;
B_H is the high barrier.

Initially it is also assumed that:

$$\begin{cases} 0 \le e \le 1 \\ 0 \le b \le 1 \\ 0 \le m \le 1 \\ e + q + m = 1 \end{cases} \quad B_H \ge B_L \ge Z$$

By varying the value of the barriers in response to market events, MLPI ensures that the volatility of the portfolio (and hence its risk) is compatible with the distance between the portfolio value and Z. A possible test is to calculate the value-at-risk of the portfolio and compare it with how much space there is between the current value of the portfolio and the zero-coupon level. In case of adverse market moves that take this distance below "safety" levels, the system generates trading signals that force the portfolio allocation into less volatile assets. The value of the high barrier determines the level at which the first trading signals are generated. The amount by which the portfolio value is below the high barrier determines the severity of the signal. The low barrier represents the level at which the entire portfolio is invested into zero-coupon bonds. The asset allocation in this case would be permanently locked to the following levels:

$$\begin{cases} e = 0 \\ b = 0 \\ m = 1 \end{cases}$$

Figure 2 shows an example of the dynamics of the barriers and the trading signal generation.

As long as the value of the portfolio is above the high barrier, no trading signals are generated and the money manager freely decides the asset allocation.

The value of the low barrier is a function primarily of the zero-coupon level. The value of the high barrier is a function of the low barrier and the volatility of the portfolio. They can be defined as follows:

$$B_L = f(Z, c)$$
$$B_H = f(B_L, \sigma, d)$$

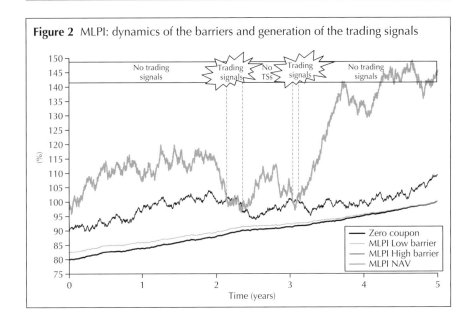

Figure 2 MLPI: dynamics of the barriers and generation of the trading signals

where:

c is the structure of coupons and/or fees embedded in the product;

σ is the portfolio volatility;

d is the execution delay in applying the trading signals.

The implementation of the functions that specify the barriers can vary but it must obey the following relations:

❑ the higher the zero-coupon bond, the higher the barriers;
❑ the higher the coupons/fees embedded in the product, the higher the barriers;
❑ the higher the portfolio volatility, the higher the barriers; and
❑ the higher the execution delay, the higher the barriers.

In other words, the following relations hold with respect to first-order derivatives:

$$\frac{\partial B_L}{\partial Z} > 0$$

$$\frac{\partial B_L}{\partial c} > 0$$

$$\frac{\partial B_H}{\partial B_L} > 0$$

$$\frac{\partial B_H}{\partial \sigma} > 0$$

$$\frac{\partial B_H}{\partial d} > 0$$

RISK MANAGEMENT

The value of the portfolio is modelled using a lognormal variable N specified as follows (for convenience time-dependant subscripts are dropped from all variables):

$$dN = (r - q)N\,dt + \xi N\,dz$$

where:

dN is the differential value of the portfolio;
r is the risk-free rate;
q is the average management fee;
dt is the infinitesimal time-step over which the process is observed;
ξ is the portfolio volatility;
dz is white Gaussian noise.

In order to determine the portfolio volatility, it is necessary to know the volatilities of all assets in the portfolio, their weights and correlations. Defining:

w_i is the weight of the i-th asset;
S_i is the value of the i-th asset;
σ_i is the volatility of the i-th asset;
C is the correlation matrix $\{\rho_{ij}\}$ of all assets;
λ is the difference between N and Z.

It follows that at all times:

$$N = \sum_i w_i S_i$$

$$\xi = \sum_{i,j} \rho_{ij} w_i \sigma_i w_j \sigma_j$$

Defining the weights at time t with W_t, a set of simple rules are defined to modify portfolio weights and hence investments into each asset class:

❑ the weights of the risky assets increase as the value of the portfolio moves away from the value of the zero-coupon bond;
❑ inversely, if market volatilities increase, the weights of the risky assets decrease.

These simple rules are summarised through the following generic function:

$$W_{t+1} = f(N_t, \lambda_t, \xi_t)$$

The value of W_t is used to determine the new portfolio volatility as indicated above and in discrete time Δt (dropping time-dependent subscripts from all variables but N), this is equivalent to:

$$N_{t+1} - N_t = (r-q)N_t\,\Delta t + \xi N_t\,\varepsilon\sqrt{\Delta t}$$

where ε is a Gaussian random variable with zero mean and unit standard deviation. Collecting homogeneous terms, the process is finally written as:

$$N_{t+1} = N_t \times \left[1 + (r-q)\Delta t + \xi\varepsilon\sqrt{\Delta t}\right]$$

This implies that the portfolio volatility ξ depends on the trajectory of value of the portfolio and can be easily calculated within a Monte Carlo simulation of each individual underlying asset. The exact implementation of this function can vary: Figure 3 shows a typical shape of the volatility function. In practice, portfolio insurance products are options with a variable strike (the zero-coupon level) on a portfolio whose volatility tends to zero as the value of the portfolio approaches the strike. The slope of the function between the barriers determines the speed at which the volatility goes to zero and hence the probability of having a sudden jump in the value of the portfolio. The risk parameters should be calibrated to reduce this risk to a minimum.

The equations reported in this section refer to the MLPI technique. This represents a generalisation of CPPI and VPPI and the equations can be readapted to represent these simpler cases.

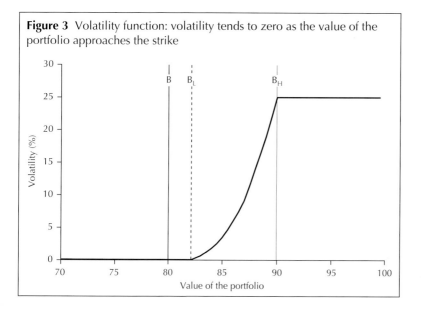

Figure 3 Volatility function: volatility tends to zero as the value of the portfolio approaches the strike

A PRACTICAL EXAMPLE

This section reports a simple example showing a comparison of a classic "option plus bond" capital-guaranteed investment with an investment based on portfolio insurance, in the specific case using MLPI.

It is assumed that in both cases the investment was made at the end of 2001, with 100% capital guarantee in five years, and paying 50 basis points per annum as structuring/management fees. The example illustrates what would be the value of the two investments in May 2004. This is approximately halfway through the life of the product, showing the active role of the dynamic barriers in MLPI.

In the case of option plus bond, the initial 100 units of capital are invested in the following way:

❑ 82 units of capital are invested into a zero-coupon bond that will pay 100 units of capital at the expiry date (five years later);
❑ the remaining 18 units of capital are invested into an at-the-money European call option on the EuroStoxx 50 index with 60% participation into the value of the index.

The asset allocation will not be modified during the life of the product, thus allowing the investor to maintain a guarantee on the full capital invested while participating in the performance of the equity market.

The calculations made for this example are based on historical values for euro interest rates, the EuroStoxx 50 index and its implied volatility.

This example is compared with a real time-series linked to an investment based on MLPI techniques. In this case, initial investments, based on market levels at the time, were split in the following way:

❏ 22 units of capital into a mutual fund investing in European stocks;

❏ 78 units of capital into a mutual fund investing in European bonds.

Using MLPI, the initial asset allocation is subject to potential changes deriving either from the money manager's market view or from trading signals issued by the system monitoring the risk of the investment on a daily basis.

The example revalues the actual asset allocation that the money manager carried out on a daily basis, with the portfolio value calculated summing up the valuations of all the mutual fund in the portfolio. There were a number of instances when the manager was required to reduce exposure as a consequence of trading signals. Figure 4 shows the comparison of the two types of capital guarantee.

As shown in Figure 4, there are cases when the value of the portfolio in the case of the MPLI investment touched the high barrier. This generated trading signals that imposed a modification of the asset allocation by reducing the percentage of risky assets.

Figure 5 shows this mechanism in detail, also displaying the percentage of investment that is allocated to equity assets. As the value of the portfolio crosses the high barrier, the money manager is forced to reduce the percentage of equity investments, from 30% as of May 2002 to 1% three months later, with the value of the index losing substantially. At that point, the value of the portfolio is at some positive distance from the high barrier. This implies that after August 2002 the money manager could, but was not forced to, start to invest again in more risky assets. The distance between the

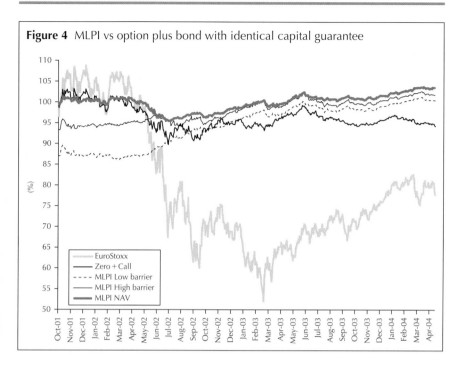

Figure 4 MLPI vs option plus bond with identical capital guarantee

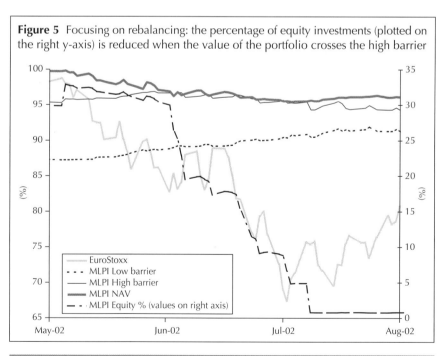

Figure 5 Focusing on rebalancing: the percentage of equity investments (plotted on the right y-axis) is reduced when the value of the portfolio crosses the high barrier

two barriers is not constant but is a function of the volatility of the portfolio: the lower the volatility, the closer the two barriers.

CONCLUSIONS
The existing techniques
Portfolio insurance has been widely used to guarantee investors' capital. Instead of relying on arbitrage and risk-neutral arguments like the Black and Scholes derivation in the world of option pricing, CPPI, VPPI and MLPI adopt insurance-like methodologies that reduce the probability of losses to a minimum. The hedging of these products is not done in the usual way by constructing a replicating portfolio, but the rebalancing mechanisms are trusted to avoid loss situations.

VPPI and MLPI are preferable to CPPI, as in the latter volatility is assumed constant throughout the life of the products and no modification to the risk profile can be carried out in case of market turbulence. Also, MLPI gives the money manager the possibility to disinvest at will, whereas CPPI and VPPI always require the highest level possible of risky assets invested.

Given that these techniques have initial 100% leverage, a substantial quantity of mutual funds will be traded and careful capital management has to be carried out in order to avoid significant capital requirements. MLPI, by allowing the structurer to work with money manager, normally requires the investment bank to buy no funds at all. The capital requirements will simply depend on the guarantee issued.

Finally, because of the initial leverage, the structurer will have to fund the position when issuing a structured bond, as the sale proceeds will be used to fund the issuer of the bond.

Future developments
The main limitation of portfolio insurance techniques is the inability to recover from a substantial market crash. If the portfolio is invested in zero-coupon bonds, this asset allocation remains constant to expiry and subsequent market rallies would be missed. New hybrid products combine the powerful concepts behind derivatives with the flexibility and dynamic management of portfolio insurance. By introducing elements of optionality in the portfolio insurance domain, it is possible to construct products that can guarantee a

minimum investment in risky assets, avoiding the case of permanent zero-coupon investments.

These products define an index as the weighted sum of an active basket and a theoretical zero-coupon bond. At time t, let:

$$I_t = w_t A_t + (1 - w_t)Z_t$$

where:

A_t is the value of the active basket;
w_t is the weight of the active basket;
Z_t is the value of the theoretical zero coupon.

Assume that the initial value I_0 is 100%. An option is issued that at expiry pays a coupon equal to:

$$\max(I_T - I_0, 0)$$

The weight of the active basket is modified daily following a rebalancing algorithm that has the following constraints:

❏ the value of w_t must be between a minimum (w_{min}) and a maximum level (w_{max});
❏ the value of w_{min} is greater than zero, therefore there will always be a part of the active basket represented in the index, regardless of the market performance;
❏ a theoretical zero-coupon bond is used, which accrues linearly on a daily basis; this has the advantage of being easily determined, making calculations simpler than in the case of traditional portfolio insurance;
❏ interest rate risk is removed because the theoretical zero-coupon bond is deterministic;
❏ the weight of the active basket increases as the value of the basket drops and decreases if the active basket gains; and
❏ the value of w_{max} can be greater than 100%.

Through this technique the investor has a simple product that benefits from dynamic rebalancing and at the same time overcomes the problem of permanent zero-coupon investments.

5

*Wrappers for Structured Products**

Robert Addison

Bespoke Financial Consulting

By their very nature structured products are made up of a number of different components. In order to be delivered to the end client in an appropriate manner, these elements need to be packaged together in a suitable wrapper. The choice of wrapper must take into account a number of different issues such as the feasibility of holding the underlying investments to the capacity of the end investor to hold such wrappers.

INTRODUCTION

For institutional clients such as investment banks, more concerned about receiving a gross payoff, this may be done using standardised over-the-counter (OTC) agreements such as those issued by the International Swaps and Derivatives Association (ISDA), while for retail investors this is likely to be in a more client-friendly form that is covered by greater regulatory protection or certain tax advantages. These agreements, or wrappers, come in a number of formats and this chapter is designed to provide a brief overview of each of the different forms of wrapper, discussing their suitability for different clients and comparing their advantages and disadvantages.

A brief history of wrappers in the UK for structured retail products

While many wrappers such as deposits have been around for a long time it was only in the early 1990s with the rise in retail

*This chapter was designed as a short practitioner's guide to wrapping structured products, highlighting some of the key features, benefits and disadvantages of some of the more common wrappers. It should not be considered as a comprehensive authority, and structured-product providers should consult a suitably qualified professional for specific advice on a particular wrapper.

structured products for the mass market that they became important as a delivery mechanism for nontraditional payoffs. It is fair to
say that structured products have now been offered in virtually
every kind of wrapper that has been made available. The main
driver has been down to innovation and a changing regulatory
climate allowing the introduction of new wrappers or amending
existing rules to strengthen or weaken the ability of existing wrappers to hold a structured product.

In the early 1990s the UK retail structured-products market was
dominated by the life companies, whose natural wrapper was the
life policy. However, this choice of wrapper has declined over the
years as others have been developed. The decline of the life policy
wrapper can be put down to a number of factors such as the unattractive headline rates (which had to be shown net of the basic rate
of tax paid by the life company and can't be reclaimed), increasingly
stringent regulation of life assurers and the tightening of the tax
regulations that made it difficult to structure or deliver a product
tax efficiently. This, together with the emergence of new regulations, markets and distribution channels, has led to structured-
product providers turning to alternative wrappers to deliver their
products.

In the past, the investment banks concentrated on offering product
payoff ideas to their clients in the hope of providing the underlying
derivative to them. The client would then use their own wrapper
solution and systems to offer this product to a wider retail audience.
However, more recently, the investment banks have begun to offer
a packaged solution, which includes both the underlying derivatives
and the wrapper.

There have been a number of reasons for doing this:

❏ a greater potential market for offering the product. Alternative
methods of distribution were found and created, meaning that
anyone with distribution could now also offer structured
products.
❏ financial ideas rarely retain their proprietary nature for long. By
having the ability to offer a complete package directly to the
market products could be launched very quickly without having
to wait for a third-party provider to have the product internally
vetted and approved.

❑ it maximises flexibility in that it allows providers and distributors access to a product range for which they don't have a wrapper.

❑ it retains some of the proprietary nature of the product and allows banks to reap higher rewards from offering the complete package benefiting from economies of scale and the opaque nature of the running costs of the wrapper. The growth of the outsourcing market for financial administration services has helped to make this possible.

THE WRAPPERS

We turn now to look specifically at some of the individual wrappers that have been used to offer structured products.

OTC agreements

In its basic form a wrapper is purely an agreement between two or more parties. For derivatives this might take the form of a highly standardised but limited set of contracts such as those traded on a regulated derivative exchange such as Eurex or the London Financial Futures and Options Exchange. However, for structured products, such derivative products need to be highly tailored to suit the individual needs of the counterparties. While these agreements can be drawn up on a bespoke basis, this is not conducive to the high-volume trading seen today and there is plenty of scope for disagreement, and hence basis risk, on the finer points of a trade (for example, in the case of a market disruption event or corporate action). So over the years an OTC standard has been put in place by an association of market participants called ISDA. Originally called the International Swap Dealers' Association (as the first series of products it covered were interest rate swaps), it has now changed its name to the International Swaps and Derivatives Association to reflect the diverse nature of the underlying assets that its members deal in. Over the years ISDA agreements have evolved to encompass interest rates, currencies, equity, commodity, energy and credit derivative products.[1]

The beauty of an OTC agreement is that it is flexible enough to encompass almost any transaction that the parties wish to consider, including most structured-product payoffs and underlying markets, as it provides the legal framework around which a commercial agreement is structured. As each market gains popularity, a standard framework is established and common definitions are agreed to minimise both the paperwork to confirm each trade and disputes over market practice. The other advantage about using an ISDA agreement is that, subject to local laws, it has the ability to net off trades and a facility to place margin using a Collateral Support Annex (CSA) incorporated within the original agreement. This has been a great aid to the interbank market as a tool for minimising credit risk and the efficient use of regulatory capital.

However, such agreements can be highly complex and, despite the ISDA framework, each one tends to be individually negotiated between the two counterparties. The agreements incorporate references to standards and definitions that are contained within separate booklets. This means that such OTC agreements are left to the interbank market, trades with corporate entities and sophisticated purchasers of hedges for structured products.

OTC agreements may also be suitable for a high-net-worth individual contemplating a substantial investment and with the means to consult independent legal advice, but the complex nature of these agreements and the legal language behind them make these agreements considered unsuitable as a wrapper for broad distribution and certainly not for retail offerings. However, their most common use outside the interbank market is by product distributors to purchase a hedge to place inside their own wrapper.

Deposits

The structured deposit was the retail banks' response to the life companies' push into the capital-protected investment market and an attempt to produce a higher-margin product when compared with interest-rate deposits. The advantage of the deposit as a wrapper is that it is simple to understand. In the UK it does not require a regulated sales force to distribute it and has a high level of regulatory protection in the form of the Financial Services Compensation Scheme.[2]

Unfortunately, it does limit the type of products that can be wrapped using a deposit to capital-protected products. However, this is no bad thing, as unprotected products have taken a battering as misselling claims have arisen during the market downturn in the early part of the new century. In addition, the majority of the retail investor base is likely to be unsophisticated and probably investing in structured products for the first time. This, combined with the fact that these products tend to be sold without advice, means that it is highly unlikely that the institutions offering these products would want to offer unprotected products in the first place.

It also requires a banking licence, which in the past has excluded a number of potential issuers from offering this product. However, with the advent of the concept of "white labelling", any product distributor or brand name with distribution power can offer such products through its network, with a bank standing behind the product offering the deposit. This means that, with clear marketing material and the appropriate authorisations, anyone with a brand name (and not necessarily one so readily connected with offering retail financial services) can provide distribution.

Bond offerings

A bond is an instrument that creates or acknowledges indebtedness. Bonds also tend to be capable of being a transferable security. In other words, unlike the case with deposits and OTC agreements, title to the bond can be transferred without the consent of the issuer. As with shares, this means that a holder of the notes has the ability to sell its holdings to another party for an agreed price. This is no guarantee of liquidity, though, and any structured-product provider considering this route should ensure that such a mechanism for sales during the life of the note and an appropriate bid–offer spread are agreed in writing with a market maker.

Most banks and financial institutions now have a debt pro-gramme in place comprising an Offering Memorandum outlining all the general terms of the programme and a pricing supplement for the specific commercial details of each debt issue. This is a very cheap and efficient way of issuing debt and as such has been the next stage in offering structured products to the wider market.

When one is considering a bond offering, thought must be given to the end purchasers of the note. For the purposes of prospectuses and offering documents, the UK distinguishes between sophisticated and professional investors with minimum investments equivalent to €40,000 and the general public for whom a much greater amount of information needs to be disclosed.

For listed bond offerings the exchange on which the bond is listed will also have rules that require a certain minimum amount of information to be provided in the prospectus regardless of the type of investor. For instance, for a product payoff linked to an equity index the exchange may require a definition of the index together with an overview of its construction methodology and some historical data on how the index has performed.

For direct bond offerings to the general public the prospectus has to comply with the Public Offers of Securities (POS) Regulations (Statutory Instrument 1537, 1995). This imposes a much heavier burden of disclosure on the issuer in the form of a full prospectus, with, among other requirements, full financial accounts for the last three years and a signed statement of responsibility for the information included by the directors of the company. This increased requirement means that it can be expensive and time-consuming to use this wrapper to offer structured products to the retail market, but, to their credit, a number of issuers have successfully launched products via this route, seeing it as the only way to provide the appropriate level of information on the nature of the investment to allow individual investors and their advisers to make an informed investment decision.

It is also important to note that, while interest and coupon payments from bonds are usually made gross between market participants and institutional investors through a settlement system such as Euroclear or Clearstream, this may not be the case for retail investors who rely on a third party to act as custodian for the bond. In some instances the custodian may be determined to be a UK collecting agent and thus may be obliged to withhold tax at the basic rate before passing the coupon on to the end investor.

Bond or investment "plans"

The alternative to issuing a fully POS-compliant bond is to offer a bond plan to retail investors. Like a mutual fund, the plan has investment objectives and a professional investment manager who selects an appropriate asset that will meet those objectives. It can best be described as a limited discretionary management agreement.

As the plan manager acts in the capacity of a professional investor, the bond issuer can rely on the simpler regulations for bond prospectuses for qualified investors. It does, however, mean an opaque structure for the end investor. While the structured-product payoff can be explained fully in the investment objectives, the plan manager is not allowed to name a specific bond issuer without falling foul of the POS regulations. The manager can, however, state the type of issuer that they are seeking to select (for example, a UK financial institution) and a minimum credit rating of the issuer (usually a Moody's or Standard & Poor's rating). The investor is therefore placing a heavy reliance on the ability of the plan manager to select both an issuer of an appropriate credit quality and in determining the tax and legal robustness of the underlying structures.

Offshore mutual funds

As with OTC agreements, the main driver behind offshore funds is to allow greater freedom for the fund manager in terms of taxation and asset allocation. Thus many hedge funds have set up in territories such as the Cayman Islands and British Virgin Islands. Closer to home, other popular offshore fund domiciles include the Isle of Man and the Channel Islands. Their being offshore does not mean that these places are devoid of regulations. Indeed, strict money-laundering regulations in the key financial centres of the world mean that the procedures for setting up companies and checking on directors and new investors offshore can be stricter than in some OECD countries, requiring additional information on the source of wealth and source of funds for particular investments.

The minimum investment in a Cayman Islands mutual fund is CI$40,000 (approximately US$50,000). They do tend to have a number of distinct advantages, the first being a low-taxation or tax-free environment, allowing gross roll-up of investments and no withholding tax, and the second being complete freedom of investment, subject to a suitable prospectus being issued and maintained.

The non-tax status is important for non-tax-paying and offshore investors who may not be able to recover taxes withheld in other jurisdictions. Taxation for onshore UK taxpayers depends on whether the fund has distributor status in the UK. While the rules changed in the 2004 budget (Inland Revenue, 2004), basically they determine whether a fund behaves like an onshore UK fund in terms of regulation and distribution of income. If it meets these requirements, then it may be treated like an onshore fund for tax purposes. If not, then any gains made in the value of fund units at realisation are treated to income tax at the investors' marginal rate of tax.

Experienced-investor funds

Recently, a number of jurisdictions more familiar to the UK investor have attempted to recapture market share from other offshore havens by introducing a new breed of fund that bridges the gap between their own existing regulations for retail funds and those territories offering no restrictions on investment activity. These are generally called experienced- or professional-investor funds.

The Isle of Man regime exempts funds from the regulatory requirements of the Isle of Man Financial Supervision Act provided that they are administered in the Isle of Man.[3] This can be done by obtaining an investment business licence to act as a licensed fund manager or outsourced to a licensed fund administrator. The fund can be incorporated in any suitable jurisdiction and the regulations are flexible on the legal form of the entity, allowing for closed companies, open-ended funds or limited partnerships. A simple offering document is required rather than a full prospectus. The burden is on the licensed manager or administrator to be satisfied that any person investing in the fund is sufficiently experienced to understand the risks associated with an investment in the experienced-investor fund. The fund is also capable of being exempt from Isle of Man taxes.

February 2004 saw the launch of Jersey Expert Funds (Collective Investment Funds (Jersey) Law, 1988). Again, as on the Isle of Man, the fund has a lighter regulatory touch, provided that investors meet certain criteria such as a minimum investment of US$100,000 in the fund, minimum net assets (excluding the main place of residence) of US$1 million or that they can demonstrate that their ordinary business is dealing in or advising on investments. There are no restrictions on investments or diversification within the fund, but the investment manager must, among other things, be regulated within an OECD member state or approved by the Jersey Financial Services Commission and have relevant experience in managing or advising on investments and strategies similar to those contemplated in the expert fund. Again, as on the Isle of Man, the administration of the fund must be carried out by a Jersey-based and regulated provider.

Closed-end company structures and special-purpose vehicles

One of the key drivers to using a closed-end company structure is tax. In the UK, equities have been clearly established as being taxed to capital gains for individual investors, and hence any structured product wrapped within such a vehicle also attracts the same tax treatment. By purchasing a share, the retail investor can take advantage of their annual tax-exempt allowance and taper relief, and can use the maximum Individual Savings Account (ISA) allowance to shelter the investment from tax (see "Tax wrappers" below). This makes it a very tax-efficient wrapper for retail investors.

Creating the company onshore in the UK tends not to be tax-efficient, as there is a double tax hit on both the company's activities and then on the income and gains made by investors. One of the exceptions to this is if the company can obtain investment trust status from the Inland Revenue.[4] This status allows the company to purchase and dispose of investments without being taxed to capital gains tax on those disposals, thus avoiding this double taxation hit for investors. However, the regulations required to achieve this status are drawn tightly, making it difficult to offer a single structured-product payoff.

The alternative, as for mutual fund structures, is to turn to the offshore market, where the jurisdiction does not seek to tax the assets and activities of the fund. While this market has been well established for the investment trust industry, it was only in the late 1990s that the structured-products market began to realise the significance of using an offshore special-purpose vehicle (SPV) structure for structured products.

Offshore companies

Again, as with offshore funds, there are now a number of jurisdictions to choose from in deciding a jurisdiction for an offshore company, and any potential product provider needs to look at the specific rules of the regulator in each regime. They may look similar but they are not all the same. For instance, protected cell companies (PCCs)[5] are a feature found in Guernsey legislation that minimises the costs of setting up additional companies, but they are not available in its close neighbour Jersey. Similarly, company rules on the type of investments and the spread of credit risks may apply in Dublin and the Channel Islands, whereas the Cayman Islands have a less restrictive regime. This freedom from investment restrictions then has to be balanced against the tax treatment and regulatory requirements to be able to offer the structured product in the country of distribution, and the perception of the jurisdiction in the eyes of potential investors. Further enhancements outside of the wrapper, such as a listing, may help to overcome some of these issues.

While many structured products using this wrapper have a natural exit point at maturity, investors seeking to exit the product earlier have to turn to the secondary market to realise their investment. While the notion of having a market maker and a liquid market is common and expected in the investment trust industry, it has been ignored for most UK structured products with little or no developed secondary market. Some providers have ensured good practice by ensuring that market makers are in place for the shares, but their specialist nature often means that the secondary market does not attract buyers, which can lead the shares to trade at a substantial discount to net asset value. This problem is also common in the investment trust market and has been tackled through various liquidity facilities such as company-initiated buyback programmes, something that to date has not been attempted by the structured-products market.

Onshore mutual funds

The majority of jurisdictions have a regulated regime for onshore mutual funds, be they unit trusts in the UK, Fond Commun de Placements (FCPs) in France or Société d'investissement à capital variable (SICAV) in Luxembourg.

Each regime has its own regulations, which were created prior to the take-off in the structured-products market and so tended to focus on traditional fund management assets and tend to have restrictive rules on the use of derivatives. This meant that it was very difficult (but not impossible) to offer structured products using those wrappers. They were also very difficult to sell in other jurisdictions, meaning that a product provider usually had to double up on costs by launching another identical fund in each jurisdiction that it marketed to.

The UK originally started off with the unit trust structure that used a trustee to hold the assets on behalf of the individual beneficial owners. The current regime for Open-Ended Investment Companies (OEICs) retains the use of unit trusts but now also allows the use of Investment Companies with Variable Capital (ICVCs).

Both structures could use derivatives in a limited manner provided that they were used for efficient portfolio management as defined in the regulations. In practice, this confined the use of derivatives to simple covered options and forwards. While this did allow some protected products to come to the market, the rules were not flexible enough to allow the majority of structured products to be considered in such a wrapper.

The introduction by the European Union (EU) of legislation known as Undertakings in Collective Investments in Transferable Securities (UCITS)[6] and in particular UCITS III[7] was an attempt to harmonise the rules on collective schemes across Europe. The idea was to make it possible to offer or "passport" a mutual fund that complied with these rules and had been approved by one EU member regulator in all other member states without the need to seek the approval of the host state.

The other major change introduced by UCITS III was an acknowledgement of the increasing importance of the use of derivatives within a fund environment. The rules for UCITS funds no longer had to comply with efficient portfolio management, giving greater scope for the use of alternative derivatives provided certain other measures were complied with, including the introduction of an appropriate risk management system to monitor derivative exposure.

These two key factors have potentially provided a great boost to the market for structured retail products. For the first time investors can obtain structured products within the same secure regulatory environment as all other onshore mutual funds. The regulations allow for pre-approval by the Financial Services Authority (FSA), transparency and price publication, and for trading to be carried out at net asset value at least once a fortnight.

The other major benefit is that structured products can now benefit from the same tax regime in the UK as onshore mutual funds, in that a gain or loss in units in the hands of the investor is treated as a capital gain rather than income. Most structured-product wrappers have a specific maturity date, which automatically crystallises a taxable event for the investor, but the OEIC is capable of rolling over into a new product within the same wrapper, thus delaying such taxable events.

At the time of writing, only a handful of structured products have been approved in the UK using this wrapper and, while the area is an exciting one in terms of new developments and the potential for innovation, it remains to be seen whether the investment banks and the fund management community will embrace this wrapper.

Qualified investor schemes (QISs)

Outside of the UCITS regime the FSA has realised that its mutual fund regulations allow little scope for investments in alternative assets and structures for the sophisticated investors such as professionals and institutional investors, and this has been clearly demonstrated by the prolific growth in offshore funds. In an attempt to maintain an innovative regulatory environment the FSA issued a consultation paper in 2003 the result of which was the introduction of QISs in the UK for promotion to those two types of investor (Financial Services Authority).

These funds will allow greater flexibility on the type of investments that can be held onshore, including property, precious metals and commodity contracts. The spread of risk and concentration is not specifically regulated but must be stated in the fund documents. The fund will also have the ability to gear up by borrowing up to 100% of its net asset value and be able to short-sell subject to providing appropriate global cover. QISs also have greater flexibility on controlling the issuance of units and limiting or deferring redemptions.

While the regulatory framework is now in place, no advice or ruling has been given by the Inland Revenue on the taxation of these structures to date. They are also unique to the UK and will not be able to take advantage of the UCITS passport rules into Europe. The real question is whether this new onshore regime is going to be flexible enough for product providers. If this is not the case, then the offshore market will remain the wrapper of choice for such offerings.

Listing

As shown above, an onshore UK fund is backed up by an extensive regulatory regime. While many structures use the offshore wrappers to give them the freedom on their investment activities, providers are also prepared to offer a higher level of comfort and disclosure to investors than required. In order to strengthen the regulatory environment of an offshore fund or company, some are able to seek and obtain a listing on an appropriate stock exchange.

Many investors confuse listing with conferring transferability or liquidity to an asset. While this may be a consequence of listing, its main purpose is to confirm acceptance by the asset manager, invest-ment adviser or product provider of a regulatory framework to which it must adhere. The provision of an appropriate level of pro-tection provides confidence to investors by providing certain min-imum standards of disclosure and conduct of affairs by issuers.

In other cases, the process of listing also allows the underlying fund or company to be considered for inclusion in a certain tax wrap-per such as an ISA (see below), or increases the appeal of a wrapper for certain investors and onshore regulated wrappers that are restricted by law or incorporation from purchasing unlisted or non-regulated investments. In the UK recognition of an exchange by the Inland Revenue and FSA confers many of these privileges. This list of recognised exchanges grows each year as new exchanges are created or existing exchanges enhance their regulations. For instance, the Inland Revenue recognised the Channel Islands Stock Exchange in December 2002 and the Cayman Islands Stock Exchange in March 2004, while the FSA recognised the Channel Islands Stock Exchange in February 2004 (Cayman Islands Stock Exchange, 2004).

The choice of exchanges is vast, but the common exchanges used for UK products tend to be the London Stock Exchange, with its more stringent rules,[8] for major product issuances, and Dublin and the Channel Islands, which are popular for smaller UK retail struc-tured products. Many European securitised products, such as war-rants and bonds linked to structured payoffs, tend to be listed where there is retail demand. A German warrant, for example, may be listed on both the primary exchange in Frankfurt and on a num-ber of other regional exchanges. The London Stock Exchange has joined the foray with its own specialised market for covered war-rants, certificates and other specialist products.[9]

As explained above, each exchange has its own rules and require-ments, so a balance needs to be made between the importance and benefits of listing on a particular exchange versus the costs of listing on that exchange. For instance, in the case of UK retail structured products, the listing may purely be a means to allow the investment to be held in an ISA rather than any perceived regulatory benefit from disclosure. The product provider may therefore be more likely to choose an exchange where the listing is a simpler and a quicker process and use the savings to offer a better payoff for investors.

Tax wrappers

Like "plans", the tax wrapper in itself is not a product offering but a regulatory environment created by legislation in which certain investments can be held in a tax-efficient manner.

While such retail client tax breaks do exist around the world, it is fair to say that the UK retail market has flourished as a result of these allowances.

For retail investors these come in the form of Individual Savings Accounts (ISAs) and formerly Personal Equity Plans (PEPs), Tax-Exempt Special Savings Accounts (TESSAs) and their successor the TOISA (TESSA-Only ISA). The other key tax wrapper is the pensions market with Self-Investment Pension Plans (SIPPs) and Small Self-Administered Pension Schemes (SSASs) being the two key schemes that might invest in structured products.

The key difference between the two is that investments in ISAs are made out of post-tax income, whereas pension investments can reclaim income tax paid on the invested amount. All returns on investments within both of these wrappers can roll up tax-free on a gross basis but any income taken out of the pension at retirement is then subject to income tax at the investor's marginal rate.

Almost all onshore wrappers are capable of being held within an ISA, but with different limits on the amount that can be invested. Closed-end companies and bonds with a term of over five years are most efficient in that they currently qualify for the full maxi ISA allowance of up to £7,000, cash deposits £3,000 and life policies £1,000.

New ISA rules have recently been introduced by the Inland Revenue on OEICs. In general terms, if it is possible to lose more than 5% of your investment in the five years from the investment date, then you can use your stocks-and-shares ISA or full maxi ISA allowance. This means that protected products with a term of greater than five years or protection of 95% or less should qualify for the full maxi ISA allowance. The Inland Revenue have a facility to pre-clear whether such investments qualify for investment in an ISA.

SELECTING THE APPROPRIATE WRAPPER

The increasing sophistication of product providers in structuring assets, together with the need to service different client segments, means that it is now possible and important to be able to offer a number of different wrappers around the same product payoff.

As can be seen from the discussion on specific wrappers, the final choice can often be a compromise between wrappers that allow flexible investment and those that offer the most regulatory protection. Regulatory protection for sophisticated and institutional investors may not be as important as a cost-efficient investment proposal, whereas the retail investor may require a greater level of protection at the expense of a higher cost.

The importance for the product provider is to issue the product in a wrapper that will maximise sales to the target market and at the same time minimise the potential reputational risk to the business model should the expected investment returns not be met for any reason.

Regulatory authorisation

Advisers are aware of the general high standards of authorisation for structured products issued in the UK. However, care needs to be taken to determine the specific issuer and its domicile and not to rely on the brand name that might accompany the product.

Closed-end companies are usually situated offshore, and so only the promotion and marketing of the product in the UK is governed by the FSA. The adviser should look to the quality of the local regulator or listing authority for comfort. This can usually be found in the main prospectus (as opposed to the mini prospectus that is usually sent out) or on the regulator's website.

For a UK OEIC, the prospectus and key-features document have to be authorised and approved by the FSA prior to issue, whereas for most other onshore wrappers no pre-clearance is required. The onshore regulated nature of the fund means that it has a statutory obligation to abide by the FSA's sourcebook for collective investment schemes. This means that many of the benefits of the product are there by way of statute rather than a benefit offered by the fund. In addition, the fund benefits from an authorised corporate director and an independent depository and custodian to ensure that the fund objectives are being met, the rules are being followed and the assets are secured.

Onshore deposit takers and life companies are also governed by the FSA and have certain rules on regulatory capital or asset diversification to comply with (see "Quality of investor protection" below). It should be noted that, while a plan manager is authorised by the FSA, the underlying bond issuer within the plan may not be.

The Financial Services Compensation Scheme offers some limited protection for closed-end companies and OEICs but this arises out of poor investment management (not to be confused with poor returns) or if an authorised investment firm goes out of business and cannot return your investments. It does not protect you against the credit quality of the assets underlying these wrappers.

Quality of investor protection

The product payoff profile is only as good as the assets that back that promise. Below is a brief examination of the basic principles in determining the quality of those promises.

Bond and deposit account wrappers give the investor 100% credit risk to the issuer, and this promise is backed by the net assets of that company. The Financial Services Compensation Scheme provides regulatory protection to onshore UK-regulated deposits, but this does have an upper limit. If there is no early exit mechanism from the product, then the investor should be satisfied that the quality is such to last the full term of the product. Note that offshore deposits may not be covered by the scheme even if they are a subsidiary of a UK bank or building society, and one should always check the specific entity offering the deposit to see if it is covered by the scheme, even if the brand name is well known. Many regulators such as the FSA now provide a comprehensive list of such banks covered by their deposit protection schemes.

Most bond products are sold via a plan manager and it is not immediately possible to see who the underlying issuer is. However, typically, the plan states that it will invest in an issuer with a certain credit rating. These are an independent analysis on the financial strength of issuers provided by companies such as Moody's and Standard & Poor's. Each rating agency has its own scoring system but in broad terms an "AAA" rating is considered to be the best risk (equivalent to UK government risk), "AA" being equivalent to a good, top, high street bank name and "A" a smaller but well-known building society. At the first opportunity the investor should establish who the issuer is (it can usually be found in the six-monthly report and accounts) and should monitor the credit quality of the company over the life of the bond. In the event of default, the investor is generally an ordinary creditor of the bond issuer. However, it is important to note that this is not always the case, and the difference can be critical. For instance, the bond could be subordinated, meaning that investors are paid out only after all other ordinary creditors. Alternatively, the bond could be asset-backed, meaning that payment from the bond depends on the performance of a specific pool of ring-fenced assets. This can be considered as good where the quality of the assets compares favourably with the strength of the company, but could be detrimental in that investors have no claim over other assets of the issuer. The investor should satisfy themselves as to the quality and diversification of those assets and whether they are collateralised or not.

In certain jurisdictions, closed-end companies have to abide by certain rules on the spread of risk as laid down by the local regulator of the domicile of the company. Typically, exposure to an individual bond issuer is capped at 20% of the company's net asset value. This rises to 30% for any derivative purchased by the company, whereas an onshore OEIC is allowed a maximum derivative exposure of only 10%, and this must be with an approved bank. This has to be monitored on a daily basis in the OEIC structure, whereas other jurisdictions allow this check to be done on a monthly basis. While the rules for other assets within the OEIC structure are more complex, they tend to require more diversification than offshore companies. Additionally, a check should be made to see that the assets are held properly by a suitable custodian, and are fully "ring-fenced" from other subfunds. Both structures are capable of being able to change the derivatives provider if at any time they decide that the credit quality of the provider has deteriorated to such an extent that it may be unable to meet its commitments.

Ongoing monitoring

Most structured products are investments made for the long term and should be considered as such. However, many advisers have an ongoing duty to monitor the performance of each investment and should consider the potential early exit mechanism of the product where the investor's changing circumstances or outlook of market conditions means that this might be required.

The investor may be locked into the product for the full term for some wrappers, such as deposits. For others there is no clearly defined or regulated exit mechanism. For bonds and life policies, a surrender price tends to be available, but this may have little bearing on the value of the underlying investment and is at the behest of the product provider. Retail investors may be penalised for unwinding their relatively small investment in the wholesale market and there is no requirement to publish a price on a regular basis.

With closed-end investment companies the investor has to find a buyer or market maker to sell their shares. As the market for those shares is invariably illiquid, shares may at times be sold only on a matched basis or potentially at a substantial discount to net asset value.

For onshore UK OEICs, a valuation based on net asset value must be given at least once a fortnight and the investor must have the ability to exit at that price. In addition, the OEIC's price must be published in an appropriate manner such as in a national newspaper, allowing investor to easily check up on the performance of their investment. Also, the fund must be able to verify the pricing of any OTC derivatives that it uses. Again, this is not just a service provided by the fund but a regulatory requirement.

Tax

Each product wrapper has its own tax treatment for the investor. For the offshore or tax-exempt investor it's important that the structured product wrapper itself should not suffer tax as they are unlikely to be able to recoup it.

For the individual UK investor a product that attracts capital gains and maximises the tax-free allowances, such as an ISA, is preferable to products that attract income tax. Consideration should also be given to products that at maturity provide the opportunity to benefit from a roll-up of capital gains.

It is also important to understand how the product is constructed to deliver the expected tax treatment to the end investor and the likelihood that that might be attacked or changed by the

Inland Revenue. Sophisticated investors who have the ability to take independent specialist advice are much better placed to take this decision than the retail public.

THE FUTURE

The changing tax, legal and regulatory framework in the UK and the rest of the world together with the innovative nature of the financial services industry means that new products and wrappers will be forthcoming in the future. Below, we examine two wrappers that the industry will exploit further in the near future.

Collateralised debt obligations (CDOs) and investment trusts

At the time of writing, the main UK regulator, the FSA, was in the process of agreeing a compensation package for misselling claims with the key parties involved in issuing Split Capital Investment Trusts. At the same time, CDOs have been moving to the fore of the institutional and high-net-worth market. The substance of these two products is essentially the same in that each has a number of different share classes with different payoff profiles and order of priority for investors. Those at the top of the priority (typically zero-coupon-preference shareholders in investment trusts and AAA-rated tranches in CDOs) have lower fixed returns but a greater level of security, while those at the lower end (typically the capital shareholders in the investment trust and the equity portion in CDOs) are paid out last but have the potential for a greater return through the gearing effect on the upside over and above the fixed returns to higher-ranked shareholders.

The use of alternative underlyings such as synthetic credit programmes or hedge funds, the targeting of different client segments and the use of rating agencies to assist in quantifying the investment risk in an objective manner have allowed the investment trust market to continue by another means.

The geared nature of the equity portion of the CDO will also allow product issuers to structure new products on underlyings that could not be hedged using the traditional options market.

Property investment funds (PIFs)

In April 2003 the UK Chancellor of the Exchequer asked Kate Barker, a member of the Bank of England's Monetary Policy Committee, to undertake a review on the responsiveness of housing supply in the UK. Her interim report[10] recommended that there was merit in considering a vehicle, similar to US Real Estate Investment Trusts, to encourage increased investment in property to increase the supply of housing in the UK.

A consultation paper has been issued on the design of such a vehicle[11] and one of the key aims is to align the taxation of this vehicle with those of holding property directly, such that it allows all the benefits of a pooled investment with those of holding property without any tax distortion between the PIF and a direct holding. If structured correctly, this vehicle can be used as a very efficient wrapper to supply a diversified property exposure into the structured-product arena.

CONCLUSION

It is clear from the above discussion that the structured product provider has a number of choices in deciding on how to present their product to clients. The final decision on the wrapper depends on a number of key factors. Some of the unique features of the UK market such as tax free investment allowances in certain conditions make the choice of wrapper even more crucial than perhaps might be the case in the rest of Europe. Individual legislation means that different wrappers provide the optimal result in each European state. However, the implementation of European legislation on funds (and maybe in the future other wrappers) has started to create a level playing field for providers and minimised the cost of cross border marketing of these products. This will further influence the choice of wrapper for issuers as EU integration continues.

1   See www.isda.org for more information.
2   Financial Services & Markets Act 2000. See www.fscs.org.uk for more information.
3   Financial Supervision (International Schemes) Regulations 1990.
4   Section 842 Income and Corporation Taxes Act 1988.
5   Guernsey Statutory Instrument: The Protected Cell Companies (Special Purpose Vehicle) Regulations, 2001.
6   Council Directive of 20 December 1985 on the coordination of laws, regulations and administrative provisions relating to undertakings for collective investment in transferable securities (UCITS) (85/611/EEC).
7   Directive 2001/108/EC of the European Parliament and of the Council dated 21 January 2002.
8   For further information on listing in London see www.fsa.gov.uk/ukla

9 See www.londonstockexchange.com/coveredwarrants

10 "A review of housing supply: Securing our future housing needs" (Interim Report), December 2003.

11 "Promoting more flexible investment in property: a consultation", March 2004.

REFERENCES

Cayman Islands Stock Exchange, press release 4 March 2004, and Section 841 Income and Corporation Taxes Act 1988 as amended.

Channel Islands Stock Exchange, press release 5 January 2004 and Section 841 of the Income and Corporation Taxes Act, 1988.

Collective Investment Funds (Jersey) Law, 1988, and Jersey Financial Services Commission: Jersey Expert Fund Guide, February 2004.

Financial Services Authority, The New Collective Investment Schemes Sourcebook.

Inland Revenue 2004 Budget, press release 17 March 2004, reference REV BN 26.

Statutory Instrument 1995 No. 1537, The Public Offers of Securities Regulations 1995.

6

Internal Asset Allocation and Currency Management for Discretionary Portfolios

Andreas Homberger

UBS

For private client portfolios a professional currency management is much more difficult than for institutional investors. The portfolios often are too small to use sophisticated and cheap currency management instruments such as futures, swaps or forwards. In addition, private investors are much less educated than institutional investors. This leads to a lot of questions to the portfolio manager with regard to currency instruments from the clients such as:

❏ why do you hold an instrument that generates losses very often?
❏ what is the instrument good for?
❏ why do you hold foreign assets at all?
❏ what does currency hedging actually mean?

INTRODUCTION*

This chapter tries to answer these and additional questions in a condensed way. In the next section, we first look briefly at the most important results from the theory on international asset allocation and the role of currencies within this framework. We then turn the attention to the relation between home bias and currency hedging. The final part of that section shows a brief asset allocation study, which illustrates the impact of the ability to hedge currencies on

*The opinions in this chapter are those of the author and do not represent the view of UBS AG.

the optimal asset allocation. In the following section, we take a closer look at empirical properties of currencies and their impact on the risk of various asset classes. In the section that follows, we first discuss habits and peculiarities of private investors and their impact on currency management. Then we discuss the most important instruments and their properties. The final section presents a conclusion in the form of a few recommendations. All calculations are in terms of Swiss francs because, from the Swiss perspective, currency management and international diversification are, due to the small size of the economy, particularly important.

Before we move on to discuss these topics, we briefly look at the anatomy of currency markets. About 200 currencies are priced and approximately 150 of them can actually be bought or sold free of restrictions. However, only about 20 currencies are liquid enough to be traded in size. Of those 20, six currencies – the US dollar, the Japanese yen, the euro, the Swiss franc, the Australian dollar and the Canadian dollar – account for 80% of the trading in the foreign exchange market.

According to the triennial BIS survey, the daily turnover in these six currencies is more than US$1 trillion per day. The foreign exchange market is by far the most liquid market. The daily turnover is about 30 times larger than the cumulated daily turnover in all global equity markets.

Since the Bretton Woods system with fixed exchange rates collapsed in 1973, the foreign exchange markets have undergone a huge structural change. Back in 1976, 25% of all foreign exchange trading was related to trade of physical goods. Today, only about 1% of all transactions are related to trade. The rest comes from investors and speculators all around the globe.

THEORY OF INTERNATIONAL ASSET ALLOCATION AND THE ROLE OF CURRENCIES

The most important assumption for international capital market models is that purchasing power parity (PPP) is violated. In its simplest form PPP states that for all goods and services that are freely tradable the law of one price should apply: the same good should have the same price everywhere in the world.

Without the assumption of violation of PPP, there would be no need for international models. When PPP is valid, real returns

(returns in excess of inflation) would be identical in all currencies and as a consequence optimal portfolios for each investor would be identical. If (relative) PPP were valid, exchange rates would only mirror inflation differentials across countries.

Portfolio selection models in an international setting as presented in its simplest form in Solnik (1974), and then extended by Adler and Dumas (1983) and Adler and Prasad (1992), reveal some very interesting results:

❑ the optimal portfolio for each investor consists in the simple model of Solnik (1974) of three parts:

1. a portfolio compromising all risky assets in proportion to the world market portfolio weights,
2. a portfolio that has short positions in foreign cash for currency hedging purposes,
3. the domestic money market account. In sum, each investor holds a combination of a partially currency-hedged world market portfolio and the domestic money market account.

❑ if the investor has liabilities, or inflation is assumed to be stochastic, the investor holds a fourth portfolio, which tracks inflation or the liability as closely as possible (liability or inflation hedge portfolio). This portfolio is investor-specific and depends on the reference currency.

❑ the currency hedge ratio (in equilibrium) is equal to one minus the risk tolerance of the investor. Because risk tolerance typically lies between 0 and 1, neither full hedging nor not hedging at all is optimal. Consistent with our intuition, a less risk-tolerant investor chooses to hedge more of the exposure in foreign currencies.

❑ the demand for long positions in the domestic money market account from domestic investors is covered by short positions from foreign investors in the domestic money market account, which are needed for currency hedging.

❑ currencies are not a zero-sum game: the currency risk premia for a pair of currencies add to the variance of the exchange rate (Siegel's paradox), ie, on average currencies have a positive risk premium.[1]

❑ by definition, the world market portfolio is universal, ie, it is the same for each investor and it does not depend on the reference currency.

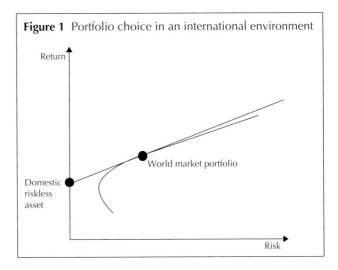

Figure 1 Portfolio choice in an international environment

❏ the hedge portfolio and the portfolio position in the domestic money market account are investor- and reference-currency-specific.

❏ if these optimal portfolios for each investor are aggregated, it turns out that the supply and the demand for all risky assets and all money market accounts are identical, ie, the capital market is in equilibrium.

To summarise, international portfolio theory suggests that each investor should blend the world market portfolio of risky assets with his domestic money market instrument. Currencies are on average rewarded with a risk premia and partial currency hedging is optimal.

Home bias and currency hedging

Home bias and currency hedging are two related issues. Cheap currency hedging facilities make it more attractive to hold foreign assets while a certain degree of home bias is justified if currency hedging is not possible or not desired.

The home bias puzzle refers to the fact that most investors tend to largely overweight domestic assets, in particular, equities, when compared with a perfectly diversified world market portfolio. This is surprising given that international portfolio theory shows that each investor should hold a combination of a (partially hedged) world market portfolio and potentially a hedge portfolio for inflation or a liability. Typically, home bias is inversely related to the size of the domestic capital market: the smaller the domestic capital market, the larger the home bias.

Financial literature provides the following explanations for home bias:

❑ domestic assets provide better hedges for home-country-specific risks such as inflation, liability risk and non-traded assets (in particular human capital) than foreign assets. In addition, many domestic companies have foreign operations and therefore foreign returns are implicit in equities of domestic companies.
❑ gains from international diversification are not sufficiently large to warrant the costs involved and legal and technical restrictions prevent more international diversification.
❑ uncertainty in means and covariances is so high that a home-biased portfolio may be optimal.
❑ investors are irrational. They have emotional preferences for domestic assets because they feel the information base is better and the investors have emotional ties to domestic companies or institutions.
❑ the difficulty with hedging foreign currency exposure justifies a certain home bias, in particular for fixed-income and other low-volatility investments.

For private investors, the last two explanations are the most relevant. It is much easier to get information on the domestic economy and domestic companies or institutions. Most newspapers and news magazines on TV have a strong emphasis on the home country.

In the past, cheap currency hedging instruments such as forwards were not available for private investors. However, as we will see below, this has changed dramatically in the recent past.

Let us now illustrate the relationship between home bias and currency with an empirical example. We look at a mixed portfolio with 50% equities, 45% bonds and 5% money market as a strategic asset allocation. The base currency is Swiss franc. In the optimisation, we have restricted some smaller markets to a zero weight and the asset class weights are being fixed *ex ante*. Expected returns are derived from the world market portfolio and a long-term covariance matrix based on the reverse optimisation technique, ie, expected returns, is inferred from the world market portfolio and the covariance matrix.[2]

Table 1 shows the result from three different optimisations:

❑ "Optimisation hedged" refers to an unconstrained optimisation where full currency hedging is allowed. The optimal asset allocation mirrors the world market portfolio; only the weights are rescaled. Foreign currency exposure is hedged with a hedge ratio of 80% (risk tolerance of 0.2).

❑ "Optimisation unhedged" refers to an optimisation where currency hedging is not possible. In this optimisation approach, the currency exposure is a direct consequence of the exposure to foreign assets.

Table 1 Unhedged vs hedged optimal portfolios from a Swiss franc perspective

CHF	Optimisation hedged	Optimisation unhedged
MM		
CHF	5	5
Total MM	5	5
Bonds		
CHF		32.58
EUR	8.02	11.85
GBP	1.77	
Nordic		
USD	25.05	
CAD		
JPY	7.98	
Far East		
Em. markets	2.17	0.56
Total bonds	45	45
Equities		
Switzerland	0.62	6.59
Europe EMU	8.08	6.12
UK	3.86	3.26
Nordic	0.23	0.55
USA	22.40	20.89
Canada	0.82	
Far East	1.80	3.45
Japan	8.61	9.14
Em. markets	3.57	
Other		
Total equities	50	50

The results show quite interesting patterns:

❑ as suggested, the impossibility of hedging foreign currency exposure leads to a substantial home bias. In the unhedged optimisation, the allocation to assets denominated in CHF is approximately 45%, while in the optimisation, where currency hedging is possible, the corresponding figure is only about 6%.

❑ in the unhedged optimisation, the home bias is much more substantial on the bond side.

❑ the allocations on the equity side are, with the exception of the Swiss market, quite similar. On the bond side, the allocations are substantially different. As we will see below, the cause is that currency risk is much more important for bonds than for equities.

EMPIRICAL EVIDENCE ON CURRENCY RISK

Before we dig into the empirical properties of currencies and their impact on equities, bonds and portfolios, it is worthwhile to define currency risk.

Currency risk is the marginal volatility (variance) that results from the translation of the returns of an asset from its base currency in a different currency. It is the additional volatility that an investor with a reference currency different from the currency of denomination of an asset has to bear if he does not hedge the foreign currency exposure.

Currency risk must not be confused with the volatility of exchange rates. Because asset returns and currency returns are not perfectly correlated, only a part of the volatility of exchange rates translates into currency risk. If the correlation between (local) returns of an asset and currency returns is negative, it is even possible that currency risk is negative, ie, the volatility of the asset is lower in a foreign currency than in local terms.

Let us now look at the historical record of currency volatility. As Figure 2 shows, currencies have been quite volatile. In most cases the annualised currency volatility is approximately 10%. A remarkable exception is the exchange rate between Swiss franc and euro. Here the volatility is only 4%. This pattern is caused by the close ties between the Swiss and the European economy. Both economies typically follow the same business and interest rate cycle and both currencies tend to move in parallel with regard to their exchange rate versus the US dollar.

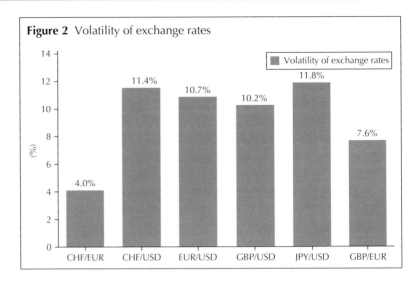

Figure 2 Volatility of exchange rates

Many empirical studies state that the importance of currency risk is inversely related to the volatility of the underlying: it is more important for bonds and hedge funds than for equities.

Figure 3 gives some simple evidence for this pattern. We compare the risk return characteristics of US bonds and equities and hedge funds when expressed in Swiss francs on a hedged and a unhedged basis.

The chart clearly shows that total volatility of US bonds is more than twice as high on an unhedged basis. For GBP and EUR bonds, the picture is similar but less pronounced. It seems that the closer two bond markets are geographically to the reference currency country, the less significant the currency risk is. The economic explanation of this pattern is that exchange rate movements are highly correlated with moves of short-term interest rates.

For equity markets, currency risk is much important. Only 10% to about 35% of total risk is actually currency risk. Again, geographical closeness leads to less currency risk. These patterns can be explained with the higher volatility of equities as such and with the fact that exchange rate movements and equity market returns have very low correlations. For equities, currency risk and, as a consequence, currency hedging are not very meaningful, anyway. This is because the listing of a company does not say very much about the currency exposure of the stock. The big Swiss food company Nestlé, for

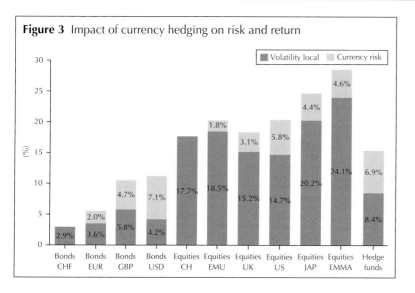

Figure 3 Impact of currency hedging on risk and return

example, makes the vast majority of its revenues and profits in foreign countries and currencies. So, in fact, a proper currency management for an investment in Nestlé requires one to know the actual exposure to all the currencies where the revenues come from. Indeed, Diermeier and Solnik (2001) show that for multinational companies listing is irrelevant for the determination of risk exposures.

CURRENCY MANAGEMENT FOR PRIVATE INVESTORS

After the theoretical considerations and a brief overview on the empirical properties of currency risk, we now turn our attention to practical aspects. The following topics are discussed in this section:

❑ particularities of private investors;
❑ strategic versus tactical hedging (including currency overlay);
❑ short- and long-term determinants of exchange rates; and
❑ suitable instruments.

Particularities of private investors

Currency management for private clients needs to take into account a few peculiarities of private investors as well as constraints relating to portfolio size and regulatory aspects:

❑ the portfolios of private clients are too small to do forwards. A forward requires a minimum size of at least 100,000 of a certain currency.

❏ private clients are not as sophisticated as institutional investors. They are not always aware of the merits of international diversification. They often struggle with loss positions in their portfolio and it may be difficult for them to see the link between a currency instrument and a position in a bond or a stock. A daily mark to market with margin payments is difficult to explain to them and it leads to a substantial administrative burden.
❏ from a regulatory perspective, short positions are often forbidden.
❏ depending on jurisdiction and tax domicile, a certain instrument may not be available for public distribution or may have adverse tax consequences.

Strategic versus tactical hedging

The strategic asset allocation defines the long-term target asset allocation of an investor. An appropriate strategic asset allocation ensures that the investor can achieve his long-term goals and it serves as the starting point for tactical asset allocation. The tactical asset allocation defines short- and medium-term deviations from the strategic asset allocation in order to capture opportunities and imbalances in the capital markets. The objective of tactical asset allocation is to enhance performance of the strategic asset allocation ("to outperform") by making the right bets at the right time. Tactical asset allocation is not mandatory. If the investor does not believe that tactical asset allocation adds value, he can stick to his strategic asset allocation.

Based on the theory from the second section above ("Theory of international asset allocation and the role of currencies"), an investor should strategically hedge currency exposure. A partial hedge in accordance with his risk tolerance is optimal. From a practical perspective, the simplest possible implementation is to define a strategic asset allocation with a constant hedge ratio. Since currency risk is much more relevant for bonds and alternative investments than for equities, we recommend hedging exposures in bonds and alternatives fully while the exposure of equities remains unhedged. For a mixed portfolio with 50% bonds and 50% equity, the hedge ratio would thus be 0.5. If the portfolio contains more equities, the hedge ratio is lower and vice versa.

With these strategic currency hedges in place, tactical currency management has a simple starting point. On the fixed-income side, the benchmark portfolio is fully hedged and it is either possible to de-hedge or to overhedge for tactical purposes. On the equity side, the starting point is an unhedged allocation; either this can be hedged or the unhedged currency position can be combined with a speculative currency position.

Although theoretically not optimal, a so-called currency overlay is a good method for implementing tactical currency allocation.[3] A currency overlay can be defined as a way of actively adjusting hedge ratios in anticipation of exchange rate moves. It is practical to first decide about the allocation to the other asset class and then to decide on the appropriate currency overlay. The currency decision is then taken separately from the investment decision and can be executed by specialist currency managers. The overlay runs alongside the asset allocation for equities, bonds and alternative investments. If the currency management is outsourced in this way, it is important to define proper risk/return objectives, risk control parameters and a performance measurement methodology.

From an instrument perspective, the simplest and most efficient instrument is an actively managed currency certificate (see below).

Short- and long-term determinants of exchange rates

As we have seen, exchange rates are quite volatile. On a historical basis, the volatility of exchange rates lies between bonds and equities. For the day-to-day currency management of private client portfolios, it is important to distinguish between short- and long-term determinants of exchange rates:

Short-term	Long-term
❏ Forward rates and interest rate parities ❏ Monetary and fiscal policy ❏ Market expectations ❏ Flows and interventions from central banks	❏ Absolute and relative PPP ❏ Balance of payments and its components such as net foreign debt, current account deficit/ surplus

On a short-term basis, currency fluctuations are often enormous. Over the longer run, currencies tend to move towards the PPP level. However, substantial deviations from PPP can last for a long time and it is very difficult to predict by when the correction towards the equilibrium level as given by PPP will eventually start.

Suitable instruments

To implement the currency hedging, we see three options:

❑ currency certificates;
❑ mutual funds with inherent currency hedges; and
❑ actively managed certificates with focus on currencies.

Currency certificates

The detailed mechanics of a currency certificate are as follows. Currency certificates are essentially the same as a currency forward. The differences are:

❑ a currency certificate requires an upfront payment and there is no physical delivery at expiry; the upfront payment is similar to a margin; and
❑ a currency certificate has an automatic stop loss build in; when this stop loss limit is reached, the certificate expires immediately.

In principle, the upfront payment can be regarded as initial margin while the stop loss can be regarded as a margin call where the counterparty does not pay the required margin and consequently the trade is closed. To keep the upfront payment as low as possible, the certificates are leveraged.[4] Over the lifetime of the certificate, the leverage is variable: when the value of the certificate falls below its initial value, the leverage increases; when the value of the certificate increases above its initial value, the leverage decreases. When a certificate is bought during its lifetime, this must be taken into account when the appropriate portfolio weight is determined. However, as with a forward, the notional amount hedged remains the same over the lifetime. This is a very important property because no daily adjustments of the hedge are required.

The leverage has to be balanced against the stop loss limit. When the leverage is very high, the stop loss limit is reached with a higher probability. As with a forward, only the notional is hedged. If the value of an underlying investment changes over time, either the hedge needs to be adjusted or a part of the position is unhedged.

Let us illustrate the mechanics of a currency certificate with an example. The following assumptions are made:

❑ the spot exchange rate between EUR and USD is 1 (USD per EUR);
❑ the currency certificate has a maturity of one year;

❑ the one-year interest rates are 2.5% (EUR) and 5% (USD);
❑ the investor is prepared to pay US$70.7 upfront for a hedge of €1,000;
❑ the investor wants to hedge the EUR exposure of €10,000; and
❑ the knockout level is at 20%, ie, when US$80 of the initial payment is lost, the trade is closed automatically; it is not guaranteed that the investor receives back the spot exchange rate corresponding to the stop loss level (slippage).

With the data given, the forward exchange rate in one year's time is 1.0243 USD/EUR or 0.9761 EUR/USD. Now a currency certificate works like this. The investor pays US$70.7 per EUR/USD bear certificate (altogether US$707 to hedge his complete exposure of €10,000). The payoff for the investor looks as in Figure 4.

From the chart we can make the following observations:

❑ when the exchange rate at expiry is identical to the forward rate, the payoff from a currency certificate is zero (as would be the case with a currency forward);
❑ if the spot exchange rate is below the forward (<1.0243), the payoff of the currency certificate is linear and identical to the payoff of a forward;

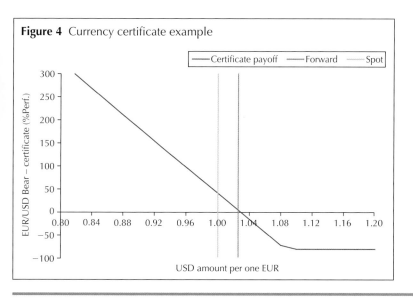

Figure 4 Currency certificate example

❑ if the spot exchange rate reaches a certain level above the forward exchange rate, the (negative) return is locked in and the certificate is sold automatically; and

❑ the floor and the steepness of the payoff curve depend on the leverage and the required stop loss level.

Currency certificates have the following advantages and disadvantages:

Advantages	Disadvantages
❑ Cheapness ❑ Maximum flexibility ❑ Relative ease of understanding ❑ Customisability ❑ Notional to be hedged is constant over the lifetime	❑ For each currency pair two certificates are required ❑ Legal and tax implications in some jurisdictions ❑ May lead to loss positions that the client does not understand ❑ Perfect hedge not possible (only notional is hedged) ❑ Strict risk control required (leverage)

Mutual funds with inherent hedge

Instead of using currency certificates, it is also possible to use mutual funds that hedge the currency exposure within the fund. This is the cheapest possible method to implement currency hedging because a fund with reasonable size can use forwards. These vehicles have the following advantages and disadvantages:

Advantages	Disadvantages
❑ Cheapest method to implement currency hedge ❑ Client is not bothered with profits and losses from currency hedging ❑ No legal issues and adverse tax implications	❑ Per reference currency and currency pair a separate fund share class is required ❑ Works only if client is willing to invest in funds ❑ Difficult to implement in an open architecture environment

Actively managed certificates with focus on currencies

Actively managed certificates are a fairly recent innovation. The idea behind them is that an investment adviser can decide actively about the asset composition of the certificate at any point in time. Trading then occurs within the certificates; there is not necessarily a need to trade the certificate itself in the client portfolio. Whenever the investment adviser thinks the currency allocation of a portfolio needs to be changed, he makes adjustments within the asset allocation of the actively managed certificate.

Actively managed certificates with a focus on currencies are very similar to currency certificates. The only difference is that, in an actively managed certificate, any number of currency certificates (or forwards) can be put together into one instrument. The upfront payment is lower than for the unpackaged combination of currency certificates because of the diversification effect between several currency pairs.

Actively managed certificates with a focus on currencies have the following advantages and disadvantages:

Advantages	Disadvantages
❑ Cheapness ❑ Low upfront payment ❑ Trading can take place at institutional prices within certificate ❑ Only one certificate per portfolio structure and reference currency required	❑ Identical or at least very similar portfolio structures required ❑ Legal and tax implications in some jurisdictions ❑ Transparency ❑ Perfect hedge not possible (only notional is hedged) ❑ Strict risk control required (leverage)

CONCLUSION

International portfolio selection models show that an investor should hold a combination of the world market portfolio partially hedged against currency risk and the domestic riskless asset. In practice, it is especially important to hedge foreign currency exposure for bond portfolios because the majority of the volatility is due to currency risk. For equities, currency risk plays only a minor role. Today, a few cheap, efficient and flexible instruments to implement currency hedging strategically and tactically are available. Thus, a modern currency management for private client portfolios (discretionary and non-discretionary) is possible today. The following rules of thumb summarise a possible approach:

❑ hedge out currency exposure for foreign bonds, hedge funds and real estate. Use a strategic hedge ratio of 100%.
❑ don't hedge currency exposure for equities strategically.

❑ regard currency management more as a risk reduction exercise than a significant return source.
❑ use currency certificates or similar cheap and efficient instruments. Don't use currency options.

1 See Adler and Prasad (1992).
2 For details regarding this approach, see Homberger (2004).
3 See Xin (2003) for a comprehensive overview of currency overlays.
4 Note that, for a forward, the upfront payment is zero by definition.

REFERENCES

Adler, M., and B. Dumas, 1983, "International Portfolio Choice and Corporate Finance: A Synthesis", *Journal of Finance*, **38(3)**, pp. 925–84.

Adler, M., and B. Prasad, 1992, "On Universal Currency Hedges", *Journal of Financial and Quantitative Analysis*, **27(1)**, pp. 19–38.

Diermeier, J., and B. H. Solnik, 2001, "Global Pricing of Equity", *Financial Analysts Journal*, pp. 37–47, July/August.

Homberger, A., 2004, "Equilibrium Risk Premia for Stocks, Bonds and Currencies", Doctoral thesis, University St Gall.

Solnik, B. H., 1974, "An Equilibrium Model of the International Capital Market", *Journal of Economic Theory*, **8**, pp. 500–24.

UBS Investment Bank, 2003, "Devisen- und Geldmarktgeschäfte", UBS Investment Bank, Zurich.

Xin, H., 2003, "Currency Overlay", *A Practical Guide* (London: Risk Books).

7

Foreign Exchange and Structured Products for Private Clients

Peter Gardner, Andrew Popper

SG Hambros

What is foreign exchange?

There are a number of ways to define foreign exchange market. At its simplest level, it can be described as follows:

> The *foreign exchange market* is the international market in which one national currency can be exchanged for another. The price at which the two currencies exchange is the *exchange rate*.[1]
>
> (Begg, Fischer and Dornbusch, 1994)

An alternative way of looking at foreign exchange is that it provides the means of converting claims on assets from one country to another.

A brief history of foreign exchange

The gold standard and Bretton Woods[2]

The *gold standard* is a method whereby each currency fixes the number of its currency units for an ounce of gold and the exchange rate between two currencies is set with reference to the number of currency units for an ounce of gold.

Pre-1914 the United Kingdom provided the gold standard and would exchange currency for gold and vice versa. The massive expense of World War One forced the UK to sell significant amounts of its gold holdings and the gold standard was temporarily abandoned.

Though the United Kingdom, among others, reintroduced the gold standard between the wars, it was not a successful policy and during World War Two the focus on hostilities prevented a new monetary standard from being established.

In 1944 the major allied powers met at Bretton Woods in the US to establish a new monetary standard. The World Bank (the Bank for Reconstruction and Development) and the International Monetary Fund (IMF) were created. The primary purpose of the IMF was to ensure that IMF members ran their balance of payments and exchange rates in an "orderly manner", and if necessary it would assist members by lending them money. The IMF was guided by the conclusions of the Bretton Woods conference, that stable exchange rates were desirable, floating exchange rates were unsatisfactory and government controls on trade and exchange were counterproductive.

The members agreed to fix par values for their currencies and make them fully convertible, effectively governments could not create new currency unless it was backed by gold at the fixed par value.

The price of gold was fixed at US$35 per ounce and it was agreed that the US dollar would be the only currency that could be directly converted into gold for monetary purposes. Other countries then set their par values with reference to the US dollar.

However, the shortcoming of this system was that the USD became the reserve asset and other countries could increase their reserves only if the US increased its supply of dollars.

From 1945 to the late 1950s there was a shortage of US dollars, which were necessary to facilitate international trade and investments. In the late 1950s the US began to run a series of current account deficits and US dollars flowed into the international monetary system. Though it was recognised that the USD was overvalued, the US decided to run a current account deficit for a number of reasons: it was fearful market intervention and deflation following its experience in the 1930s and it was under pressure from other countries not to devalue the USD, as their reserves were held in dollars.

As the central banks began to accumulate large reserves of dollars, they started to exchange some of these reserves for gold at the set price of US$35 per ounce.

By the mid-1960s foreign central banks held more US dollars than the US Treasury held in gold reserves, and by 1971 the US had run up a cumulative deficit of US$56 billion, partly financed by a decrease in its gold reserves.

Foreign central banks became nervous and in August 1971, prompted by a request from the United Kingdom that the US cover some US$3 billion of its reserves against loss, President Nixon and his senior financial advisers met to make what would become a major decision.

The end of the gold exchange standard

The US announced that it would no longer exchange the US dollar holdings of foreign central banks for gold and it would apply a tariff of 10% on all imports.[3]

The international monetary system was in turmoil and after closing for a number of days it reopened to a floating exchange rate system with no established rules.

In December 1971 an agreement was reached on new exchange rates against a devalued dollar. Exchange rates were fixed again at the start of 1973, but in both instances currency speculators felt the levels had been set incorrectly and invested in what they believed were undervalued currencies. This of course became self-fulfilling as their investments added to the strength of those currencies.

In mid-1973 the major currencies began to float and established the foreign exchange system that exists today.

ERM to the euro

In 1979, the establishment of the European Monetary System introduced the European currency unit (ECU), the forerunner of the euro. In addition it introduced the Exchange Rate Mechanism (ERM), which gave member currencies an exchange rate band within which their currencies could fluctuate with relevance to the ECU, the unit of the European Community's internal budget. The UK did not enter the ERM until September 1990.

By 1992, volatile currency markets put the ERM under enormous pressure and a number of currencies were no longer able to keep within the ERM limits. On "Black Wednesday", March 1, 1992, the British pound and Italian lira were forced out of the system and the Spanish peseta was devalued. The British chancellor, Norman (now Lord) Lamont, raised interest rates from 10% to 12%, then 15% (though this second rise was later reversed) and spent billions of pounds to try to support the value of sterling. The measures failed and Britain was forced out of the ERM.

In addition to creating the European Union from the European Community, the Maastricht Treaty signed in 1991 also set out the path for monetary union in Europe. The progress towards the euro was set out in three stages:

1. From July 1990 to December 1993, controls over the movement of capital were lifted and the ERM bands were narrowed. European central banks started to coordinate their efforts and economic policies.
2. From January 1994 to December 1998, there was further convergence of members' economic and monetary policies. The European Central bank was established and the exchange rates for conversion to the euro were fixed.
3. From January 1999, the euro was launched, first as an electronic currency and then notes and coins were launched across the member states.

Greece met the convergence criteria in January 2001 and joined the other members of the euro zone; the UK, Denmark and Sweden remain outside the euro.[4]

Current exchange rate regimes

In the current international monetary system, exchange rate regimes can generally be divided into the following two broad regimes:

Floating exchange rate regimes. Most economists regard free-floating exchange rates as ensuring efficient markets. Under floating exchange rate regimes, governments allow their currencies to be fully convertible against other currencies, ie, without any government intervention. Thus the exchange rate can be considered the price of the currency in another currency and is thus set at the equilibrium point between supply and demand as governed by normal economic rules.

Supply and demand is governed by international trade and investment. In its simplest form, demand is driven by the demand for foreign goods, services, investments and assets; supply is driven by the sales of goods, services, investments and assets to foreigners.

Fixed exchange rate regimes. Under fixed exchange rate regimes, a government will agree to maintain the convertibility of its currency against other currencies at a fixed rate. The government will therefore intervene to defend the exchange rate where necessary.

If the government wishes to change the fixed rate, it may devalue (reduce) or revalue (increase) the exchange rate.

Common forms of fixed exchange rate regimes are pegged currencies. Most currencies of developing countries are fixed (pegged) against a major currency (normally the USD, but the euro and the IMF's "Special Drawing Rights" SDRs are also used).

KEY DETERMINANTS OF FOREIGN EXCHANGE RATES
Balance of payments

Possibly the most important determinant of short-term exchange rate fluctuations is balance of payments capital flows. The balance of payments is defined as:

> A summary of all economic transactions between a country and all other countries for a specific time period, usually a year. The balance-of-payments account reflects all payments and liabilities to foreigners (debits) and all payments and obligations received from foreigners (credits)."[5]
>
> (Gwartney, Stroup and Sobel, 2000)

In a free and liquid market, the quantity demanded always equals the quantity supplied, thus total debits = total credits (the balance of payments).

The balance of payments can be divided into current account transactions (with a current account deficit or surplus) and capital account transactions (likewise with a capital account deficit or surplus).

Current account
Current account transactions relate to all payments (and gifts) related to the buying and selling of goods and services and income flows for the current period. The current account balance of payments includes:

❑ *visible trade* (also referred to as merchandise trade), which relates to imports and exports of goods;

❏ *invisible trade*, which refers to the import and export of services; and

❏ *income flows*, including transfer payments relating to foreign aid and international budget commitments (eg, to the EU) as well as the flow of income from investments (eg, dividends from foreign securities); unilateral transfers (or monetary gifts) are also included.

Capital account

Capital account transactions relate to changes in the ownership of real and financial assets. This includes:

❏ *financial investments* such as the purchase and sale of foreign securities; and

❏ *lending arrangements*, such as loans to and from foreigners and foreign corporations.

Thus the balance of payments, current and capital account flows to and from a country will determine the supply and demand for a country's currency, which will in turn set the price at which the currency is exchanged. Taken further, current and capital flows always net to zero. This means that trade/current account deficits can exist only if financed by capital inflows. However, if the deficits are financed by short-term borrowing or official borrowings, this may have a negative impact on the currency.

Capital account flows will always dominate currency movements in the short run due to international capital mobility.

The impact of monetary and fiscal policy

Monetary policy. The impact of monetary policy on exchange rates can be mixed and is often uncertain. For example, consider an unanticipated increase in the money supply as a result of a decrease in interest rates.[6] We would expect this to stimulate economic growth, which will have several consequences. If economic growth leads to inflation, this will cause the currency to depreciate, as the real interest rate will be further eroded, causing capital to flow out of the country, leading to a capital account deficit.

Likewise if economic growth leads to increased incomes, this may cause consumers to spend part of their increased income on imports, causing the current account to weaken.

Figure 1 Impact of monetary and fiscal policy on exchange rates

	Effect on the exchange rate	
	Monetary policy	Fiscal policy
Unanticipated expansion	Depreciation	*Appreciation*
Unanticipated restriction	*Appreciation*	Depreciation

Therefore the currency may weaken, followed by a readjustment, as imports become more expensive.

However, in the longer run economic growth will cause a currency to appreciate as capital flows into the country from investors seeking investment opportunities that take advantage of this growth, such as purchasing domestically listed securities or investing in domestic businesses.

Fiscal policy. As with monetary policy, the impact of fiscal policy on exchange rates is also mixed and often uncertain. Let us consider an unanticipated restrictive fiscal policy. This will have a twofold effect. First, consumer demand will decrease, causing a fall in inflation and a fall in imports, causing a current account surplus, forcing the currency up. Second, borrowing will decrease, leading to a fall in real interest rates and capital outflows, and a capital account deficit. As mentioned previously, given international mobility, the capital account effect will dominate the current account surplus, causing the currency to depreciate.

Other factors
Interest rates and "hot money"
If a government raises interest rates, it will attract "hot money" in the short term. This capital inflow will be driven by investors seeking the higher yields offered by the increased interest rates. This inflow of funds will increase demand for the local currency and cause it to appreciate.

Trade barriers and quotas

By imposing trade barriers, quotas and other protectionist policies, a government is effectively restricting the flow of imports and exports between its own country and its trading partners. In controlling trade the government will indirectly affect the supply and demand for that country's currency, which is largely determined by international trade.

Natural resources

An increase in or discovery of additional natural resources can cause a currency to appreciate. For example, if a major deposit of oil were found in a country, that country's currency would appreciate as foreign investors sought to exploit or take advantage of the newly discovered resources.

Currency block membership

As mentioned previously, currencies may peg their exchange rate to another major currency (eg, the US dollar). Thus, factors affecting the currency against which they are pegged have to be taken into account.

If a country decides to join or abandon a currency bloc, this will obviously have an impact on its exchange rate, depending on where investors and speculators feel that the currency's true value lies.

Investor sentiment, political events and terrorism

Investor sentiment, political events and more recently terrorist acts can have a major short-term impact on the exchange rate of a currency. Elections, opinion polls, and comments from senior government representatives can have a significant impact on exchange rates. This was amply illustrated in the 1990s when exchange rates moved on the comments of Eisuke Sakakibara, Japan's deputy finance minister for international affairs known as "Mr Yen".

And it has been illustrated more recently, when rates have moved following comments on the state of the US economy by Allan Greenspan, chairman of the US Federal Reserve.

Of course in the post-9/11 world, singular terrorist acts can have a profound effect on investor sentiment and the way investors choose to invest their money, which of course has repercussions on exchange rates.

Inflation and purchasing power parity

As mentioned above, inflation has an important impact on exchange rates and this is a significant factor in the determination of exchange rates in the long run.

This is referred to as purchasing power parity and can be simply illustrated as follows. Let us assume that a basket of goods costs £100 in London and that same basket of goods costs US$200 in New York. Then, in an free, open and liquid market and excluding other factors, we would expect the exchange rate to be £1 = US$2.

Now if the UK has an inflation rate of 1% and the US has an inflation rate of 10%, in one year's time, the basket of goods costs £101 in London and US$220 in New York. Thus we expect the exchange rate to be £1 = US$2.18.

The short-term supply-and-demand factors and investor sentiment as discussed above may disguise this overall trend, but inflation and purchasing power parity gives long-term direction to exchange rates. If a country has an inflation rate that is continually higher than that of its trading partners, its currency will depreciate in the long run.

CURRENCY INSTRUMENTS
Spot transactions
Spot rates

The spot rate is the exchange rate for an immediate currency exchange, ie, it is the rate you would receive or pay if you wished to sell or buy another currency for what is generally the earliest possible delivery.

The most common way of quoting the spot rate is European quotation. Under this convention, the US dollar is the fixed currency and a variable number of units in the other currency are quoted against the US dollar. For example:

European Quotation   USD/JPY   USD 1.00 = JPY 110.60

A few currencies use American quotation, where the US dollar is the variable currency. This is the common form of quotation for EUR/USD and GBP/USD (commonly known as cable). For example:

American Quotation   GBP/USD   GBP 1.00 = USD 1.786
                     (cable)

The quotation can also be classified as direct, where the foreign currency is the fixed currency and indirect, where the domestic currency is the fixed currency.

The spot rate will normally be quoted as a bid–ask spread:

$$\text{GBP/USD spot rate}$$
$$\text{Bid–Ask}$$
$$1.7855–1.7865$$

The bid price will be the price that the client will be paid if he sells sterling; the ask price is the price the client will pay if he buys sterling. It should be noted that more exotic and illiquid currencies will have greater spreads. When the market is volatile, the spread may also increase.

Settlement for spot transactions is normally t + 2 (two business days after trade date).

Cross rates

Since generally currencies are quoted against the USD or major currencies, cross rates are derived as the effective exchange rate between two currencies less frequently traded against each other and thus where no direct market exists.

The cross rate is calculated by using the exchange rate for each currency against a common currency. Due to liquidity and stability, the USD is the most widely used currency for cross rates.

For example, to obtain the rate between the South African rand and the Uruguayan peso, where the currencies are not directly traded against each other, we would use a cross rate against the US dollar, against which both currencies are traded:

$$\text{USD } 1.00 = \text{ZAR } 6.8637 \text{ and}$$
$$\text{USD } 1.00 = \text{UYU } 29.4850$$

This implies (assuming no spread)

$$\text{ZAR } 6.8637 = \text{USD } 1.00 = \text{UYU } 29.4850$$
$$\text{ZAR } 6.8637 = \text{UYU } 29.4850$$
$$\text{ZAR } 1.00 = \text{UYU } \frac{29.4850}{6.8637}$$

So the rate is ZAR/UYU is 4.2958.

In this example, we have assumed there is no spread. However, in reality, the spread across ZAR/UYU will be greater as two currency transactions are involved, thus incurring two sets of transaction costs. First US dollars are purchased with the South African rand and then these US dollars are used to purchase the Uruguayan pesos.

Currency forwards

A forward transaction is the agreed exchange of two currencies for future delivery. A currency can trade in the forward market at a premium, where it is stronger in the forward market, or at a discount, where *t* is weaker in the forward market. Rates can also be traded at par in the forward market, ie, at the same rate as currently traded in the spot market.

The premium is subtracted from the spot in order to obtain the forward rate, whereas the discount is added. The forward rates are determined by interest rate differentials as illustrated in this example.

Consider an investor who holds pounds and needs US dollars. Assume that, instead of trading at the spot rate, the investor places his pounds on deposit for 12 months and borrows the required amount of US dollars for the same period. For simplicity we will assume the amount is £100.00.

The spot rate is £1.00 = US$1.786

1. The investor places the £100.00 on deposit at 4.00% for 12 months, receiving £104.00 in 12 months.
2. The investor borrows US$178.60 (£100 × 1.789) at a rate 1.00% for 12 months, resulting in a final payment of US$180.39.
3. The effective forward exchange rate when the investor pays back his US dollar loan with the proceeds from his sterling deposit is GBP/USD 1.735 (180.39/104).

As we can see in this example (albeit somewhat simplified) that the forward rates are easily derived. In this example the US dollar, which strengthened, is trading at a premium in the 12-month forward market.

The relationship between exchange rates and interest rates as derived above can be easily expressed using the interest rate parity formulae:

$$\text{Forward rate} = \frac{1+R_v}{1+R_f} \times \text{Spot rate}$$

Where:

R_v is the interest rate for the variable currency and R_f is the interest rate for the fixed currency.

Note that R_v and R_f must be calculated at the appropriate rate for the forward period. For example, if we were considering the six-month (180-day) forward, and if the USD six-month interest rate was 1.15%, then the rate used will be $180/360 \times 1.15\% = 0.575\%$.[7]

Currency futures

Forward currency contracts are agreements between two financial institutions (banks) or a financial institution and a client. By contrast foreign exchange futures are agreements to buy or sell on a recognised exchange a specified amount of a currency for another at a set rate on a set future date. Foreign exchange futures contracts are also traded actively prior to the future settlement date.

Another difference between the forward and futures market (excluding their size) is that, while forward market transactions are largely bespoke/over-the-counter (OTC), futures contracts are standardised and traded on an exchange. One of the counterparts in a currency futures contract is always the exchange.

The futures market is also more regulated (the forward market being self-regulating) and most futures market contracts are not settled by actual delivery (around 1%), whereas more than 90% of forward contracts *are* settled by actual delivery (see Kolb, 2000).[8]

The forward market is significantly larger and dominates the futures market.

Currency options

Currency options differ from futures in that they provide the investor with the *right*, not the obligation, to buy or sell a specified amount of a currency for another at a set rate on a set future date (European option) or at any point up to or on the set future date (American option).

Options like futures allow investors to hedge their currency exposure, and obtain leveraged exposure to currency movements, but they also allow investors to trade volatility, that is to take a position not on the direction of a currency movement, but rather how volatile that currency movement will be.

In addition to OTC options, exchange-traded options, first introduced in 1973 by the CBOE (Chicago Board Options Exchange), are also traded. While exchange-traded options are less flexible than OTC options, which are by definition bespoke, exchange-traded options are more liquid and transparent due to their market listing and standardised prices and expiration dates.

Investors will pay a premium to purchase an option (go long the option), which will go to the counterpart writing the option, or the seller of the option. The option gives the investor the right to buy (a call option) or the right to sell (a put option) a currency in the future at the terms specified by the option.

The profiles in Figure 2 show the profiles of a simple call and put position. The horizontal axis shows the movement in the price of the underlying (with the option strike price at 100); the vertical axis represents the investor's profit or loss (in all cases with a premium of 5).

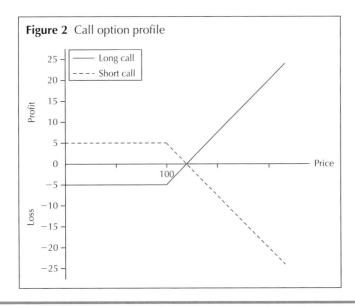

Figure 2 Call option profile

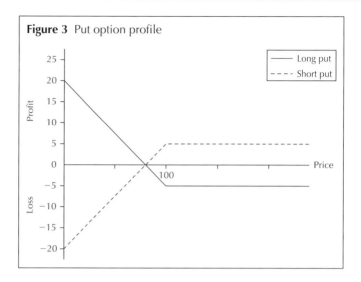

Figure 3 Put option profile

Note: While Figures 2 and 3 show the simplest option profiles, by buying, selling or writing a combination of options with different strikes, maturities, etc, it is possible to create very complex option strategies. However, it is not the purpose of this chapter to discus these advanced strategies. Exotic options such as barrier options, look-back options and so forth are also not discussed in detail here.

A further note: Currency warrants are effectively securitised option strategies with an exchange rate as the underlying (normally straight call or puts) that are tradable on a stock exchange.

Currency swaps

In essence currency swaps are agreements to exchange currencies on one day, followed by the reverse exchange of currencies on another date in the future.

Currency swaps allow an investor or company to borrow funds in one currency, yet pay back the interest in another currency, effectively enabling the investor or company to change their underlying currency exposure.

Here is an example. Client A borrows £6,000,000 from the bank at a rate of 6.00% for five years. It swaps this for US$10,680,000 and pays 4.00% interest on the USD for five years. After the five years the swap is reversed.

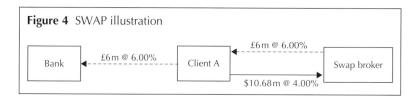

Figure 4 SWAP illustration

Three separate sets of transactions will take place for the swap:

1. The first currency exchange – Client A exchanges £6.00 million with the SWAP broker and in return receives US$10.68 million.
2. The exchange of interest payments – Client A pays 4.00% on US$10.68 million and receives 6.00% on £6.00 million.
3. The reciprocal currency exchange at maturity – Client A returns the US$10.68 million and receives £6.00 million.

This is a very simple illustration of a fixed-for-fixed currency swap; there are more complex currency swaps where the exchange may be fixed-for-floating or floating-for-floating.

STRUCTURED PRODUCTS
Capital-guaranteed products
Capital-guaranteed products provide access to foreign exchange market returns while guaranteeing the repayment of the initial capital at maturity. Capital-guaranteed foreign exchange products are simply constructed using zero-coupon bonds to provide the capital at maturity, together with simple or complex option strategies.

The amount invested in the zero-coupon (deposit) at inception is the net present value (NPV) of 100% of the initial capital at maturity. The remaining portion of the initial investment is used to invest in the options strategy, which will generate the additional returns at maturity.

The more money available to invest in the options strategy, the greater the potential returns. Thus, by decreasing the amount of money to be invested in the zero-coupon, we increase the potential returns of the strategy. This can be done in three ways:

1. Increasing the maturity of the product
2. Decrease the capital guarantee (to say 95%)
3 The higher the interest rates the lower the amount needed to invest in zero-coupons to guarantee the capital at maturity.

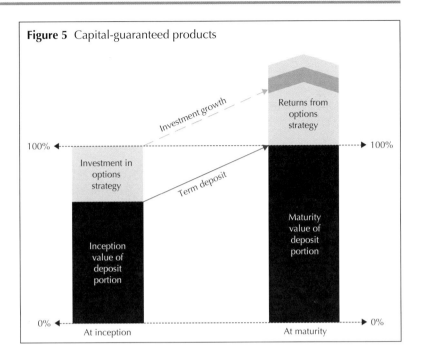

Figure 5 Capital-guaranteed products

There are a number of different combinations that can be used to meet client objectives and the following section illustrates just some of the more widely used strategies available. (These generic products will also be available from a range of companies, here specific SG product names are used)

Propulsive deposit
The propulsive deposit is a deposit account, that has the following basic characteristics:

❑ 100% capital guarantee at maturity;
❑ a predefined currency pair and target spot rate is set on start date;
❑ a guaranteed minimum yield can be included in the structure (optional);
❑ a progressively higher yield is payable above the minimum yield, leveraged on the appreciation of the currency pair, provided that the spot rate of the currency pair is above a given rate at maturity;[9]
❑ flexibility to determine the level of risk by altering the range and target spot rate; and
❑ short-term deposit.

The guaranteed minimum yield applied to deposits will always be below the prevailing money market interest rate. However, there is significant potential to outperform this rate should one currency in the currency pair appreciate against the alternate currency, beyond the target spot rate.

For example:

Currency pair:	GBP/USD
Deposit currency:	GBP
Term:	3 months
Target spot rate:	1.82
Participation/leverage:	180%
3-Month money market rate:	4.25% per annum
Guaranteed minimum yield:	1% per annum
Capital guarantee:	100% at maturity
Maximum potential yield:	unlimited
Margin (to the bank):	50 bps per annum

There are two possible outcomes, in terms of the yield payable on the deposit, depending on the spot rate at maturity.

1. If the GBP/USD exchange rate is above 1.82 at maturity, then you will receive a yield higher than the minimum guaranteed. The more the GBP appreciates against the USD above the target spot rate, the higher the yield. For example, if at maturity the spot

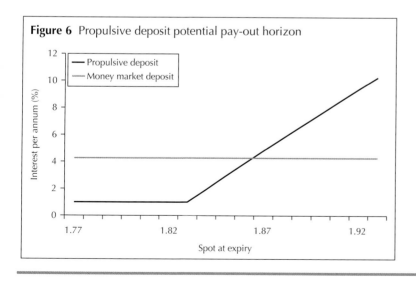

Figure 6 Propulsive deposit potential pay-out horizon

rate is 1.85 the yield applied will be 2.92% per annum, and if at maturity the spot rate is 1.90 the yield will be 7.58% per annum.

2. If the exchange rate goes below 1.82 at maturity then the investor will only receive the guaranteed minimum return of 1% per annum.

Turbo deposit
The turbo deposit is a deposit account, which has the following basic characteristics:

❑ 100% capital guarantee at maturity;
❑ a predefined currency pair and range is set on start date;
❑ a guaranteed minimum yield can be included in the structure (optional);
❑ a progressively higher yield is payable above the minimum yield, provided that the spot rate of a predefined currency pair is above a given rate throughout the term and is within the range at maturity;[10]
❑ flexibility to determine the level of risk by altering the range and target spot rate; and
❑ short-term deposit.

The guaranteed minimum yield applied to deposits will always be below the prevailing money market interest rate. However, there is significant potential to outperform this rate should one currency in the currency pair appreciate against the alternate currency, within a predetermined range.

For example:

Currency pair:	EUR/USD
Deposit currency:	EUR
Term:	2 weeks
FX range:	1.1750 to 1.2000
3-Month money market rate:	2% per annum
Guaranteed minimum yield:	1% per annum
Capital guarantee:	100% at maturity
Maximum potential yield:	7.01% per annum
Margin (to the bank):	30 bps per annum

There are two possible outcomes, in terms of the yield payable on the deposit, depending on the trading range during the life of the deposit and the spot rate at maturity.

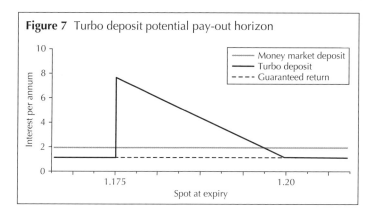

Figure 7 Turbo deposit potential pay-out horizon

1. If the EUR/USD exchange rate is above 1.1750 throughout the term and below 1.2000 at maturity, then the investor will receive a yield higher than the minimum guaranteed. The more the USD appreciates against the euro within this range, the higher the yield.
2. If the exchange rate goes below 1.1750 at any time during the term or is above 1.2000 at maturity then the investor will receive only the guaranteed minimum interest rate of 1% per annum.

Dolphin deposit
The dolphin deposit is a similar concept to the turbo deposit but offers a different reward structure:

❑ 100% capital guarantee;
❑ a predefined currency pair and range are set on the start date;
❑ a high variable yield will be paid on the deposit provided that the currency pair spot rate remains below a given level throughout the term; the exact yield will depend on the spot rate of the currency pair at maturity;
❑ a fixed yield will be paid provided that the spot rate of the underlying currency pair reaches or exceeds a predetermined level at any time during the term;
❑ a yield of zero is applied if the underlying spot rate is below a given level at maturity;
❑ flexibility to determine the level of risk by altering the range and target level; and
❑ short-term deposit.

As with the turbo deposit, on the start date of the deposit period a predefined currency pair and range will be established. Provided that the spot rate of the currency pair remains within the range over the deposit period, a yield will be paid depending on the appreciation of one currency in the currency pair against the alternate currency.

As opposed to the turbo deposit, there is no minimum yield on the account. If, however, the spot rate goes above a predetermined level, the yield may be higher than the prevailing money market interest rate.[11]

For example:

Currency pair:	EUR/USD
Deposit currency:	EUR
Term:	1 year
FX range:	1.20 to 1.32
3-Month money market rate:	2.00% per annum
Yield if spot greater than 1.32:	2.50% per annum
Capital guarantee:	100% at maturity
Maximum potential yield:	8.91% per annum
Margin (to the bank):	45 bps per annum

There are three possible outcomes, in terms of the yield on the deposit, depending on the trading range during the life of the deposit and the spot rate at maturity.

1. If the spot exchange rate trades below 1.32 during the term and is less than 1.20 at the maturity date, then 0% per annum will be the yield applied on the deposit.

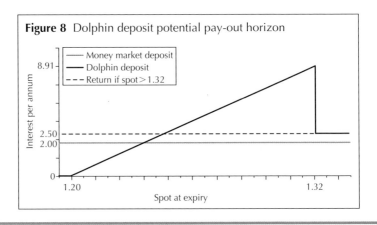

Figure 8 Dolphin deposit potential pay-out horizon

2. If the spot exchange rate trades anywhere below 1.32 during the term, and is between 1.20 and 1.32 at maturity, then a yield will be paid depending on the spot exchange rate at maturity. The more the euro appreciates in terms of USD within the range, the better the yield.
3. If the spot rate trades at or above 1.32 at any point during the term, then the investor will receive a fixed yield of 2.50 per annum, which exceeds the money market rate stipulated in this example.

One-touch-barrier deposit

The "one-touch-barrier" deposit offers capital protection and the potential to achieve an enhanced yield provided that the spot rate of a specific currency pair remains within a predefined range. If the underlying spot rate trades outside of the range at any point during the deposit term then the yield will be 0%.

The key characteristics of the deposit are as follows:

❏ 100% capital-guaranteed;
❏ predetermined maximum and minimum return;
❏ flexible and tailored range choice;
❏ repayment is always in the original currency; and
❏ short-term deposit.

For example:

Currency pair:	GBP/USD
Deposit currency:	GBP
Term:	1 year
FX range:	1.63 to 1.96
Spot:	1.78
Yield if in range:	12% per annum
Yield if range breached:	0%
Capital guarantee:	100% at maturity
Margin (to the bank):	50 bps per annum

There are two possible outcomes, in terms of the yield on the deposit, which is dependent on the spot rate of the currency pair remaining within the trading range during the life of the deposit.

1. Provided that the GBP/USD spot rate remains within the range of 1.63 to 196 over the term, the investor will receive the maximum yield of 12% per annum.

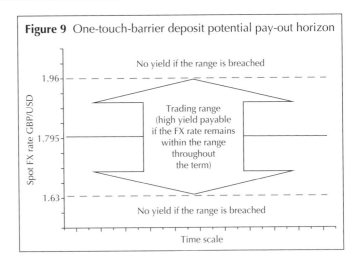

Figure 9 One-touch-barrier deposit potential pay-out horizon

2. If, however, the spot rate should touch or breach either of the outer limits of the range (ie, 1.63 or 1.96) at any time during the term then 0% yield will be applied.

In both scenarios the investor will receive their initial capital in full at maturity.

Daily accrual deposit
The "daily accrual" deposit operates in a very similar fashion to the "one-touch-barrier" deposit, but daily accrual deposits pay a yield that is accrued on the basis of each day that the underlying spot rate of the currency pair trades within a range. If the spot rate trades outside of the range on any given day then no yield is accrued for that day.

The key characteristics of the deposit are as follows:

❑ 100% capital-guaranteed;
❑ pre-determined maximum and minimum return;
❑ the fixed daily yield for each day that the spot rate of the currency pair trades within the range spreads the risk;
❑ returns of previous days are always maintained;
❑ repayment will always be in the original currency;
❑ flexible and tailored range choice; and
❑ short-term deposit.

For example:

Currency pair:	GBP/USD
Deposit currency:	GBP
Term:	1 year
FX range:	1.69 to 1.87
Spot:	1.78
Yield:	Maximum 7.00% per annum
Capital guarantee:	100% at maturity
Margin (to the bank):	40 bps per annum

Based on the above example, the investor would be paid a daily yield for every day the GBP/USD spot rate remained within the range over the term, with a maximum yield of 7.00% per annum.

If however the spot rate trades outside the range, no interest would be yielded on those days. Based on the above example, the following illustrates the returns applicable, based on the number of days that the spot rate remains within the range:

90 days	1.75%
180 days	3.45%
300 days	5.76%
365 days	7.00%

There are any number of possibilities for return on the deposit, dependent on the number of days that the spot rate trades within the range.

Irrespective of the number of days within the range, the investor will receive capital in full at maturity.

Wedding cake deposit

The "wedding cake" deposit operates in a very similar fashion to the "one-touch-barrier" deposit. However, it gives the ability to set two predetermined ranges. If the underlying spot rate of a predefined currency pair remains within the first range over the deposit term, then a higher yield is paid. If the underlying spot rate touches the outer limits (or "barriers") of the first range, then the second range will come into effect (which will include the first range) and, provided that the rate remains within the second range thereafter, a lower yield is paid. If the underlying spot rate trades at any time during the deposit term outside of the second range, then 0% yield will be applied.

The key characteristics of the deposit are as follows:

❏ 100% capital-guaranteed;
❏ predetermined maximum and minimum return;
❏ flexible and tailored range choice;
❏ repayment is always in the original currency; and
❏ short-term deposit.

For example:

Currency pair:	EUR/USD
Deposit currency:	EUR
Term:	6 months
FX range – Range 1:	1.14 to 1.26
Range 2:	1.11 to 1.29
Spot:	1.20
Yield if in Range 1:	6.50% per annum
Yield if in Range 2:	2.50% per annum
Yield if Range 2 breached:	0%
Capital guarantee:	100% at maturity
Margin (to the bank):	50 bps per annum

There are three possible outcomes, in terms of the yield on the deposit, which is dependent on spot rate of the chosen currency pair remaining within the ranges during the life of the deposit.

1. Based on the above example, should the spot rate trade within Range 1 during the whole term then the investor will receive a yield of 6.50% per annum.
2. If however the spot rate breaches Range 1 at any time during the term, but trades within Range 2, then the investor will receive a yield of 2.50%.
3. If the spot rate breaches both Range 1 and Range 2 at any time during the term then no yield would be applied to the deposit.

Irrespective of the outcome, the initial capital will be repaid in full at maturity.

Double scoop deposit
The "double scoop" deposit also operates in a very similar fashion to the "one-touch-barrier" deposit. It is 100% capital-guaranteed and offers the potential for a higher yield than the interest rate available on standard fixed deposit.

A currency pair and range are chosen at the start of the deposit term, and provided that the underlying spot rate remains within the range then a high yield will be applied. If however the range is breached at any time during the deposit term then there is the added advantage of being able to reset a range around the barrier that has been breached. If the range is breached for a second time then a minimum yield is applied (which may be zero). Given that this is a more cautious strategy the potential returns are generally lower than for a one-touch-barrier deposit.

The key characteristics of the deposit are as follows:

❑ 100% capital-guaranteed;
❑ predetermined maximum and minimum return;
❑ a predefined second range is set around the breached barrier, giving a "second chance";
❑ flexible and tailored range choice;
❑ repayment is always in the original currency; and
❑ short-term deposit.

For example:

Currency pair:	GBP/USD
Deposit currency:	GBP
Term:	6 months
FX range:	1.705 to 1.855 (±7.5 cents from spot)
Spot:	1.78
Yield if in range:	8.00% per annum
Capital guarantee:	100% at maturity
Margin (to the bank):	50 bps per annum

There are two possible outcomes, in terms of the yield on the deposit, which is dependent on the chosen currency pair spot rate remaining within the trading range during the life of the deposit.

1. If the GBP/USD exchange rate remains within the range of 1.705 to 1.855 throughout the term then a yield of 8.00% will be applied. If however the GBP/USD exchange rate were to breach the lower or upper limts of 1.705 or 1.855 at anytime during the term, then the range would be reset around the broken limit (ie, a lower-limit breach of 1.705 would reset a range of 1.63 to 1.78 and an upper-limit breach of 1.855 would reset a range of 1.78 to 1.936.) Should the exchange rate then remain within the new

range until maturity then the investor will receive the bonus of 8.00% per annum in addition to their original capital.

2. If the range is breached for a second time then 0% yield would be applied irrespective of the outcome; the initial capital will be repaid in full at maturity.

Bespoke products and variants

As mentioned previously, the above examples refer to the more commonly traded foreign-exchange-structured products, but there are many variants of these structured products and bespoke products are often created to meet a specific client's need or request.

Additionally, "naked" or non-capital-guaranteed products can be created, whereby the client risks losing part or all of their initial investment.

Most product providers will create bespoke products whereby the investment amount is above a specified amount (normally around €1,000,000 or the equivalent for capital-guaranteed products).

Dual-currency accounts

The globalisation of world markets has had a significant impact on how people conduct their business and personal finances. Many people now hold cash in multiple currencies awaiting reinvestment and, although traditional deposit accounts are available for these funds, the interest rates that they earn are often unattractive. One innovative structure that can be used under these circumstances is a dual-currency account.

Dual-currency accounts offer investors returns significantly higher than money market deposits in exchange for the potential risk that the capital invested may be converted into an alternate currency.

The yield applicable on this type of account will vary depending on the deposit currency and alternate currency ("currency pair") chosen, plus the volatility in the market at the time. In exchange, the investor takes the risk that their initial deposit (plus yield) may be repaid in an alternate currency at a predetermined conversion rate. Ideally, the alternate currency should be one in which the investor has assets or have a requirement for in the future.

At the start of the deposit term, a predefined target level ("strike price") is selected for the underlying currency pair. At maturity the investor will receive a predefined yield whatever the outcome. However, their capital will be repaid in the original currency or alternate currency, depending on whether or not the target level is achieved.

Dual-currency accounts have the following characteristics:

❑ predefined currency pair selected at inception;
❑ a fixed high yield will be paid whatever the outcome;
❑ ability to have capital and yield paid in an alternate currency;
❑ there are no capital guarantees associated with dual-currency accounts and the initial capital is at risk in deposit currency terms should the investment be converted into an alternate currency; and
❑ short-term deposit.

The following example illustrates further how the account operates:

Deposit amount:	GBP 200,000
Alternate currency:	USD
Currency pair:	GBP/USD
Spot price:	1.50
Strike price:	1.51
Guaranteed yield:	10.10% per annum
Term:	31 days

There are two possible outcomes on maturity of the deposit:

1. If the spot rate between GBP/USD is lower than US$1.51, then the investor will receive back their initial deposit of £200,000, plus a yield of £1,715.62 (10.1% per annum for 31 days, total = £201,715.62).
2. If the spot rate is equal to or higher than US$1.51, then the sterling deposit plus yield will be redenominated into USD at the strike price. (Capital plus interest of £201,715.62 converted at US$1.51 = US$304,590.59).[12]

PRIVATE CLIENT CURRENCY INVESTING

Private clients will generally invest in currency-structured products from one of two perspectives: either to hedge currency exposure or speculate on currency movement.

First, the client may have an asset or liability in one currency and hedge their exposure to that currency using a structured product

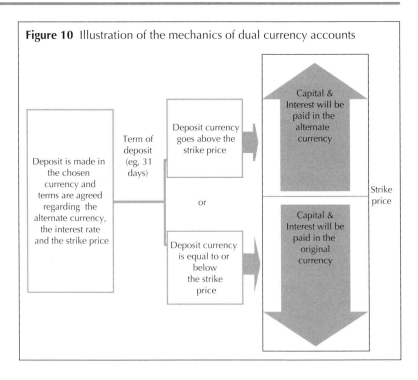

Figure 10 Illustration of the mechanics of dual currency accounts

(though some more sophisticated private clients may trade directly in options or warrants).

Second, the client may wish to speculate on the directional movement or the volatility of a currency pair and invest in a product that exploits this.

Of course, arbitrage trading, where derivatives and structured products are used to exploit trading inefficiencies to create riskless profit, can also motivate investments. However, due to the narrow margins involved, these trades generally necessitate large amounts and are not normally undertaken by private clients.

It goes without saying that the most important factor in deciding what currency investments to make on behalf of a client or advising on which investments to make is the risk tolerance and investment appetite of that client. It is important to understand the level of risk that a client is willing to accept if they have foreign currency exposure, which would drive any hedging strategy. Likewise, it is important to understand the level of risk the client is willing to accept on their principal investment if undertaking a speculative trade. The amount at risk in relation to the total net worth of a client is also a key element in determining the suitability of a currency strategy.

Hedging

Currency hedging, whereby clients seek to reduce the risk from unfavourable exchange rate movements of a currency, can be simple or extremely complex. It can range from passive, less costly hedging strategies to active strategies, which are more expensive.

A client relationship manager (CRM) or private banker (PB) should first determine their client's overall risk appetite and their foreign currency exposure. Once this has been determined the client's tolerance to unfavourable movements of their currency exposure should be assessed.

Once the client's risk appetite, and currency exposure and tolerance have been agreed, a hedging strategy should be determined. This may conclude with the need for total hedging away of all risk, partial or selective hedging, or a stop loss strategy where the client will accept a limited amount of currency fluctuations, but requires protection beyond a certain point.

Having the hedging strategy has been determined, suitable structured products or those that can be used to effect the strategy over the required timeframe should be assessed and finally invested in by/for the client.

Detailed below are examples of hedging strategies using the various currency derivatives discussed previously:

Example: Hedging using forward or futures
Example: A UK-based client, whose reference currency is in GBP, would like to hedge the value of their portfolio of US investments against adverse movements in the US dollar. Any increase in the GBP/USD exchange rate will cause the GBP value of the portfolio to decrease.

For example, current portfolio value is US\$5,000,000, the GBP value is £2,777,778 with a GBP/USD rate of 1.80. If at maturity the rate has increased by 5% to 1.89, the GBP value of the portfolio will decrease to £2,645,503 (a corresponding loss of 5%).

If the client is long a GBP/USD future with a strike of 1.80, they will have made 5% on the future, as they will exchange their dollars

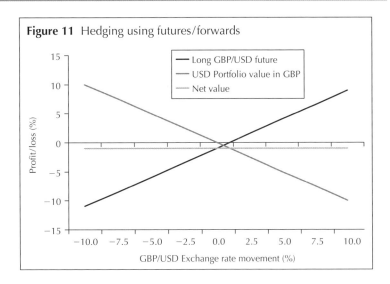

Figure 11 Hedging using futures/forwards

and buy sterling at a price of US$1.80, whereas the market price is US$1.89.

As the loss in the portfolio value is offset by the future/forward, this results in a constant portfolio value, irrespective of currency movements.

This is illustrated by Figure 11. Note the graph includes a 1% cost for the forward/future.

Example: Hedging using options
Using the same example discussed above, the client could have hedged their exposure on the USD portfolio buy buying a long call option on GBP/USD.

The decrease in the GBP value of the portfolio caused by a weakening dollar (rise in the GBP/USD rate) would be offset by an increase in the value of the call option. In this example we have assumed a premium of 2.5%, which will be the client's maximum loss.

Note this is purely one example of a hedging strategy using options, and more sophisticated strategies can be used that better match individual client requirements.

Hedging using structured products
Currency exposure may of course be hedged using structured products, which may be used to provide a full or partial hedge. For

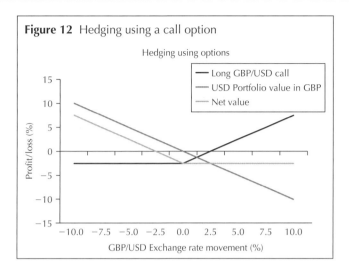

Figure 12 Hedging using a call option

instance, in the above example, the client could have invested in a structured product that gave a return based on the appreciation of GBP/USD, therefore effectively hedging the loss in GBP value of their USD portfolio with the return from the structured product.

Speculative

In addition to hedging their currency exposure, private clients occasionally speculate on exchange rates. Speculative investors seek investment returns that are greater than those available from cash and in return are prepared to accept some risk. The potential risk can be limited to the opportunity cost of what the investor would have received had they placed the money on cash deposit, or the investor may choose to place part or all of their capital invested at risk.

As mentioned previously, the client may speculate on either the directional movement or the volatility of a currency pair, in which case the direction of movement can be irrelevant. The client could choose to invest in a structured product or derivative strategy that meets their investment requirements, though generally only more sophisticated private clients would choose to invest directly in a derivative strategy.

Example: Speculating using forwards or futures
Speculating on directional currency movements. Suppose the client believes that the USD is overvalued with respect to GBP. The spot

rate for GBP/USD is 1.78 and the 1 September futures contract price is 1.82.

The client can speculate by making the following trades:

1. The client purchases (goes long) a 1 September GBP/USD futures contract at 1.82.
   Suppose the spot now moves to 1.85 after one month, and the futures contract price moves to 1.92.
2. The client sells the 1 September futures contract for 1.92, realising a profit of US$0.10 per futures contract.

However, if the investor felt that USD was undervalued with respect to GBP, they could of course speculate by undertaking the reverse trade: selling (going short) the futures contract and later closing their position by buying the futures contract.

It should be noted that forwards and futures cannot be used on their own to speculate only on currency volatility regardless of market direction.

Example: Speculating using options
Speculating on directional currency movements. Using the same example discussed above, the client could meet their investment objectives by investing in options.

Assume that when GBP/USD spot is at 1.78, a three-month GBP/USD call option with a strike of 1.80 is trading at US$0.05.

1. The client goes long the call option at a price US$0.05.
   Suppose the spot now moves to 1.85 after one month, and the call option price moves to US$0.10.
2. The client sells the call option for US$0.10, realising a profit of 50%.

If the investor felt that USD was undervalued, they could speculate on the downward movement of the exchange rate by purchasing a put option.

Speculating on exchange rate volatility. Discussed below and illustrated in Figures 13–16 are the simplest option strategies that can be used to speculate on volatility. Only straddle and strangle strategies are discussed; more complex strategies such as butterflies and condors can achieve more bespoke goals but are perhaps more suited to options traders rather than private clients.

The client may either speculate that there will be movement in the exchange rate, but they are unsure of the direction of movement (ie, volatility is increasing) or that the exchange rate will be stable over their investment horizon (ie, volatility is decreasing).

Increasing volatility: the long straddle. A long straddle is an options strategy suitable where the investor expects considerable volatility in the exchange rate and feels that the options are underpriced with respect to the expected volatility.

The strategy consists of purchasing a call and a put of the same maturity and the same strike price. The long straddle strategy's returns are illustrated in Figure 13.

Increasing volatility: the long strangle. An alternative options strategy that also benefits from increasing volatility is a long strangle. This is a cheaper strategy than a long straddle (the option premiums will be lower). However, the exchange rate will have to move further before the strategy becomes profitable.

The long strangle strategy's returns are illustrated in Figure 14.

Decreasing volatility: the short straddle. A short straddle is the opposite strategy to a long straddle. The strategy is suitable for investors who believe that the exchange rate will remain steady

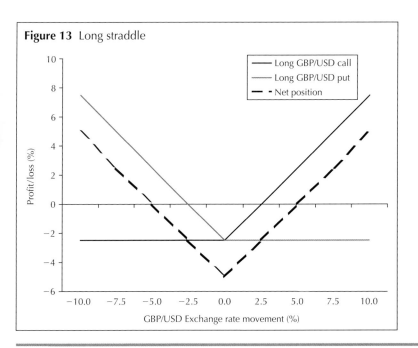

Figure 13 Long straddle

Legend:
— Long GBP/USD call
— Long GBP/USD put
— · Net position

Y-axis: Profit/loss (%)
X-axis: GBP/USD Exchange rate movement (%)

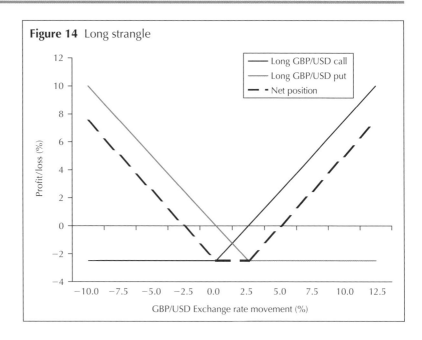

Figure 14 Long strangle

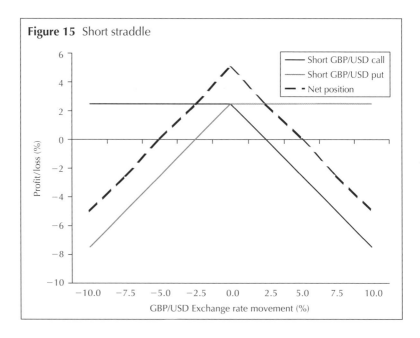

Figure 15 Short straddle

within a narrow range and that the options are overpriced with respect to the expected lower volatility.

The strategy consists of selling a call and a put of the same maturity and the same strike price. The short straddle strategy's returns are illustrated in Figure 15.

Decreasing volatility: the short strangle. An alternative options strategy that also benefits from decreasing volatility is a short strangle. This strategy is profitable for a wider range than a short straddle. However, the returns are lower as the options sold are cheaper.

The short strangle strategy's returns are illustrated in Figure 16.

Speculating using structured products

By speculating using forwards and futures options, the client is placing the capital invested at risk.

Movements in forwards and futures prices generally correlate to movements in the underlying currency pair and, if the exchange rate collapsed against the client's expectation, they could lose their money. Likewise if an option expires out-of-the-money, the option will expire worthless and the client will lose the capital invested.

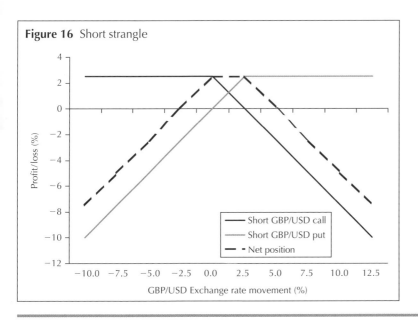

Figure 16 Short strangle

The benefit of investing using structured products is that the client's principal investment can be fully or partially protected. Structured products therefore allow the client to speculate on currency movement without risking their initial capital or a limiting the risk to a known maximum potential loss.

As discussed previously, the most common structured products use a zero-coupon bond together with an options strategy, which could be one of the simple strategies discussed above or a more complex strategy, including using exotic options.

There is an abundance of structured products available that can meet a client's exchange rate investment needs. As can be seen from the examples presented in this chapter, structured products could be used to trade on exchange rate directional movement or exchange rate volatility. Of course with bespoke products able to be constructed for relatively small amounts (€1 million+), products can be made to be as creative as the client or investment adviser's thinking.

1   *Economics*, 4th Ed. 1994, David Begg, Stanley Fischer & Rudiger Dornbusch.
2   Note that this draws on Walmsley (2000) and Ball and Wendall (1996).
3   Excepting imports from Canada.
4   The other members of the euro zone are Austria, Belgium, Finland, France, Germany, Ireland, Italy, Luxembourg, The Netherlands, Portugal and Spain.
5   *"Economics: Private and Public Choice"*, 9th Ed. 2000, James D Gwartney, Richard L Stroup and Russell S Sobel, The Dryden Press .
6   If it were anticipated, the foreign exchange markets will already have factored this policy into the current exchange rate.
7   Note that the UK uses 365-days day count convention whereas most other countries use 360.
8   *"Futures, Options, & Swaps"*, 3rd Ed. 2000, Robert W Kolb, Blackwell Publishers.
9   Dependent on the currency pair chosen, this may be the reverse based on which currency the currency pair is represented in.
10 Dependent on the currency pair chosen, this may be the reverse based on which currency the currency pair is represented in.
11 This will be dependent upon market conditions.
12 Dependent on the currency pair chosen, this may be the reverse based on which currency the currency pair is represented in.

REFERENCES

Ball, D. A., and W. H. McCulloch Jr, 1996, *International Business: The Challenge of Global Competition*, 6th Edition, Richard D. Erwin, A Times Mirror Higher Education Inc. Company.

Begg, D., S. Fischer, and R. Dornbusch, 1994, *Economics*, 4th Edition, McGraw Hill Book Company.

Gwartney, J. D., R. L. Stroup, and R. S. Sobel, 2000, *Economics: Private and Public Choice*, 9th Edition, The Dryden Press.

Kolb, R. W., 2000, *Futures, Options, & Swaps*, 3rd Edition, Blackwell Publishers.

Walmsley, J., 2000, *The Foreign Exchange and Money Markets Guide*, 2nd Edition, John Wiley & Sons Inc.

8

Fixed-Income Structured Products

Lode Roose, Kristien Meykens, Hans Duquet

KBC Asset Management

This chapter deals with structured products on fixed-income underlyings (interest rates, bonds, etc). As will be made clear in the coming sections, the market in fixed-income-linked structured products is characterised by a very wide variety of products. The aim of this chapter is to give the reader a basic understanding of this market. It is not intended to be complete or deal with all the technicalities in depth.

The chapter consists of seven sections:

❑ the first describes the interest rate sensitivity of a bond and explains the concept of (modified) duration.
❑ then we look at the workings of some basic interest rate derivatives: interest rate futures and interest rate swaps (IRS).
❑ the following section deals with some basic interest rate options, such as calls on interest rate futures and swaptions.
❑ we then turn to an overview of how structured products can be put together, as well as a schematic cashflow diagram.
❑ the following section deals with the problem of interest rate sensitivity of most of the structured products, and describes an innovative variant of an exotic interest rate option: the Bermudan Accreting Swaption (BAS).
❑ the next section explains the basics of interest rate option pricing.
❑ finally an overview of the market in fixed-income-linked structured products is given and illustrated by some recently launched structures.

INTEREST RATE RISK OF A BOND

In this section we discuss the interest rate risk for bonds that have no call provision or default risk, so the cashflow schedule is fully known in advance.

The price of a bond equals the sum of the present values of all future cashflows of the bond. Assuming annual coupons, the price of a bond is given by the formula:

$$P = \sum_{t=1}^{T} \frac{C_t}{(1+z_t)^t}$$

with:

P: price of a bond

T: maturity of the bond

C_t: bond cashflow at time t (for $t = T$, C_t = coupon$_T$ + notional)

z_t: spot interest rate (discount or zero rate) for the cashflow at time t.

As can be seen from the above formula, the price of a bond is sensitive to changes in interest rates. If interest rates move up, the price of a bond decreases and vice versa. The impact of interest rate movements on the price of the bond depends on the specific characteristics of the bond, being its time to maturity and its cashflow schedule. In general, the higher the maturity and the lower the coupon rate, the higher will be the proportional impact of interest rate movements on the bond price.

The measure for the interest rate sensitivity of the price of a bond to changes in interest rates is called "duration". As illustrated below, this measure is analogous to the beta concept for stocks, which measures the sensitivity of a common stock to changes in the stock index.

The current yield to maturity on a bond is defined as that discount rate (one single number) that equates the present value of the bond's cashflows to its price. It is the discount rate that has to be applied on all future cashflows in order to obtain the current price of the bond.

$$P = \sum_{t=1}^{T} \frac{C_t}{(1+y)^t}$$

with:

y: the current yield to maturity.

The Macaulay duration of a bond is the weighted average of the maturities of the future cashflows, where the weight on each maturity equals the present value of the corresponding cashflow calculated using the current yield to maturity of the bond as the discount rate.

$$D_{\text{Macaulay}} = \frac{\sum\limits_{t=1}^{T} t \cdot \dfrac{C_t}{(1+y)^t}}{P} = \frac{\sum\limits_{t=1}^{T} t \cdot \dfrac{C_t}{(1+y)^t}}{\sum\limits_{t=1}^{T} \dfrac{C_t}{(1+y)^t}}$$

It is clear from this formula that for a zero-coupon bond Macaulay's duration equals maturity and that for coupon paying bonds Macaulay's duration is less than the maturity and proportionally declines if the coupon rate is higher.

If we take the derivative of the price of the bond with respect to $1 + y$, we find that:

$$\frac{dP}{d(1+y)} = -\sum\limits_{t=1}^{T} t \cdot \frac{C_t}{(1+y)^{t+1}}$$

Or,

$$\frac{dP}{d(1+y)} = -\frac{1}{1+y} \sum\limits_{t=1}^{T} t \cdot \frac{C_t}{(1+y)^t}$$

As,

$$\sum\limits_{t=1}^{T} t \cdot \frac{C_t}{(1+y)^t} = P \cdot D_{\text{Macaulay}}$$

we can write that:

$$\frac{dP}{d(1+y)} = -\frac{1}{1+y} P \cdot D_{\text{Macaulay}}$$

$$\frac{dP}{P} = -\frac{d(1+y)}{1+y} \cdot D_{\text{Macaulay}}$$

The modified duration is defined as the Macaulay duration divided by one plus the current yield to maturity of the bond.

$$D_{\text{Modified}} = \frac{1}{1+y} D_{\text{Macaulay}}$$

It is clear that the modified duration measures the proportional sensitivity of a bond's price to a small absolute change in its yield. Thus, if modified duration is, for example, 3, a one-basis-point increase in the yield results in a 0.03% drop in the bond price.

$$\frac{dP}{P} = -D_{\text{Modified}} d(1+y) = -D_{\text{Modified}} \cdot dy$$

The (modified) duration concept is valid only for small yield changes (in fact it is the tangent line to a nonlinear graph of the price/yield relationship as shown in Figure 1). There is an inverse, convex relationship between yield and duration. As a consequence, in case of substantial yield changes, the modified duration under-estimates the interest rate sensitivity of the bond and we need to add a correction to the duration approach that takes into account this convexity (see Figure 1). This correction is equal to convexity multiplied by the square of the yield change.

So, everything taken together, the interest rate risk is measured as follows:

Percentage price change = −modified duration × yield change
+ convexity × (yield change)²

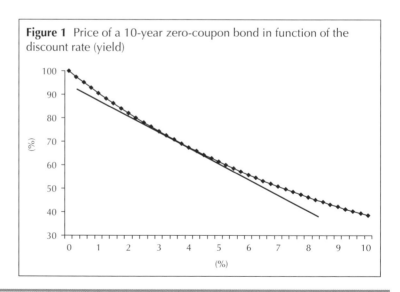

Figure 1 Price of a 10-year zero-coupon bond in function of the discount rate (yield)

$$\frac{\mathrm{d}P}{P} = -D_{\text{Modified}} \cdot \mathrm{d}y + \text{Convexity} \cdot \mathrm{d}y^2$$

Interest rate derivatives such as futures, swaps and options offer a possibility to change the interest rate risk of a portfolio without doing (costly) bond transactions. Below we will offer an explanation of these instruments and their use.

INTEREST RATE DERIVATIVES

For an explanation of interest rate options, see the next section.

Interest rate futures

A futures contract is an agreement between a buyer/seller and an established exchange, in which the buyer/seller agrees to take/make delivery of a certain asset at a certain moment in the future. Most financial futures contracts have settlement dates in March, June, September or December. A futures position can either be liquidated prior to the settlement date (by taking an offsetting/inverse position in the same contracts) or be executed on the settlement date by delivery of the underlying.

The buyer of a futures contract will make a profit if the futures price increases; the seller will make a profit if the futures price decreases. When a position is taken in a futures contract, there is no need to put up the entire amount of the investment. Instead, only a limited amount – the "initial margin" – has to be put up as a guarantee, allowing managers to create leverage. This can be used to speculate on price movements, but also to reduce price risk.

Economically, a forward contract is the same as a futures contract. However, the two differ in some important respects:

❑ futures contracts are standardised, with regard to delivery dates and quality requirements for the deliverable, whereas a forward contract is not standardised (terms are negotiated individually between buyer and seller);

❑ futures contracts are traded on organised exchanges, while forward contracts are over-the-counter (OTC) instruments with no or very limited secondary markets;

❑ futures contracts are not intended for delivery, while the opposite holds true for forward contracts;

❑ futures contracts are marked to market at the end of each trading day, while forward contracts are more often valued on a *pro rata* basis; and

❑ for futures contracts, there is only minimal credit risk (clearing house), while forward contracts are exposed to the risk that either party may default on its obligations.

For hedging interest rate risk in long-term portfolios, bond futures are the most important kind of interest rate futures, because they relate to longer-term instruments (bonds), where the interest rate risk is higher. The contracts in government bond futures in most countries are modelled on contracts for US Treasury Bond futures.

To explain bond futures in more detail, we will use the example of a US long bond future. The underlying is the hypothetical US$100,000 par value of a 20-year 8% coupon bond. The price and yield of the Treasury Bond future contract are quoted in terms of this hypothetical bond. However, for delivery purposes, the seller of the futures contract has the choice between several real Treasury Bonds that are considered acceptable. Because the economic characteristics of the bonds that can be delivered do not exactly match the (hypothetical) economic characteristics of the underlying of the bond future, a conversion factor is determined, which is constant throughout the trading period of the contract. The amount paid by the buyer of the bond delivered by the seller is:

$$\text{notional} \times \text{futures contract settlement price} \times \text{conversion factor} + \text{accrued interest.}$$

Bond futures are often used to hedge the interest rate exposure of a position. This means that they are used as a temporary substitute for positions to be taken in the cash market at a later date. A short hedge (selling of bond futures) is used to protect against a decline in the cash price of a bond. A long hedge (buying of bond futures) is used to protect against an increase in the cash price of a bond.

Example
A mutual fund has a big investor entering the fund on day *D* for value on day *D* (subscription date) + 5 (the money to finance a

cash transaction will only be available in five days). The matching cash transaction is carried out for value on day D (transaction date) + 3 and so can take place only on day D (subscription) + 2. However, the net asset value (NAV) at which the investor can enter the fund is calculated based on the rates of day D (subscription). The mutual fund is therefore exposed to the risk of an increase in the prices of the bonds it wants to buy between day D (subscription) and day D (subscription) + 2. To hedge this risk, it can buy bond futures. If there is a rise in the price of the bonds it wants to buy, it will make about the same profit on the (long) bond futures position.

Interest rate swaps (IRS)

In an IRS, two parties exchange periodic interest payments. The amounts are based on the notional amount (principal) and equal the applicable interest rate multiplied by the notional amount. The only cash that is actually exchanged represents the interest payments, not the notional amounts. An IRS can be used to alter the cashflow characteristics of the assets or liabilities of a portfolio or change the duration of a portfolio.

Economically, the same effect can be obtained by using other methods, such as a package of forward contracts or appropriate positions in bonds. However, IRS are a more transactionally efficient vehicle for accomplishing the objectives. Forward contracts would each have to be negotiated separately. Also, IRS offer more liquidity than forwards or bonds, and the maturities of forward and futures contracts are not as long as for IRS (for an IRS, a maturity of more than 15 years can be obtained).

In the most common type of swap, one party agrees to pay the other party fixed-interest-rate payments on fixed dates (fixed-rate payer), while the other party agrees to make floating-interest-rate payments relative to a certain reference interest rate (floating-rate payer). For example, on a certain notional amount and during a period of 10 years, party A will pay to party B annually a fixed coupon of 4%, while party B pays to party A a quarterly coupon of Euribor. Party A is a fixed-rate payer/floating-rate receiver, while party B is a floating-rate payer/fixed-rate receiver.

The value of an IRS will vary with market interest rates. If, in our example, after the conclusion of the contract, 10-year interest rates go up to 5% and party A wants to sell its position, the party taking over this position will have to pay one percentage point less than in the market to receive a quarterly payment of Euribor. Party A will get compensation for this benefit. The inverse happens if interest rates go down.

❑ the position of the fixed-rate payer (= floating-rate receiver) is similar to a short bond futures position or to having a long position in a floating-rate bond and borrowing the funds to finance the floating-rate bond on a fixed-rate basis: a profit will be made if interest rates rise and a loss incurred if interest rates fall.
❑ the position of the fixed-rate receiver (= floating-rate payer) is similar to a long bond futures position or to having a long position in a fixed-rate bond and financing that at a floating rate: a loss will be incurred if interest rates rise and a profit made if interest rates fall.

The value of an IRS equals the balance of the present value of both legs: receiving minus paying. All cashflows are discounted at the zero-coupon rate applicable to the time period when the cashflow will be realised. The value of an IRS will change as interest rates change.

Duration as a measure of the interest rate sensitivity of a fixed-income security is also important here. From the perspective of the party who pays floating and receives fixed, the IRS position can be viewed as long a fixed-rate bond and short a floating-rate bond. The duration of this position is the duration of the fixed-rate bond minus the duration of the floating-rate bond. As the last duration will be very small, the duration of the fixed-rate bond (leg) will be dominant.

INTEREST RATE OPTIONS
Interest rate options can be written on cash instruments or derivatives (futures, swaps). Options on futures or on swaps ("swaptions") are far more popular than options on cash instruments.

For futures, if the option is a call option, the buyer has the right to buy one designated futures contract at the strike price. That is, the buyer has the right to acquire a long position in the designated contract. If this right is exercised by the buyer, the writer acquires a corresponding short position in the futures contract. A put option on a futures contract grants the buyer the right to sell a designated futures contract to the writer at the strike price. Accordingly, the option buyer has the right to acquire a short position in the designated futures contract. If the buyer exercises that right, the writer acquires a corresponding long position in the designated futures contract.

How the mechanism works

Suppose the investor buys a *call option* on some futures contract in which the strike price is 85. Assume that the futures price is 95 and the buyer exercises the call option. When the option is exercised, the call buyer gets a long position in the futures contract at 85. The call writer is assigned the corresponding short position in the futures market at 85. The futures positions of the buyer and of the writer are immediately marked to market by the exchange. Because the prevailing futures price is 95 and the strike price is 85, the holder of the long futures position (the call buyer) will realise a gain of 10, while the holder of the short futures position (the call writer) will incur a loss of 10. The call writer pays the exchange 10, and the call buyer receives 10 from the exchange.

Suppose the investor buys a *put option*, and the current futures price is 60 rather than 95. If the buyer exercises this option, he would have a short position in the futures contract at 85 (strike price) and the option writer would have a long position in the futures contract of 85. The mark-to-market value of the exchange will result in a gain for the put buyer of 25 and a loss for the put writer of the same amount.

The price of an interest rate option depends on the price of the underlying instrument, which in turn depends on the interest rate applying to the underlying instrument. Thus, the price of an interest rate option depends on the interest rate applying to the underlying instrument. Consequently, the interest rate sensitivity or duration of an interest rate option can be determined. The modified duration of an interest rate option is equal to: (modified duration of the underlying instrument) × (*delta*) × (price of the underlying instrument/ price of the option). The delta is the price responsiveness of the option to a change in the price of the underlying instrument. The last term refers to the leverage. The higher the price of the underlying instrument relative to the price of the option, the greater the leverage (= the more exposure to interest rates for a given investment).

Since the delta of a call option is positive, the modified duration of an interest rate call option will be positive. Thus, when interest rates go down, the value of an interest rate call option will rise. A put option has a negative delta. Thus, the modified duration is negative and, when interest rates rise, the value of a put option will also go up.

Two of the main derivatives products in the interest rate market are interest rate caps/floors and swaptions.

An interest rate cap is an OTC derivative that is designed to provide protection against an increase in interest rates above a defined cap (strike). It can be considered a "payer IRS", whereby each exchange payment is executed only if it has positive value. A cap can be viewed as a portfolio of call options on interest rates or a portfolio of put options on discount bonds. An interest rate floor is defined analogously to an interest rate cap. It is designed to provide protection against a decrease in interest rates below a defined floor (strike). A floor can be viewed as a portfolio of put options on interest rates or a portfolio of call options on discount bonds.

An option on a swap ("swaption") gives the buyer the right to enter into a swap agreement by a specified date. For example, a company knows that in six months it will enter into a five-year floating-rate loan agreement with resets every six months and knows that it will want to swap the floating interest payments for fixed interest payments to convert the loan into a fixed-rate loan. At a cost, the company could enter into a swaption giving it the right to receive the six-month LIBOR and pay a certain fixed rate of interest, for example 4% per annum for a five-year period starting in six months. If the fixed rate on a regular five-year swap in six months turns out to be less than 4% per annum, the company will choose not to exercise the swaption and will enter into a swap agreement in the usual way. However, if it turns out to be greater than 4% per annum, the company will choose to exercise the swaption and will obtain a swap at more favourable terms than those available in the market. A swaption can be constructed for all kinds of periods and maturities and is an OTC contract.

STRUCTURED FUNDS
Introduction
Fixed-income derivatives can be structured and sold to investors (institutional investors, private banking clients, retail clients and

so on) in several ways: as notes, as (mutual) funds and in any other investment vehicle. The technicalities and pricing issues relating to the embedded derivatives are similar for all types of packaging insofar as they relate to the same underlying derivatives.

In the next few sections, we will see how structured funds are set up, focusing solely on technical and pricing issues. It is important to note that the conclusions of the analysis also hold true for all the other packagings, too.

How do structured funds work?

Structured funds have two investment objectives:

❏ to give the investor back a guaranteed amount, as a percentage of his starting capital. For capital-protected funds, this percentage is 100; for non-capital protected funds, 0. Any percentage between 0 and 100 is possible for funds offering partial capital protection (or limited loss potential).
❏ to pay the investor, on top of the guaranteed amount, an additional amount made by the fund. The extra amount these funds make will depend on the change in value of the "underlying", such as stock market indices, shares, interest rates, currencies, credit events and inflation, on the final maturity and/or on interim maturity dates.

The workings of structured funds are explained in the cashflow diagram shown in Figure 2.

1. The investor invests capital in the fund.
2. The fund puts the capital into a fixed-income investment (time deposits, government bonds, asset-backed securities).
3. The fixed-income investments generate interest income for the fund.
4. The fund uses this income to buy options (in general: all kind of OTC options; in this analysis: interest-rate OTC options, fixed-income derivatives). At the inception of the fund, the present value of the interest income is the same as the present value of the options.
5. On the final maturity date, the fund will receive the capital from the time deposit account and

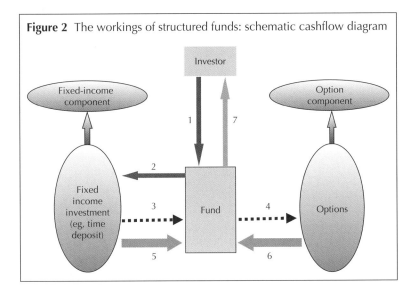

Figure 2 The workings of structured funds: schematic cashflow diagram

6. the capital gain realised on the options (or loss if there is no (full) capital protection).
7. The investor will get xx% of his capital back on the final maturity date, along with any potential gains on top of this guaranteed amount.

The investor does not have to keep his units in the fund until the final maturity date. The NAV are accurately calculated (see below) and published on a regular basis, and, when shares are purchased or sold, settlement is made at the appropriate NAV.

After the inception of the fund, the calculation of the NAV boils down to valuing the fixed-income component and the option component of the fund (as can be seen from Figure 2). The NAV of the fund is thus made up primarily of two important elements:

❑ the present value of the initially invested capital at maturity (present value of a zero-coupon bond paying the initially invested capital at maturity); and
❑ the present value of the option strategy underlying the structure (present value of the expected capital gain in the case of a capital-protected fund; the present value of the expected capital gain or loss in the case of a fund without a (full) capital guarantee).

Prior to the final maturity date of a fund, its NAV may fluctuate and may be affected by all kinds of external factors such as interest rate fluctuations, changes in the value of the underlying, market volatility and the residual lifetime of the option.

The guarantee regarding capital protection and the rates of return are valid only on the final maturity date.

This chapter deals with fixed-income structured funds, ie, funds where the underlying of the option is an interest rate, a combination of interest rates or a combination of interest rates and instruments belonging to other asset classes (hybrids). Examples are given in the final section.

CAPITAL-PROTECTED FUNDS AND THE PROBLEM OF INTEREST RATE SENSITIVITY: THE BAS (BERMUDAN ACCRETING SWAPTION)

Most of the fixed-income-linked structured products are set up as capital-protected funds.

As mentioned earlier, a good deal of the NAV of capital-protected funds is accounted for by the present value of a zero-coupon bond. The main valuation risk of a zero-coupon bond lies in its interest rate sensitivity, as shown in Figure 3. This effect will only be temporary and will have disappeared completely by the final maturity date.

In Figure 3 an example is given of a 14.5-year capital-protected fund issued at a point in time characterised by a flat yield curve at 5%. In this case, the present value of the zero-coupon bond equals $1/(1.05 ^ 14.5)$ or $\pm49.3\%$, as indicated by the line "Initial value of the zero-coupon bond".

At inception, the interest rate sensitivity of this zero-coupon bond is depicted by the line "Value of the zero-coupon bond". If interest rates rise, this value drops and vice versa (the x axis shows a parallel shift in the yield curve, the y axis shows the present value of the different instruments).

This implies that the NAV of a capital-protected product is subject to shifts in the yield curve and may fluctuate considerably prior to maturity as a result of changing interest rates. On the one hand, the investor would benefit from a decline in interest rates. On the other, he is exposed to the risk that interest rates might go up, especially with products that have long maturities. When interest rates rise, the NAV of the fund can drop substantially even though

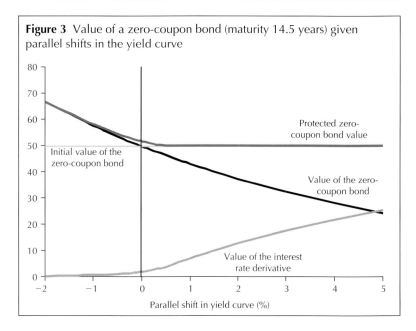

Figure 3 Value of a zero-coupon bond (maturity 14.5 years) given parallel shifts in the yield curve

the present value of the option component remains constant (or even rises).

As investors in fixed-income-related capital-protected products generally have a defensive investment profile, the interest rate risk of the zero-coupon bond should be hedged.

The aim is to find an interest-rate-dependent option/derivative that offers protection against rising interest rates, without impacting potential intermediate profits due to a decline in interest rates, and this at an acceptable cost. Thus we want to create a floor under the evolution of the zero-coupon bond (see also Figure 4).

In fact, an interest rate derivative is needed whose interest rate sensitivity is shown by the upward-sloping line "Value of the interest rate derivative". If this interest rate derivative is added to the existing zero-coupon bond, the total value of the portfolio (fixed-income component of the fund) is depicted by the "floored" line, "Protected zero-coupon bond value".

Fixed-income derivatives that can be used to mitigate the zero-coupon interest rate risk are, for example, caps and payer swaptions (see "Interest rate options" above). However, none of the "standard" derivatives helps to offset the zero-coupon interest rate risk perfectly (either at inception or during the lifetime of the fund/zero-coupon bond).

A perfect hedge of the fixed-income component of the fund can be achieved by adding an exotic fixed-income derivative to the fund, more specifically a Bermudan Accreting Swaption (BAS). A BAS is a special (exotic) type of swaption: an option on an IRS with early exercise opportunities, whereby the notional amount grows over time ("accreting" notional). The Bermudan feature allows investors to exercise their rights at one of several previously agreed points in time between inception and maturity: the exercise dates.

There are two main types of BAS – a payer BAS and a receiver BAS – just as there are two main types of swaptions: a payer swaption and a receiver swaption.

In a payer swaption, the buyer acquires the right to enter into an IRS, where he makes fixed-interest-rate payments periodically (eg, every six months) from start to maturity (this interest rate is fixed at the start of the swaption), while the swap counterparty (seller of the swaption) has the obligation to make floating-rate payments (eg, Euribor payments) periodically from start to maturity if the buyer of the payer swaption decides to exercise his right to enter the swap.

If interest rates increase, the value of this swaption will increase, as the expected floating-rate payments will go up while the fixed-interest-rate payments remain constant.

In order to perfectly offset the zero-coupon bond interest rate risk, a "fine-tuned payer BAS" has to be included in the product. The specificity of the fine-tuned payer BAS lies in the fact that the notional amount varies periodically (eg, from month to month) as a function of the initial expected zero-coupon bond evolution ("accreting"). Furthermore, the fixed rate, although fixed in advance, is not constant during the entire maturity, but also varies periodically (eg, from month to month) depending on the forward curve.

The option can be exercised periodically (eg, each month). However this right can be exercised only once for the full notional amount.

The reason for making use of these specific accreting and fixed-rate schemes lies in the fact that the interest rate sensitivity of the resulting "fine-tuned payer BAS" is perfectly inverse to the interest rate

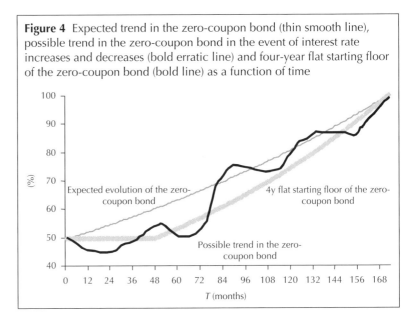

Figure 4 Expected trend in the zero-coupon bond (thin smooth line), possible trend in the zero-coupon bond in the event of interest rate increases and decreases (bold erratic line) and four-year flat starting floor of the zero-coupon bond (bold line) as a function of time

sensitivity of the zero-coupon bond (at inception and subsequently, ie, during the lifetime of the fund/zero-coupon bond).

The impact of combining this type of BAS with a zero-coupon bond is shown in Figure 4.

The thin smooth line shows the expected changes in the value of the zero-coupon bond in the future in function of the yield curve existing at the start of the structure (for a 14.5-year capital-protected product (see also Figure 4)). In practice, the trend in the value of the zero-coupon bond is much more capricious, as indicated by the bold erratic line (as an example of a possible trend). If interest rates rise, the value of the zero-coupon bond will drop, and vice versa. If at some point in time interest rates head up sharply, the value of the zero-coupon bond will go down and may lie well below the value of the zero-coupon bond expected at the inception of the product. Including this type of BAS in the portfolio (fixed-income component of the fund) will create a floor under the realised value of the zero-coupon bond. This floor is the expected evolution of the value of the zero-coupon bond value.

The cost of the BAS as described above – ie, for a "perfect hedge" of the interest rate risk of a zero-coupon bond – is relatively high compared with the present value of the option component at the inception of the fund.

In order to reduce the cost of the BAS, the protection level/floor might be lowered. For example, the floor might be kept constant for the first few years, as is shown by the bold smooth line in Figure 4 (where we assumed a four-year flat floor). In this case, the fixed rate payable by the buyer of the payer swaption is kept at zero during the first few years, but is substantially higher than the forward rates after that, and will increase to 100% at maturity. The BAS will become cheaper because, even though the same total amount of interest is paid, the buyer of the BAS would, in the event that the swaption is exercised, have to pay a higher amount in this case than if there were no "flat start" (the "perfect hedge").

In fact, the BAS can be thought of as a portfolio of weighted European swaptions, each one associated with an exercise date of the BAS. The reset dates of the underlying IRS correspond to the exercise dates of the BAS. Since the investor has the right to enter into just one of the underlying IRS, the start and the length of the IRS he will enter into depends on when the option is exercised.

The price of a BAS swaption should at least be equal to the maximum of the individual swaption prices for all exercise dates. Hence, a lower boundary (and good approximation) for the price of the BAS is formed by the price for the most expensive individual swaption. An upper boundary (but not a good approximation) for the price of the BAS is the sum of the individual swaption prices.

It is quite clear that the price of the BAS depends not only on the construction of the floor, but also on some technical pricing parameters, such as the interest rate curve at the start, implied swaption volatilities or implied volatility skews.

An example of a BAS scheme (fixed-payment scheme and notional scheme) is given below, for a five-year maturity with no "flat floor start". The buyer of the payer BAS has the right (once and for the full notional amount) to exercise the option monthly, starting in one month. If he exercises the option, he has to pay the fixed rate according to the schedule as shown in Table 1, while the swaption counterparty has to pay the one-month Euribor. Both strings of payments are calculated on the basis of the accreting notional schedule as shown in Table 1.

Table 1 Example of the BAS scheme

Calculation period (months)	Fixed rate (%)	Notional as a % of total capital invested (%)
1	End of first month: first exercise date	
2	2.163	83.8291
3	2.185	83.9803
4	2.198	84.1434
5	2.214	84.2975
6	2.231	84.4530
7	2.246	84.6153
8	2.263	84.7737
9	2.280	84.9495
10	2.295	85.1056
11	2.311	85.2575
12	2.334	85.4272
13	2.610	85.5989
14	2.666	85.7851
15	2.724	85.9757
16	2.782	86.1773
17	2.841	86.3837
18	2.899	86.6019
19	2.954	86.8041
20	3.013	87.0178
21	3.071	87.2509
22	3.126	87.4742
23	3.184	87.6869
24	3.243	87.9428
25	3.355	88.1725
26	3.418	88.4190
27	3.481	88.6877
28	3.542	88.9364
29	3.606	88.2077
30	3.668	88.4847
31	3.730	89.7582
32	3.793	90.0372
33	3.857	90.3408
34	3.916	90.6311
35	3.978	90.9072
36	4.040	91.2287
37	3.920	91.5358
38	3.973	91.8348
39	4.025	92.1490
40	4.080	92.4581
41	4.133	92.8039
42	4.184	93.1022
43	4.238	93.4376
44	4.292	93.7897
45	4.344	94.1251
46	4.397	94.4659

Table 1 (continued)

Calculation period (months)	Fixed rate (%)	Notional as a % of total capital invested (%)
47	4.449	94.8236
48	4.493	95.1634
49	4.298	95.5316
50	4.340	95.8852
51	4.381	96.2204
52	4.424	96.5834
53	4.467	96.9514
54	4.511	97.3123
55	4.553	97.7146
56	4.595	98.0607
57	4.639	98.4612
58	4.680	98.8545
59	4.721	99.2144
60	4.763	99.6047
		100.0000

An illustration of how the BAS can be used to obtain interest rate protection in a structured fund is shown in the final section.

PRICING FIXED-INCOME DERIVATIVES

Fixed-income (or interest rate) derivatives, whose values and pay-offs are dependent in some way on the level of one or more yield curves, are much more difficult to price than, say, equity options, for a number of reasons, the most important being the following:

❑ the probabilistic behaviour of interest rates is much more complicated than the probabilistic behaviour of a stock or stock index, for example.
❑ for pricing more exotic interest rate derivatives, it is necessary to develop a model that describes the probabilistic behaviour of the entire yield curve. Hence, different volatilities for each interest rate and correlations between the different interest rates also have to be taken into account.
❑ not only the expected payoff but also the discount factors used to discount the expected payoff will determine the value of the option.

There are a lot of models available for pricing interest rate derivatives. However, none of them can be used for all the different kinds of derivative. Furthermore, there is no model that is accepted as a "standard" by the entire industry. Below is a short overview of the most important existing models. This is only a general overview and it is certainly not the intention to describe the models in great detail or to provide an exhaustive list.

There are two main ways to value interest rate derivatives: on the one hand using simple valuation models where bond prices can be obtained with closed formulae, on the other hand, using interest rate models, or term structure models.

Simple valuation models

Simple valuation models are appropriate for basic interest rate derivatives whose payoffs depend only on the value of a single variable (forward rate, swap rate, bond price, etc) observed at one particular point in time. These models assume a lognormal probability distribution of the variable at that point in time. The big advantage of these models is that they provide a closed-form solution for the option value.

The Black–Scholes model, as published in 1973, has become the market standard for pricing calls and puts on stocks or stock indices. It has been extended so that it can be used to value options on foreign exchange, on futures contracts, etc.

The extension of the Black–Scholes model that is most widely used in the area of interest rates is Black's model. The key assumption made in Black's model is that the variable underlying the option is assumed to be lognormal at the maturity of the option (the same assumption as the one underlying the underlying Black–Scholes stock price option model). In the case of a European bond option, Black's model assumes that the underlying bond price is lognormal at the option's maturity. For a cap, Black's model assumes that the interest rate underlying each of the caplets is lognormally distributed. In the case of a swaption, Black's model assumes that the underlying swap rate is lognormally distributed.

Black's model formulae can be found in every handbook about interest rate derivatives. Shown below is the model for pricing European options.

The following assumptions are made, with V_T being the value of the underlying variable at point T in time:

1. The probability distribution of V_T is lognormal, ie, the probability distribution of the variable underlying the option at point T in time is lognormal.
2. The standard deviation of $\ln V_T$ is $\sigma\sqrt{T}$.
3. Interest rates are nonstochastic.

The formula for the price (the present value) of a call option c, with payoff being $\max(V_T - X, 0)$ at time zero is:

$$c = e^{-rT} \cdot [F \cdot N(d_1) - X \cdot N(d_2)]$$

where:

$$d_1 = \frac{\ln(F/X) + \sigma^2 \cdot T/2}{\sigma \cdot \sqrt{T}}$$

$$d_2 = \frac{\ln(F/X) - \sigma^2 \cdot T/2}{\sigma \cdot \sqrt{T}} = d_1 - \sigma \cdot \sqrt{T}$$

with:
  T: maturity of the option
  F: futures price of V at maturity T, ie, $F = V_T$
  X: strike price of the option
  r: zero-coupon yield for maturity T
  σ: volatility of F
  $N(x)$: cumulative standard normal distribution of x.
  The price of a put option, the value, p, is given by:

$$p = e^{-rT} \cdot [X \cdot N(-d_2) - F \cdot N(-d_1)]$$

Extensions of Black's model exist and can be used (besides the above-mentioned formulae for bonds, caps and swaptions) to value accrual swaps (where payoff accrues only when the floating reference lies within a certain range) and spread options (where the payoff is dependent on the spread between two interest rates).

A convexity adjustment is necessary when the derivative is structured so that its payoff does not reflect the way in which interest is normally paid. In this case, the future interest rate should be assumed to be the forward rate plus a convexity adjustment.

Interest rate models

The simple valuation models as described above do not describe the way in which interest rates evolve over time. The interest rate is assumed to be nonstochastic and the only assumption about the interest rate is that, at some point in time T, it is lognormally distributed. Consequently, these simple models cannot be used to value many of the interest rate derivatives that are popular in many structured products at this point in time (as automatically redeeming structures, callable structures, etc).

The limitations of these simple models can be overcome by using more complicated models, which do construct an evolution of the total yield curve or term structure over time. These models are fittingly called yield curve models or interest rate models, and describe the probabilistic, stochastic nature and behaviour of all rates over time. As a consequence, they are the most complicated models. They take into account movements of the entire yield curve and should take into account individual interest rate stochastics (different volatility assumption for each of the interest rates) as interrelated interest rate stochastics (correlation assumption for each pair of interest rates).

Interest rate models can be split up into short-rate models on the one hand and market models on the other.

Short-rate models

Short-rate models describe the evolution of the short rate, r, sometimes referred to as the instantaneous short rate. By using interest rate conversion equations it is possible to obtain the term structure of interest rates at any given time from the value of r at that time and the risk-neutral process for r. Once the risk-neutral process for r is defined, the initial term structure of r and how it can evolve over time is fully defined.

The big advantage of these models is their analytical tractability (bond and/or option prices can be calculated explicitly) or numerical ease of implementation.

In short-rate models with time-homogeneous parameters (constant over time), the initial term structure is an output of the model rather than an input. This is a big disadvantage for short-rate models, although they are useful for understanding potential relationships between variables in the economy. Because the initial term structure is an output of the model, it might be different from what is observed in the market (and inconsistent with reality). An improvement would be to make the parameters time-varying. In that case, the initial term structure would be an input of the model (via the time-dependent drift function: see below).

One-factor short-rate models. In a one-factor model, the process for r involves only one source of uncertainty. This means the entire yield curve is specified by a single variable, the short rate. Usually, the short rate is described by an Ito process, ie, $dr(t) = m(r,t)\,dt + s(r,t)\,dz(t)$, with $r(0) = r_0$, and m being the instantaneous drift and s the instantaneous standard deviation.

Some of the best-known one-factor short-rate models are:

- ❏ Vasicek model $m(r,t) = a \cdot [b - r]$ $s(r,t) = \sigma$
- ❏ Cox, Ingersoll & Ross (CIR) $m(r,t) = a \cdot [b - r]$ $s(r) = \sigma \cdot \sqrt{r}$
- ❏ Hull and White $m(r,t) = a \cdot [b(t) - r]$ $s(r,t) = \sigma$
- ❏ Black and Karasinski $m(r,t) = r \cdot [n(t) - a \cdot \ln r]$ $s(r,t) = \sigma \cdot r$

In these models a, b and σ are constants and $b(t)$ and $n(t)$ are deterministic functions of time.

Vasicek, CIR and Hull–White assume that r is mean-reverting ($m(r) = a \cdot (b - r)$). When r is high, mean reversion tends to cause it to have a negative drift; when r is low, mean reversion tends to cause it to have positive drift. There are of course compelling economic arguments in favour of mean reversion, and hence these models are to be preferred above models not incorporating this mean reversion. The problem with Vasicek and Hull–White is that the short-term interest rate, r, is normally distributed ($s(r) = \sigma$) in the future, and hence, can be negative. This problem is solved by the CIR-model, which implies positive interest rates ($s(r) = \sigma \cdot \sqrt{r}$). In this model the short rate is characterised by a non-central chi-squared distribution. The drawback of negative rates is also solved by the lognormal Black and Karasinski model. However, this model is not analytically tractable and prices have to be computed numerically.

Two-factor short-rate models. One-factor models still prove to be useful when the product to be priced does not depend on the correlations of different rates but depends at every instant on a single rate on the whole interest rate curve. In general, when correlation plays a more relevant role, one needs to use a multifactor model, eg, a two-factor model. Two-factor short-rate models are models in which the process of interest rate r involves two sources of uncertainty. For example, the two-factor Gaussian Vasicek model. Brennan and Schwartz developed a model where the process for the short rate is linked to a long rate, which in turn follows a stochastic process. Besides a stochastic process for the interest rate, Longstaff and Schwartz (1992) include a stochastic process for volatility.

Market models
The disadvantage of the short-rate models presented is that they do not reproduce the initial term structure automatically. By choosing the proper parameters, the fit can be made better, but it is usually not exact and in some cases may lead to significant errors. Furthermore, it is difficult to achieve a clear understanding of the covariance structure of the forward rates. Therefore, most models (and most widely used by traders, structurers, etc) are market models, which are designed to be exactly consistent with today's term structure.

HJM model: An alternative to short-rate models is the Heath, Jarrow and Morton (HJM) model, which models the behaviour of instantaneous forward rates. It fits the initial term structure of interest rates exactly and permits a volatility structure as complex as desired. The HJM can use several independent risk factors and is described by following equations:

$$df(t, T) = m(t, T) \, dt + \sum_i \sigma_i(t, T, f(t, T)) \, dz_i(t)$$

$$m(t, T) \, dt = \sum_i \sigma_i(t, T, f(t, T)) \left[\int_t^T \sigma_i(t, u, f(t, u)) \, du \right]$$

with:
$m(t, T)$: drift term
$\sigma(t, T, f(t, T))$: volatility term
$f(t, T)$: instantaneous forward rate
$dz(t)$: Brownian motion

The advantage of the HJM model is the freedom it allows in choosing the volatility term structure. The disadvantages include the fact that the instantaneous forward rate is not directly observable in the market and that there is no analytical solution. A Monte Carlo approach or non-combining tree is needed.

LMM and SMM model: More recently, the HJM model has been modified by, among others, Brace, Gatarek and Musiella (BGM), to apply to non-instantaneous forward rates. This modification has come to be known as the lognormal LIBOR Market Model (LMM). The LMM model prices caps with Black's cap formula, which is the standard formula used in the market. The version where three-month forward rates are modelled is widely used. This version allows the model to replicate observed cap prices that depend on three-month forward rates exactly. In another version, the lognormal Swap Market Model (SMM), forward swap rates are modelled. Since the SMM model prices European swap options with Black's swaption formula, the model replicates observed market swap option prices exactly. Note that the LMM model and SMM model are not compatible, since the forward LIBOR rates and the forward swap rates cannot be lognormal at the same time. In the LMM model, analytical approximations for swaption prices are available. The main difficulty with the market models is (as is the case for the HJM model) that they are difficult to implement other than by using Monte Carlo simulation. As a result, they are computationally slow and difficult to use for American- or Bermudan-style options.

Calibration

The difficulty with each of the above models is that the model must fit the current market data available (yield curve) and that the parameters must be calibrated such that the model prices match the prices observed in the market for various liquid instruments such as swaps, caps, floors and liquid bonds.

The matching of the prices of various liquid instruments observed in the market can be done using minimisation procedures for a specific function that must be minimised.

The function to be minimised is typically:

$$\sum_{i}^{n}(U_i - V_i)^2 \quad \text{or} \quad \sum_{i}^{n}\frac{(U_i - V_i)^2}{U_i}$$

where

n: number of instruments used to calibrate the model parameters

U_i: market price of the i-th instrument used for calibration purposes (cap, swap, bond, etc)

V_i: model price of the i-th instrument used for calibration purposes.

STRUCTURED FIXED-INCOME PRODUCTS:
THE UNDERLYING OPTION STRATEGIES
Overview of the structured fixed-income market

It is impossible to give a detailed and exhaustive overview of all types of fixed-income derivative structures that have recently been launched. We can only give some idea about the variety and richness of the market by providing a general classification and outlining recent trends and by describing some recently issued structures.

The most logical way of classifying fixed-income derivative structures is along three different lines:

1. the fixed income instrument(s) underlying the option;
2. the payoff structure (type of option applied to the underlying); and
3. the maturity of the option (taking into account early redemption features).

It is clear that any type of payoff formula can be applied to any (set of) underlying. Likewise, any maturity (and early redemption features) can be applied to any combination of underlying and payoff formulae.

The combination of underlying, payoff structure and maturity determines the conditions that can be offered to the investor. These conditions are determined by the market environment (yield curves, volatilities, correlations and so forth) and are set in such a way that the present value of the cashflows paid by the fund is equal to the present value (price) of the option sold by the option (swap) counterparty.

For the underlying of the option, a single underlying interest rate or bond (short-term or long-term in any currency), a basket of interest rates or bonds (fixed-income multi-asset option) or a basket of interest rate variables and variables of other asset classes (hybrid options) can be used. The only limitation is the liquidity of the underlying market, which has to be high enough in order to effectively hedge the option.

As regards the fixed-income multi-asset option, the multiple underlying interest rates (or bonds) may be denoted in the same currency (for example, intra-yield curve spread options (such as a payoff dependent on the difference between the ten-year euro swap rate and the two-year euro swap rate)), or in different currencies (for example, inter-yield curve spread options (such as a payoff dependent on the difference between the six-month Euribor and the six-month USD LIBOR rates)).

Hybrid options are characterised by an underlying basket that consists of variables belonging to different asset classes. Interest rates or bonds can be combined with stocks or stock indices, commodity indices (eg, a call on a basket of a government bond, a stock index and a commodity index), forex, inflation (eg, yearly lock-ins based on an interest rate, but floored at inflation), credit events (eg, payoff related to interest rates, or bond returns, stepping down in function of the number of credit events linked to a basket of companies), or any other type (or combination of types) of underlying.

The payoff of the structure shows even more variation. "Simple interest rate derivatives" such as calls and puts on the underlying, caps or floors, or swaptions are of course frequently used. Furthermore, some more exotic payoff structures are also widely used in structured notes and funds: knockout options, barrier options, range accruals, spread options, floating reverse structures, step-up structures and so on.

The maturity of the option may vary from very short (just a few days) to very long (up to 20 years or even longer). Recently, early redemption features have often been used in the interest rate derivatives market. Callable features, where the note or fund can be called early at the issuer's sole discretion at some predetermined point(s) in time, are very frequently used. Also, puttable features are possible, although less used, where the investor can decide to terminate the structure early at some predetermined point(s) in time. A recent innovation is the "target automatic redemption" structure, where the early termination of the structure depends on an objective measure (such as the total amount of coupons paid out).

Some examples

The following examples show how the structurers of these fund try to meet the demands of the market environment (yield curve environment) and investors.

The first example concerns the KBC Maxisafe Interest structure, a product for very defensive investors. It takes into account the low-yield-curve environment (and hence expectations of higher long-term rates in the future).

In the last three examples, some products are shown that exploit the current steep yield curve, and take account of investors' expectations that short-term euro yields will remain low. These examples also illustrate two of the recent market trends: the frequent use of callable structures and the "target automatically redeeming structures" innovation.

KBC Maxisafe Interest structure (long-term structure with yearly, floored lock-in of the long-term interest rate)
Payoff feature. The Maxisafe/Multisafe Interest structure has two investment objectives: first of all full capital protection at maturity; secondly, additional "gains" dependent on the interest rate market via an interest-rate-linked option.

Specifically, the payoff of the option component depends on the level of the 10-year euro swap rate at well-defined observation dates and on a minimum yearly lock-in or floor that is fixed at the start. Each year, at the start of each interim period, the higher of either the floor or the 10-year euro swap rate at that moment, whichever is higher, is locked in. The floor can be zero, but (up till now) not negative. Hence, negative lock-ins are (at present) not possible. At maturity, the investor will receive the arithmetical sum of all gains locked in annually for all the interim periods.

The periodic floor offers the investor a guaranteed minimum return. Furthermore, the structure enables the investor to benefit from a higher return if the 10-year euro swap rate moves up. This periodic lock-in can be considered a fixed coupon plus a call on the underlying interest rate with deferred payment. Via a string of simple call options on the underlying interest rate, 100% of the increase in that rate can be offered.

Some variants on this theme are possible: the predetermined floor can be different for several interim periods, the participation rate can be lower than 100% – for instance 90% or 80% – or the underlying interest rate may differ – for instance the 10-year REX rate, the five-year euro swap rate, etc. The conditions of a particular fund are tailor-made depending on the requirements of the clients and the market conditions.

BAS feature

As demonstrated earlier, the NAV of a capital-protected fund is largely dependent on the zero-coupon bond-value component of the NAV. This is also the case for this fund. The NAV of this fund, without interest rate protection, is depicted by the thin line in the graphs below (NAV analysis after one year and two years, depending on the parallel yield shifts for the complete yield curve).

As this fund aims to attract very defensive investors, a Bermudan Accreting Swaption (BAS, see "Capital-protected funds and the problem of interest rate sensitivity: the BAS (Bermudan Accreting Swaption)" above) is included in the portfolio. The effect of including the BAS is depicted by the bold line in Figures 5 and 6.

The fund used in this analysis is the KBC Maxisafe Interest 6 fund, which has a maturity of 14.5 years and a yearly lock-in equal to the maximum of 90% of the 10-year German government

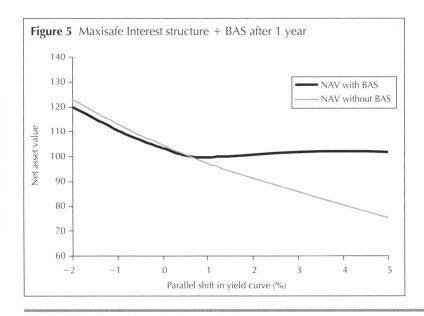

Figure 5 Maxisafe Interest structure + BAS after 1 year

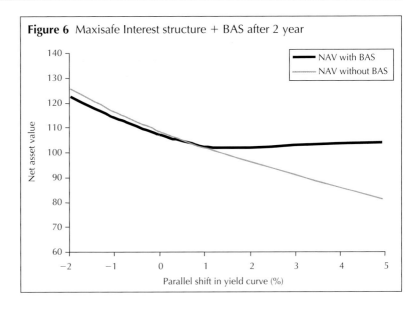

Figure 6 Maxisafe Interest structure + BAS after 2 year

rate (REX) and a floor of 4.8% for the first six periods and 3% for the last eight periods.

KBC Multisafe Exclusive Step Up 3 (callable range accrual on six-month Euribor)
This structure has a maximum maturity of nine years. Besides offering a capital guarantee at maturity, the fund pays yearly coupons to the investor.

The first coupon is fixed at 4.5%, the next coupons (for Years 2 to 9) are determined by the formula:

$$\text{coupon}_t = \text{MaxCoupon}_t \times \frac{n}{N}$$

where:

❑ n = number of observation dates in the (yearly) period, where the six-month Euribor rate is below a certain level, fixed in advance for that period, the so-called StepUpBarrier_t
❑ N = total number of observation dates in the (yearly) period.

Table 2 shows, per period (from 2 to 9), the value of MaxCoupon_t and StepUpBarrier_t.

Table 2 Conditions for the structure KBC
Multisafe Exclusive step up 3

Period$_t$	MaxCoupon$_t$ (%)	StepUpBarrier$_t$ (%)
Period 2	6.0	4.00
Period 3	6.0	4.00
Period 4	8.0	4.75
Period 5	8.0	4.75
Period 6	10.0	5.25
Period 7	10.0	5.25
Period 8	12.0	5.75
Period 9	12.0	5.75

The structure is callable yearly at par by the option counterparty (the counterparty selling the option to the fund), this starting at the end of the second year. It is clear that the counterparty will call the structure, in which case it will be terminated early at par for the investor, if the present value of the option is higher than the present value of Euribor payments used by the fund to buy the option (see Figure 2).

The variable periodic coupons can be considered a series of forward-starting accrual swaps plus a callable feature (option on a string of options).

*KBC Click Interest Target 2 (target automatic redeeming
reverse structure on 12-month euro swap rate)*
This structure has a maximum maturity of seven years. Besides offering a capital guarantee at maturity, the fund pays yearly coupons to the investor.

The first coupon is fixed at 7%; the next coupons (for Years 2 to 7) are determined by the formula:

$$\text{Coupon}_t = \max(0\%, 11\% - 2 \times \text{12-month EUR swap rate})$$

So, the yearly coupon is higher if the one-year swap rate remains low. If this underlying rate increases dramatically, the coupon level will be floored at 0%.

The fund is redeemable early after each coupon payment. The early redemption feature is triggered automatically (hence the term "Target Automatic Redeemable") if the sum of the coupons paid reaches 15%. In this case, the last coupon is capped such that the sum of the coupons paid is exactly equal to 15%.

The variable periodic coupons can be considered a series of forward-starting reverse floaters floored at zero, plus an autocallable feature (option on a string of options).

KBC Click Interest Callable 1 (callable leveraged reverse structure on 12-month euro swap rate)
This structure has a maximum maturity of nine years. Besides a capital guarantee at maturity, the fund pays yearly coupons to the investor.

The first two coupons (after one year and two years) are fixed at 4.75%, the next coupons (for Years 3 to 9) are determined by the formula:

$$\text{Coupon}_t = \max\{0\%, 3 \times [(5\% + 0.25\% \times (t - 3)) - \text{12-month EUR swap rate}]\}$$

So, the yearly coupon equals three times the difference between a fixed percentage (5% for Year 3 and afterwards increased by 0.25% per year) and the 12-month euro swap rate. Hence, if this underlying rate remains low, the investor can expect high coupons; if this underlying rate increases dramatically, the coupon level is will be floored at 0%.

The structure is callable yearly at par by the option counterparty (the counterparty selling the option to the fund), this starting at the end of the second year. It is clear that the counterparty will call the structure (in which case it will be terminated early at par for the investor), if the present value of the option is higher than the present value of Euribor payments used by the fund to pay for the option (see Figure 2).

The variable periodic coupons can be considered a series of forward-starting step-up reverse floaters floored at zero, plus a callable feature (option on a string of options).

REFERENCES

Brigo, D., and F. Mercurio, 2001, *Interest Rate Models, Theory and Practice* (Berlin: Springer Finance).

Campbell, J. Y., A. W. Lo and A. C. Mackinlay, 1997, "The Econometrics of Financial Markets" (Princeton, N.J.: Princeton University Press).

Clewlow, L., and C. Strickland, 1998, *Implementing Derivatives Models* (West Sussex: John Wiley & Sons).

Hull, J. C., and A. White, 1996, "Using Hull–White Interest Rate Trees", *Journal of Derivatives*, Winter 1996.

Hull, J. C., 2000, *Options, Futures and Other Derivatives*, 4th edn (Prentice-Hall: N.J.).

Hull, J. C., and A. White, 2000, "The General Hull-White Model and Super-Calibration", Working Paper.

Hull, J. C., and A. White, 2000, "Forward Rate Volatilities, Swap Rate Volatilities and the Implementation of the Libor Market Model", Working Paper, in *Journal of Fixed Income*, **2**, 46–62.

James, J., and N. Webber, 2000, *Interest Rate Modelling* (West Sussex: John Wiley & Sons).

Lee, H., 2000, *Interest Rate Risk Models – Similarities and Differences* (London: Risk).

Longstaff, F. A., and E. S. Schwartz, 1992, "Interest Rate Volatility and the Term Structure: A Two-Factor General Equilibrium Model", *Journal of Finance*, **47(4)**, 1259–82.

Ong, M. K., 1997, "Volatility and Calibration in Interest Rate Models", in I. Nelken (ed), *Volatility in the Capital Market* (Chicago, IL: West Glenlake).

Rebonato, R., 1996, *Interest Rate Option Models* (2nd Ed, 1998) (New York: John Wiley & Sons).

Rebonato, R., 2002, *Modern Pricing of Interest Rate Derivatives – The Libor Market Model and Beyond* (Princeton, NJ: Princeton University Press).

9

Hedging with Inflation Derivatives

Allan Lane; Stanley Myint

Independent; Royal Bank of Scotland

With inflation being such a hot topic of discussion lately, there has been an accompanying boom in the demand for inflation-linked (IL) products. Inflation permeates all levels of the economy, from the world's central banks, through large and small corporates, all the way down to the individual. The importance of inflation is truly global. Pressure on Japanese retail prices continues downwards; in the US Alan Greenspan, head of the Federal Reserve Board, famously reduced interest rates as an "insurance policy" against deflation; while in the euro zone the inflation level of member states remains a key criterion for membership of European Monetary Union (EMU).[1] Indeed, some members have experienced low, or even negative inflation, which could become a difficult hurdle for any accession country to get past before they can sign up.

INTRODUCTION

Welcome to the world of post-millennium economics. As with many other popular themes from economics, the concept of inflation/deflation is hardly a new one, so much so that many of the issues around the subject are now taken for granted. The derivatives markets have until recently been conspicuously sluggish in their appetite for providing risk management solutions tailored to inflation. During 2003 the market appeared to burst into life. This is an example of a recent trend towards derivatives being linked to broad economic parameters, ("economic derivatives"). A number of market participants offer a range of contracts whose payoff directly depends on inflation indices such as the Retail Price

Inflation (RPI) in the UK and the Harmonised Index of Consumer Prices (HICP) in Europe, but to some extent these products are still at their embryonic stage.

In this chapter, we shall explore the reasons for the growth of the inflation derivatives market and examples of their use, and shall touch upon some of the pricing and risk management issues.

A BRIEF HISTORY OF THE IL BOND MARKET

Before going on to explore the range of derivative instruments that are traded within the market, it will prove useful to take a look at the way the underlying index-linked bond market has evolved over the last 20 years. The issuance of such bonds was led by the UK, when in 1981 the Bank of England launched its first index-linked government bond. It was some 17 years before the Agence France Tresor issued a 10-year bond with a series of cashflows linked to the level of the French Consumer Price Index (excluding tobacco), before subsequently issuing some additional bonds linked to the European HICP index. The UK was also the first market that actively traded swaps on the back of the RPI and LPI (Limited Price Inflation) indices.[2] As a final note, one should highlight that both Australia and Canada were issuers of index-linked bonds in 1985 and 1991 respectively, providing the basis for their own inflation swaps market.

Currently, a wide range of inflation indices exists, most obviously on a country-by-country basis, but often within a single country as well. For example, as a trading bloc, Europe comprises a set of countries each of which measures its consumer price index in its own way. To allow for comparisons of inflation on country-by-country basis, each participating member also constructs the Harmonised

Table 1 Main IL bonds markets

	Canada	France	Sweden	UK	US
First issue date	1991	1998	1994	1981	1997
Maturities	2021–36	2009–32	2008–28	2004–35	2007–32
Number of indexed bonds	4	6	6	10	12
Notional outstanding (USD bn)	13	64	23	73	141

Source: DMO, Bloomberg

Inflation Index, HICP. To reflect the level of inflation on a pan-European basis, a weighted average of these national indices is known as Monetary Union Index of Consumer Prices (MUICP) for those countries that have signed up for full monetary union. When Denmark, Sweden and the UK are included in that average, it is known as the European Index of Consumer Prices (EICP) index. In the US, the main index of interest is the Current Consumer Price Index (CPI-U), which essentially is the level of inflation as measured within the urban areas. Another variation by which alternative measures can be constructed is to include/ exclude such key items as tobacco or mortgage payments.

This wide range of inflation indices has, as of recently, been accompanied by a corresponding set of IL government bonds. For instance, there are currently 6 government bonds linked to euro-zone inflation, with maturities from 2008 to 2032, issued by France, Italy and Greece. In addition to that, there is a number of issues linked to domestic inflation indices. There is an even higher number of issues in the UK and US (see Table 1). Increasing number of available points on the inflation curve is one of the reasons for increased trading in inflation derivatives.

WHY THE DEMAND FOR IL DERIVATIVES?

There are a number of separate reasons why inflation-related products have become more popular over the last few years, combining to create a level of market activity that has outstripped that of the previous five together.

Global inflationary trends: Although globalisation has helped inflation to trend down, both the cyclical nature and the structural changes associated with the economic environment have produced inflation pressures on a country-by-country basis. For example, the reasons for locking into a long-term real interest rate may apply to one European country but not another.

Pension fund legislation: Structural change within the European pension fund industry caused by a shift in government led policy initiatives, increasing the gap between the supply and demand for IL issues.

Increased bond issuance: Over the last decade or so there has been a gradual increase in the number of IL securities issued by both governments and corporates. This increased range of underlying securities was always a prerequisite to the development of the derivatives market.

Private finance initiatives: In a number of government-led private finance initiatives, local governments have underwritten infrastructure projects with IL payments, which directly lead to a number of IL bond issues.

Fund management requirements: Within the asset management and hedge fund community, there has been an increase in the use of IL instruments in their quest to optimise portfolio returns.

Within the UK market it was primarily government-led legislation that stimulated much of the demand for index-linked gilts. The Private Finance Initiative saw many local and national government agencies fund their infrastructure projects by working in conjunction with the private sector, often using a securitisation vehicle to repackage the index-linked revenues. Furthermore, the government had undertaken a wholesale reform of the pensions industry, first with its Minimum Funding Requirement initiative, included as part of the 1995 Pensions Act. More recently the accounting profession enacted the accounting standard FRS17.

On the back of this regulation came a variation of the RPI, where, within the insurance and pension fund sector, there naturally arose the need to match their LPI-linked exposures. In contrast to the case of RPI-linked exposures, these liabilities contained an embedded cap and floor that protected against extreme moves in the inflation rate. Suddenly, what started as a simple inflation swap had changed into a complex structure with embedded option features.

This extra activity within the UK coincided with the creation of the single European market, which by pure accident occurred in one of the more pronounced equity bear markets of the last 50 years. The diminishing equity returns provided the opportunity for the Medium-Term Notes (MTN) market to offer a number of inflation-dependent structures to the retail investor base. By the end of the first quarter of 2003, this new category of MTN had arrived by storm and was only surpassed in volume by interest-rate-linked MTNs. It had been possible to structure these notes so that they provided more attractive features than those of a pure equity-linked note, insofar as they hedged for the effect inflation would have on the capital investment.

During the previous two years, there has been a period of dramatic reductions in nominal interest rates, so investors started looking more carefully at inflation. It was as though inflation had become an asset class in its own right. With inflation noticeably higher in some European countries than others, retail demand for these products continues to vary across national frontiers. As the facts and figures were collated for the second quarter of 2003, it appears that the initial ardour for inflation-related MTNs was starting to cool. Because of the global events that were to dominate the first half of 2003 – the war in Iraq and the rapid outbreak of the SARS epidemic – the prediction for rising inflation, was replaced by a fear of impending deflation.

In the UK, the government has been instrumental in galvanising the demand with its reform of the pension industry. A similar reform is starting to take shape in mainland Europe, explaining why most of the biggest players in the inflation market have set their sights on Europe.

WHO ARE THE MARKET PARTICIPANTS?

To simplify one's understanding of the IL derivatives market, it helps to identify the sectors that pay or receive inflation.

Who needs to hedge against inflation? Parties whose revenue or cost is linked to inflation have different motivations to use these products. This link can be explicit. For example, the water regulators in England and Wales, OFWAT, limit increase of water prices to RPI ± margin. In a similar fashion, property companies often have rental increases contractually linked to inflation. On the other hand, every producer or retailer of goods that figures in the consumer basket has an implicit link of revenues to inflation. Food retailing is a particularly good example for this, as the inflation index has a significant exposure to food items. Whether the link to inflation is explicit, implicit or both, as long as inflation dependence is significant, (and not offset elsewhere), it is worth considering whether to reduce it via IL derivatives.

Table 2 Main participants in the inflation markets

Inflation receivers	Inflation payers
❑ Pension funds ❑ Insurance companies ❑ Hedge funds ❑ Retail investors	❑ Utilities (water companies, gas companies, etc) ❑ Retailers ❑ Property companies and housing associations ❑ Local government entities (PFI-based projects, eg, railways, roads, healthcare, etc)

One cannot address all of the customer's requirements by only using IL bonds, and, as a consequence, this increase in demand has naturally led to the development of a variety of products that provides:

❑ increased liquidity
❑ customized cashflows:

　❑ better cashflow and timing matching
　❑ wider range of inflation indices
　❑ ability to hedge monthly index fixings

❑ ability to provide exposure to multiple asset classes, via hybrid structures (eg, an MTN paying the best of an equity or inflation index)

Potential users of inflation derivatives largely come in the following categories: pension funds and life insurers, utilities, retailers, property companies, hedge funds and finally individuals. The economic fortune of all these types of user depends on the level of inflation, although for different reasons.

Pensions and life insurance policies are normally linked to inflation. Traditionally funds used to invest a majority of their assets in stocks and bonds, which do not have obvious inflation dependence. This creates a mismatch of assets and liabilities, which can be hedged with inflation derivatives. This mismatch has become more obvious given the recent regulatory requirements to mark it to market. Consequently, in the UK, we have recently seen an increase in the use of inflation derivatives by pension funds and life insurers.

As mentioned earlier, regulators often restrict the growth in prices that a utility company can charge to the inflation rate plus or minus a margin. Those utilities have an explicit link to inflation and

have reasons to worry about low inflation or even deflation, causing their revenues to fall. This can be offset in two ways. First, the
company can use IL funding (ie, issue an IL bond). Alternatively,
through the use of inflation derivatives, it can hedge synthetically.

Retailers' income is also linked to inflation, insofar as the products
they are selling reflect the composition of the consumer basket used
to define inflation. This is particularly relevant for food retailers. We
can see this by starting from the relationship that Food Sales = Food
Price × Volume Sold. Since food items are a significant portion
of the consumer basket, the food price is expected to have a high
correlation with inflation. On the other hand the volume of food sold
is relatively insensitive to the state of the economy, as these are
"essential items". From there follows the empirically observed high
correlation between the rate of inflation and food sales.

Similarly, many property companies have an (explicit or
implicit) inflation link in their future rents. Therefore, property
companies are increasingly a user of inflation derivatives. However,
in a dynamic and booming property market, incomes of large property companies show relatively little correlation with inflation and
depend more on the specifics of their property portfolio. As we all
know, property and rents depend as much on "location, location,
location", as on the overall measure of inflation.

With the dramatic rise in the number of hedge funds operating
within the market has come an accompanying interest in inflation.
Acting as another source of market risk, IL bonds and swaps provide another tool by which a fund manager attempts to improve
the return on his or her portfolio.

Finally, the last category of potential users of inflation derivatives are consumers, as it is their habits and needs that form the
basis for the inflation measures. For reasons that partly have to
do with psychology and partly with the fact that salaries can be
considered a natural hedge against inflation, people still rarely
hedge against inflation (as opposed to, say, car theft or fire).
Nevertheless, IL products have been a popular retail investment.
For example in Italy, retail investors have been able to buy equity-
linked notes, whose principal was protected against inflation and
the equity downside.

To this we can add other categories of users whose cashflows are
linked to inflation explicitly or implicitly: the Private Finance

Initiative (PFI) and similar infrastructure companies in Europe (railways, roads, healthcare, local authorities and supranationals). We expect that, over time, the number and type of inflation derivative users will grow, but there are also structural constraints on market growth.

Of the categories of inflation players, the only natural receivers of inflation are pension funds and insurers. However, the relative size of the market is severely biased towards a desire to receive inflation. For example, in the UK, estimates based on extrapolating the structure of liabilities of a typical corporate pension scheme give a figure of about £400 billion of liabilities that are linked to inflation, most of it unhedged. This is to be compared with the IL bond market at about £100 billion, of which 90% is index-linked gilts. Therefore, there is a significant mismatch between potential payers and receivers of inflation, that only the derivatives market can bridge.

THE MOST FAMILIAR IL DERIVATIVES

The following list shows the four most basic types of inflation product. In the next section we discuss how these can be combined in IL structures adjusted to user needs.

Zero-coupon swaps

Zero-coupon swaps constitute an example of what is known as a "pure" inflation swap (see Oppon and Alibert, 2003). This is a simple swap that involves the exchange of a pair of cashflows at the maturity date of the swap.

❑ Maturity of swap — n years
❑ Notional of swap — N
❑ Inflation index at year j — $I(j)$
❑ Fixed rate of swap — rf
❑ Payer's leg — $N \times \{(1 + rf)^n - 1\}$
❑ Receiver's leg — $N \times \{I(n)/I(0) - 1\}$

Year-on-year swaps

Year-on-year swaps provide another example of a pure inflation swap. This swap involves the exchange of cashflows on an annual basis.

❑ Year-on-year rate (annual) – ryoy
❑ Payer's leg – $N \times$ ryoy
❑ Receiver's leg – $N \times \{I(1)/I(0) - 1\}$
   $\times \{I(2)/I(0) - 1\} \ldots$
   $\{I(n)/I(0) - 1\}$

Synthetic index-linked bonds

These bonds are typically issued by companies with exposure to long term index-linked debt, and, more often than not, the cash-flows are swapped into LIBOR. The index fixings are subject to the same time lag as the equivalent government index-linked bond.

❑ Fixed based coupon – cf
❑ Coupon paid at year j – $\text{cf} \times I(j)/I(0)$
❑ Notional paid at maturity – $N \times I(n)/I(0)$

Real annuity swaps

This type of swap allows a user to swap an index-linked set of cash-flows, for a set that compound up in size with a predetermined growth rate.

❑ Payer's leg – $N \times I(j)/I(0)$
❑ Receiver's leg – $N \times (1 + \text{rf})j$

Examples of IL derivatives

Case study: Hedging a pension liability via a synthetic RPI swap

A corporate pension fund needs to hedge its liabilities, which are linked to inflation. Option one is to buy IL gilts or IL corporate bonds and hedge the credit risk via a credit default swap. Due to the shortage of IL debt, this is easier said than done. The alternative is for the pension fund to buy a synthetic package consisting of a vanilla gilt and the IL swap, whereby the fund receives inflation and pays the gilt coupon. The net result is that the corporate receives a stream of cashflows adjusted by inflation. In this way, the desired economic exposure is achieved. An additional advantage of this strategy is that, unlike in the underlying IL bond market, details of the IL swap (coupon dates, amortising schedule, etc) can be matched to the preferences of the fund.

Case study: Pre-hedging an IL bond issue

A corporate plans to issue an IL bond in two months' time, but is concerned about the possible rise in IL gilt yields. The price of a new IL issue is a function of the IL gilt yield at the time of issue and the corporation's credit spread:

$$\text{Yield of issue} = \text{IL gilt yield} + \text{credit spread}$$

Pre-hedging using the IL gilt lock would allow the corporate to hedge the IL gilt yield element of the issue. The corporate enters into a cash-settled contract for differences, based on IL gilt yields, which pays out in the event that yields rise. The bank effectively "shorts" the IL gilt on behalf of the corporate, for settlement on any day up to the maturity date of the IL gilt lock, ie, the expected issue date of the bond. On the issue date, the bank buys the IL gilt on the corporate's behalf and provides cash settlement if yields are higher. If yields are lower, the corporate provides the difference. The rationale is that, if IL gilt yields rise, the price of IL gilts will fall. This will give a profit on the "short" IL gilt position, which equals the present value of the increase in the funding costs associated with this rise.

Case study: Optimal portfolio restructuring via IL swaps

A corporate has income contractually linked to inflation. So far, it was funded 50% through floating bank loans and 50% through fixed-coupon bonds. However, the residual dependence of income to inflation has not been hedged. From the portfolio perspective, this funding is suboptimal, as the corporate could achieve a better return, with the same amount of risk if it diversified its sources of funding into inflation-linked. Using portfolio optimisation techniques, the optimal short-term mix of funding is found to consist of 30% IL, 20% fixed and 50% floating debt. There are two ways to restructure the portfolio to achieve this mix. If the corporate needs additional funding, it might consider issuing an IL bond, which can often give very attractive financing levels. Alternatively, if there is no need for additional financing, the corporate enters into an IL swap for 30% of overall debt, whereby it pays IL cashflows and receive fixed.

Case Study: Structured finance property sale and leaseback

A corporate whose income is linked to inflation sells part of its property portfolio to a special-purpose vehicle (SPV). It receives an upfront sale price from the SPV, which is financed via structured debt. The bank takes senior and mezzanine positions in the loan to the SPV, while the equity tranche is retained by the corporate. In order to use the properties, the corporate then pays IL rental streams to the SPV, which it hopes to hedge via its IL revenue stream. Finally, the SPV enters into an inflation swap whereby it pays out the HICP uplifts to the investment bank, and receives fixed.

MODELLING INFLATION – FROM BOOTSTRAPPING THE INFLATION CURVE TO AN EXTENDED HJM MODEL
Fisher's hypothesis

In modelling inflation, one of the key ideas that underpin the subject is the Fisher hypothesis, which bridges the gap between nominal interest rates and the expected level of inflation. There are a number of ways in which this relationship can be expressed, but in its original form Fisher postulated that the expected level of inflation $I(t)$, can be represented as the difference between the level of real interest rates, $r(t)$, and nominal interest rates $\hat{r}(t)$:

$$I(t) = r(t) - \hat{r}(t)$$

Alternatively one can represent the relationship in terms of forward rates (see Manning and Jones 2003),

$$\{1 + F^n(t:T_1,T_2)\} = \{1 + F^r(t:T_1,T_2)\} \times \{1 + F^i(t:T_1,T_2)\}$$

where the quantities $\{1 + F^k(t:T_1,T_2)\}, k = n, r, i$ represent the forward nominal rate, real rate and inflation rate as measured at time t, between the times T_1 and T_2 respectively.

With such a simply stated relationship among stochastic quantities, it is not surprising to discover that when tested with empirical data the hypothesis often breaks down. Indeed, over the last decade or so the level of real interest rates has not remained static as the inflation risk premium has ebbed and flowed with the changing views of the market.

In its modern form, it is more appropriate to suggest a weaker version of the proposition that states that the difference between inflation and the nominal to real interest rate gap is proportional to the so-called inflation risk premium.

It is perhaps worth noting that the notion of real interest rates is not purely a theoretical construction: inflation is of particular interest to investors. Indeed, they need to worry about the level of real interest rates, particularly if they invest for a substantial period. Of course, any investor will expect a higher inflation risk premium if the deposit is held for any considerable length of time. As inflation eats away at the effectiveness of one's saving account, on both the nominal amount invested and on the interest accrued, then it also eats away at any outstanding debt. Why pay off your debt early if inflation is going to make any future debt become more manageable?

Bootstrapping the curve

The methodology that is used to construct the inflation curve is driven by the collection of market instruments for which the current price is known. In the mid-1990s, when the government-backed PFI deals provided much of the activity in the index-linked gilts arena, very little choice was available. Bond prices were pretty well the only game in town.

As the supranational-backed issues subsequently hit the markets a few years later, this had a notable impact on the inflation swaps market, and offered the possibility of also using the swaps market as a source of input prices. These bond issues came to the notice of other swap houses, and in turn was of more benefit to the pension fund industry, which was better able to match its own liabilities.

In an era before the swaps market had really increased in depth, the "real rates" method of bootstrapping the curve was more commonplace (see Evans, 1998). This approach used the data from the nominal interest rates market, combined with the traded prices of index-linked bonds to construct the real rates curve. This curve was in turn used to imply the level of forward index values.

In contrast, once the swaps market was deep enough to provide good market prices, and the market convention was to quote swap rates in terms of forward index values, the "projection" or "compensation" method became possible. Using this technique, one instead constructed the level of forward index rates, and then implied the corresponding term structure of real interest rates.

There are a number of technical issues that one must deal with if the resulting curve is to be good enough to trade off. These include the issue of seasonality, which may or may not be adjusted by the issuing body, or the difficulties that arise because the published index levels are provided by the central banks with an accompanying time lag – three months in the US and Europe, and eight months in the UK.[3]

More extensive models

Up until this point, it has sufficed to tackle the issue of pricing straightforward inflation-swap-based structures. As with their counterparts in the interest rate markets, these models essentially comprise a bootstrapping algorithm to construct the forward inflation curve.

Pricing LPI swaps, with their embedded optionally is an entirely different prospect. One needs a model that includes the feature of inflation rate volatility. This provides an interesting challenge, but, as is often the case with models, one prefers the simplest model with the maximum scope. At first sight it would seem that any model used to value inflation derivatives would need to also be able to consistently value interest rate derivatives. Such a constraint would suggest the model would need to simultaneously treat real interest rates and nominal interest rates as stochastic variables, so requiring at least a two-factor model. Although this is strictly the case, it is possible to construct a user-friendly one-factor model for some categories of inflation swaps.

The Hughston pseudo-FX model

By the same token, if you would like a single model that can be used to value all types of contingent claims, whose payoff depends on either real or nominal interest rates, a particular inflation index, or indeed any combination of the above, expect your model to be a tad more complicated.

One of the more innovative, and certainly more general, treatments was that formulated by Lane Hughston (1998). As a model built on the back of the Heath, Jarrow and Morton framework, Hughston's approach was to give an interpretation to the inflation index as a pseudo-FX rate whose role was to convert an amount of money denominated in the real economy, to the same amount denominated in the nominal economy. Both the real interest rate curve and the nominal interest rate curve are treated as multifactor

HJM processes, coupled with an inflation index that is modelled as a lognormal process.

More recently, Jarrow and Yildirim (2002) applied a particular case of Hughston's model to the US inflation market, where the payoffs are written against government-linked Treasury Inflation Protected Securities, known as TIPS. They chose to model the short rates of both the nominal and real interest rate curves as correlated random processes, which in turn are each correlated to the CPI-U index. The resulting three-factor model provides a fairly promising approach that is applicable to a wide set of financial contracts. When taking such a sophisticated approach to modelling inflation, one is tempted to be a little bit wary of a construction that, using first principles, treats the inflation index as a continuous time model, when in reality these indices are published only on a monthly basis. This is an example of the type of problem that one encounters when valuing contracts on economic indices and may well be a worthy area for quantitative research over the next few years.

CONCLUSION

Given the broad range of counterparties who have fundamental exposure to inflation, IL derivatives are not a "flavour-of-the-month" product and will develop over time into a broadly used instrument for managing risk. The IL derivative product range has been central in bridging the gap between what is a diverse pool of issuers and investors. It is fair to say that the success of these products has itself led to a more efficient underlying IL bond market.

The euro zone market is now very active in IL swaps, and, once the number of accompanying IL bond issues increases to the levels seen in the UK or the US, the pricing of these transactions will continue to be very much driven by a supply-and-demand approach. As this European market moves into the next stage of development, where already there is clear evidence of an increase in the volume of two-way flows, the requirement for more sophisticated pricing models will go hand in hand with the tighter pricing bounds found in the market.

Currently it is impractical to use a full-blown model for pricing IL derivatives in the spirit of the HJM model as applied to the Interest Rate Exotics Market. Given the realities of the actual market datasets available, the difficulties associated with the calibration stage of using such models would most likely outweigh the benefits of such an approach. Nonetheless, the experience from other classes of derivatives tells us that, as the number of underlying products, the number of users and their sophistication increase, more sophisticated pricing and risk management techniques are most likely on the horizon.

The IL derivatives market has clearly come of age, and could act as a catalyst for other instances of economic derivatives. From this will follow more appropriate modelling and statistical methods that are better suited to products where the underlying economic indicators are published only on a monthly basis. We are witnessing the dawn of a new area of quantitative research – the IL derivatives research.

1   The criteria as set out in the 1992 Maastricht Treaty actually requires any member country to manage its inflation rate so that it does not exceed the average of those three countries with the lowest inflation rate by more than 1.5%.

2   "Limited price inflation" can appear in a number of forms, but of particular interest was that definition resulting from the 1990 Social Security Act, which essentially defined LPI as price growth on a year-on-year basis, as the RPI rate capped at 5% and floored at 0%.

3   These include details such as the fact that not all indices are seasonally adjusted – for example the RPI index isn't, unlike the HICP index.

REFERENCES

Evans, M., 1998, "Real Rates, Expected Inflation, and Inflation Risk Premia", *Journal of Finance*, **53**(1), p. 187, February.

Hughston, L. P., 1998, *Inflation Derivatives*, Working Paper (London: Merrill Lynch).

Jarrow, R., and Y. Yildirim, 2002, "Pricing Treasury Inflation Protected Securities & Related Derivatives using an HJM model", Cornell University and Syracuse University mimeo.

Manning, S., and M. Jones, 2003, "Modelling Inflation Derivatives – A Review: The RBS Guide To Inflation-Linked Products", *Risk*, September 2003.

Oppon, J., and C. Alibert, 2003, "Inflation Derivatives: The RBS Guide To Inflation-Linked Products", *Risk*, September 2003.

10

Commodities, Term Structures and Volatility

Michael Lewis

Deutsche Bank

Investors are familiar with the returns generated from equity and bond ownership, which come in the form of dividends and coupons. In this chapter Deutsche Bank examine the various components of commodity returns. Deutsche Bank also introduce the concept of convenience yield, which is a key variable in determining term structures and volatility levels across commodity markets. Deutsche Bank then examine the key properties of commodities and discuss why their integration into an investor asset allocation process not only enhances returns but also raises the Sharpe Ratio.

THE TERM STRUCTURE OF COMMODITIES

The forward curve for foreign exchange rates is simply calculated by the difference between short- and long-term interest rates. In commodity markets, the process is more complicated since forward curves also have to contend with, among other things, changes to production costs, weather and inventory levels. In terms of market definitions, when the spot price of a commodity is higher than the forward price the market is in backwardation. Conversely, contango is where the spot price is lower than the forward price. These two types of term structure are best represented by the current WTI crude oil and gold price forward curves (see Figure 1).

COMMODITIES OFFER NATURALLY OCCURRING RETURNS

Investors are familiar with the returns generated by equity and bond ownership, which come in the form of dividends and

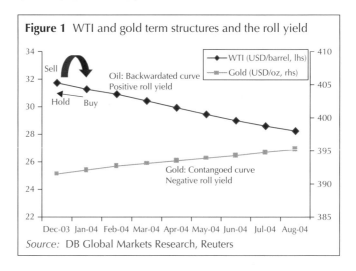

Figure 1 WTI and gold term structures and the roll yield

Source: DB Global Markets Research, Reuters

coupons. However, for commodities, returns traditionally come from three sources:

$$\text{Total returns} = \text{Spot return} + \text{Roll yield} + \text{Collateral yield} \qquad (1)$$

The spot return is simply a result of commodities' becoming more, or less, expensive over time. In terms of the roll yield, where the price of a commodity is higher for shorter delivery dates, an investor earns a positive roll yield by buying the future, waiting for the price to appreciate as the delivery date approaches, then selling and using the proceeds to reinvest at a cheaper price at a future date. Such a strategy is highlighted in Figure 1. The final source of return is the collateral yield, which is the return accruing to any margin held against a futures position, and which Deutsche Bank proxy with the US T-bill rate.

THE COMPOSITION OF RETURNS

The composition of returns for the six components of the Deutsche Bank Liquid Commodity Index (DBLCI) are detailed in Table 1. The persistence of backwardation in the crude oil market, and hence the positive roll yield, helps to explain why the main source of returns within the DBLCI, and for most other commodity indices, is largely

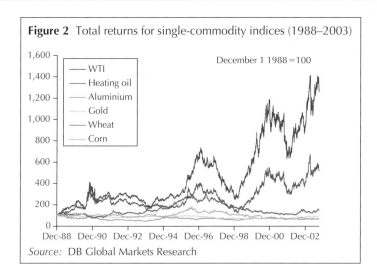

Figure 2 Total returns for single-commodity indices (1988–2003)

December 1 1988 = 100

WTI
Heating oil
Aluminium
Gold
Wheat
Corn

Source: DB Global Markets Research

concentrated in the energy sector. Figure 2 highlights how energy products have significantly outperformed all the other components of the DBLCI over the past 16 years.

WHAT DRIVES THE TERM STRUCTURE?

While energy markets are typically characterised by backwardated markets, this is not the case for the precious and industrial metals markets. For a majority of the time, the spot price for industrial metals is typically below the future price, that is, the market is in contango. These differing term structures between the energy and metals complexes can be explained by the theory of storage and the existence of convenience yield. The relationship between the forward and spot price is defined as:

$$\text{Forward price} = \text{Spot price} + \text{Interest rate} - (\text{Convenience yield} - \text{Storage costs}) \quad (2)$$

Formula 2 relies on the fact that, by storing rather than selling the commodity, one surrenders the spot price, but incurs interest rate and warehousing costs. However, offsetting these costs are the benefits accruing from holding inventory, or what is called the *convenience yield* (see Working, 1949).

Table 1 Commodity returns, storage and the convenience yield*

1988–2003	Total returns (%)	Spot returns (%)	Roll returns (%)	Collateral returns (%)	Storage costs (%)	Convenience yield (%)	Days of stock	Effect of shortage
WTI	19.58	4.78	8.82	4.88	20.00	**33.70**	**20**	Severe
Heating oil	12.59	3.48	3.79	4.88	20.00	**28.67**	**20**	Severe
Aluminium	–2.48	–3.16	–4.04	4.88	6.33	7.17	**90**	Medium
Gold	–0.39	–0.97	–4.18	4.88	0.03	**0.73**	**16,700**	Mild
Wheat	2.96	–0.63	–1.17	4.88	11.40	**15.11**	**90**	Severe
Corn	–2.38	–0.58	–6.47	4.88	10.91	**9.32**	**70**	Severe

*Returns, storage costs and the convenience yield are average per annum figures
Source: DB Global Markets Research

THE CONVENIENCE YIELD

A holder of inventories in a particular commodity generates a convenience yield. This is the flow of services and benefits that accrue to an owner of a physical commodity, but, not to an owner of a contract for future delivery of the commodity (see Brennan and Schwartz, 1985). This can come in the form of having a secure supply of raw materials and hence eliminating the costs associated with stock-outs.

Rearranging Formula (2) implies that:

$$\text{Forward} - \text{Spot} = -\text{Roll yield}$$
$$= (\text{Interest rate} -$$
$$[\text{Convenience yield} - \text{Storage cost}])$$

or,

$$\text{Convenience yield} = \text{Roll return} + \text{Storage costs}$$
$$+ \text{Interest costs} \qquad (3)$$

To solve for the convenience yield, one now has only to estimate the fixed costs of storage for each commodity. For this Deutsche Bank use industry estimates (see Table 2). Since storage costs are fixed, the share of costs accounted for by storage will be a function of the spot price. For example, in 1989 the average WTI spot price was US$19.60/barrel. Fixed costs for storing a barrel of oil amount to US$0.04/barrel per month and consequently for that year fixed costs were US$4.80 (0.04 x 12) or 24.49%. Over the 1989–2003 period, storage costs have amounted to an average of 20% per annum. Deutsche Bank repeated this exercise for the other five components of the DBLCI and the results are presented in Table 2.

With this ammunition Deutsche Bank are able to calculate the average convenience yield for each commodity, since it will be the sum of the roll return, storage and interest rate costs (see Table 1). Deutsche Bank then compare the convenience yield to the days of above-ground stocks, that is the amount of time it would take to run out of available *commercial* supplies if production ceased and consumption growth remained unchanged.

These results show that convenience yields trend higher for those commodity markets that have low levels of inventories. Put another way, the convenience yield rises as the market's precariousness increases. This makes intuitive sense, since in tightening market

Table 2 Estimated fixed storage cost for various commodities

1989–2003	Storage cost (USD/month)	Average cost per annum (%)
Crude oil (WTI)	0.40/barrel	20.00
Heating oil	3.00/tonne	20.00
Aluminium	7.80/tonne	6.33
Gold	0.004/oz	0.06
Wheat	3.33/bushel	11.40
Corn	2.00/bushel	10.91

Source: Industry estimates, DB Global Markets Research

conditions consumers attach a greater benefit to the physical ownership of a commodity. Oil is the most obvious example, since if production ceased today the economic and financial consequences would be felt within a matter of days, if not hours.

The gold market is at the other extreme. It would take several years for the world to exhaust available gold reserves on current demand trends. This reflects the fact that annual gold consumption amounts to approximately 320 tonnes per annum while total above-ground stocks total more than 145,000 tonnes. In the absence of additional new mine supply, the world would consequently only run out of gold after 16,700 days or sometime after 2048. As a result, any disruptions to gold mine production would have only a marginal effect on the convenience yield. This positive relationship between convenience yield and consumption of stock per day is highlighted in Figure 3.

It is worth remembering that the convenience yield will vary over time as and when there is an increase in stocks above or below "requirements". Indeed, the convenience yield is likely to rise very sharply when there is a reduction of stocks below requirements (see Kaldor, 1939). Commodities subject to sudden changes in inventory levels due to supply or demand shocks are particularly vulnerable in this regard.

Such shocks help to explain why certain markets are more prone to move from contango to backwardation in a very short space of time. One can therefore consider the slope of the forward-price term structure as an indication of the current supply of storage such that a continuing decline in inventory levels implies an even steeper backwardation and vice versa.

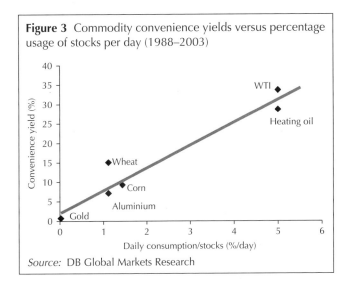

Figure 3 Commodity convenience yields versus percentage usage of stocks per day (1988–2003)

Source: DB Global Markets Research

EXPLAINING BACKWARDATION AND CONTANGO VIA THE CONVENIENCE YIELD

Rearranging one of the formulae derived earlier to solve for the roll yield – that is the difference the spot and forward price – Deutsche Bank find that:

$$\text{Roll yield} = \text{Convenience yield} - \text{Interest rate} - \text{Storage cost} \tag{4}$$

Consequently, where the convenience yield exceeds the interest rate and storage costs, it implies a positive roll yield or a backwardated market. This is the main feature of the crude oil market and underpins why commodity investment and in particular investment in the energy sector is a highly profitable strategy to undertake. The likelihood that this situation will change over the medium term is slim. Oil dependency ratios for the major industrialised economies, although lower than the 1970s, have been relatively stable over the past 10–15 years.

Moreover, not only is geopolitical risk on the rise, sustaining the energy market's precariousness and hence its backwardation feature, but, on a fundamental basis, the oil market is unique in that more than 60% of global oil reserves are controlled not by corporations but by governments, most of whom reside in the Middle East.

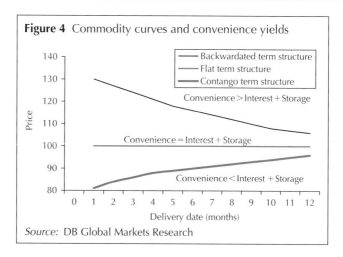

Figure 4 Commodity curves and convenience yields

Source: DB Global Markets Research

Conversely, where the convenience yield is low and over-whelmed by interest rate and storage costs, the roll yield will be negative. A negative roll yield indicates that the spot price is lower than the futures price and is a typical feature of the precious and industrial metals market (see Figure 4).

THE IMPLICATIONS FOR THE INDUSTRIAL METALS COMPLEX

What has been noteworthy over the past year is that as global reflation has taken hold, inventory levels across the industrial metals complex have been falling. In the case of copper, lead and nickel, inventory levels on the LME have more than halved over the past twelve months. This implies that the convenience yield on the physical ownership of these metals has risen significantly. This has encouraged the industrial metals term structure to move into backwardation and volatility levels to rise as market precarious-ness increases.

COMMODITY VOLATILITY AND THE CONVENIENCE YIELD

This leads to another important characteristic of commodity mar-kets, namely the positive correlation between the convenience yield and commodity volatility. This reflects the fact that as inven-tory levels decline so market precariousness increases and markets become more vulnerable to demand–supply shocks (see Figure 5).

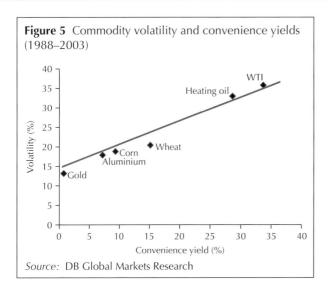

Figure 5 Commodity volatility and convenience yields (1988–2003)

Source: DB Global Markets Research

Consequently, those commodities with high convenience yields, such as crude oil, have high levels of volatility and vice versa.

This rising level of volatility is best demonstrated by the recent behaviour of implied aluminium volatility. Figure 6 plots the implied aluminium volatility curve from April 2004 and compares it with the curve a month earlier as well as against its five-year history. The shaded boxplot for each month shows:

❏ the inter-quartile range (box);
❏ the 5–95 percentile range (whisker); and
❏ the median of the five-year history (dashed line) for implied volatility out to 27 months.

As Deutsche Bank have seen from other markets where market deficits have appeared and inventory levels have fallen rapidly, this not only increases the precariousness of an individual industrial metal market, but it also elevates volatility risk, which is starting to appear in the aluminium market.

Consequently, commodities with a high convenience yield consequently tend to be characterised by:

❏ low inventory levels;
❏ backwardated term structures; and
❏ higher volatility levels.

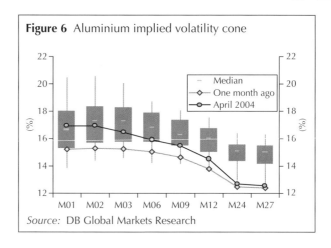

Figure 6 Aluminium implied volatility cone

Source: DB Global Markets Research

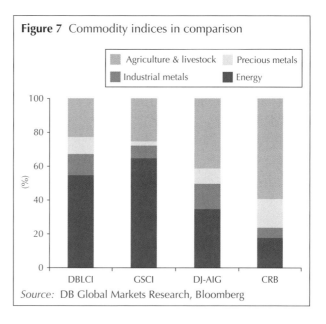

Figure 7 Commodity indices in comparison

Source: DB Global Markets Research, Bloomberg

Since energy markets have high convenience yields and back-wardated term structures, it suggests that any commodity expos-ure should be heavily skewed towards the energy sector. This is borne out by the performance of the various commodity indices, a selection of which are highlighted in Figure 7.

This outlines the sector components of the Deutsche Bank, Goldman Sachs, Dow Jones-AIG and Commodity Research Bureau commodity indices. Typically, the weights for a particular commodity index are determined by world production and inventories in these sectors. For simplicity, Deutsche Bank believe it is preferable to have only a small number of commodities within an index, as this facilitates its replication in an investor's portfolio. A smaller number of components also need not increase the volatility of the basket.

Deutsche Bank tested this assumption by investigating the volatility of a series of indices with fewer and fewer components. This was accomplished by taking the Goldman Sachs Commodity Index (GSCI), which contains 25 commodities, removing the lowest-weighted commodity and redistributing that weight among the remaining components. It was found that decreasing the number of basket components had only a gradual effect on the volatility of the basket. It was only when the number of components fell below four that there was a significant increase in volatility risk (see Figure 8). As a result, a commodity index with five or six commodities does not expose the index to any elevated level of

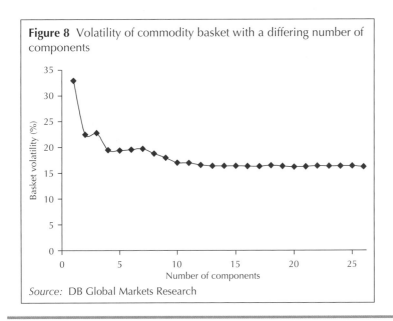

Figure 8 Volatility of commodity basket with a differing number of components

Source: DB Global Markets Research

Table 3 Sectors and weights of the DBLCI

Commodity	Symbol	Exchange	Notional weight (%)
Energy			
Sweet light crude oil (WTI)	CL	NYMEX	35.00
Heating oil	HO	NYMEX	20.00
Precious metals			
Gold	GC	COMEX	10.00
Base metals			
Aluminium	MAL	LME	12.50
Grains/softs			
Corn	C	CBOT	11.25
Wheat	W	CBOT	11.25

Source: DB Global Markets Research

volatility risk, compared to an index with a larger number of constituent parts.

This analysis helps to determine not just the optimum number of commodities for inclusion in an commodity index but also the requirement that energy must form the lion's share of the index. The sectors and weights of the DBLCI are detailed in Table 3.

In order to extract additional returns from the base DBLCI, Deutsche Bank constructed the DBLCI-Mean Reversion index (DBLCI-MR), which takes advantage of the fact that commodities tend to trade within wide but defined ranges because:

❏ as prices of commodities rise, new production capacity is brought on line to benefit from high and rising prices;
❏ moreover, as prices rise additional supply becomes available from alternative sources that were previously considered uneconomic;
❏ in certain markets, quota systems that attempt to control supply come under strain as the rewards for cheating rise, most notably in the crude oil market; and
❏ as prices rise, demand for a commodity tends to fall as it faces competition from cheaper sources.

The net effect is to keep commodity prices bound around their long-run average price. One measure of the degree of mean

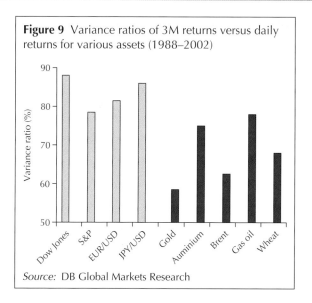

Figure 9 Variance ratios of 3M returns versus daily returns for various assets (1988–2002)

Source: DB Global Markets Research

reversion of an asset is its "variance ratio". This compares the asset's volatility when measured over a long period (quarterly) with the volatility of returns over a short period (daily). The lower the value, the more mean reversion the instrument exhibits. If one examines the 3M returns versus daily returns for various assets from 1988–2002, one will see that commodity prices possess variance ratios significantly lower than 1.0, demonstrating mean reversion (see Figure 9).

The DBLCI-MR index capitalises on this recurring characteristic of commodities and overweights those commodities that are trading cheaply compared with their long-run average and underweights those commodities that are trading richly. The intended result is to generate extra returns from holding a diverse portfolio of assets while lowering the volatility of returns.

Over the last few years, commodities have been one of the best-performing asset classes. The DBLCI-MR has shown an annual return of 13% per annum since 2000, which is in sharp contrast to the performance of equities. Over a longer period of time, returns have been similarly strong – almost 13% total return per annum in USD terms (see Table 4). The performance in euro terms has been equally impressive.

Table 4 Performance of indices (1988–2003)

	DBLCI-MR (%)	S&P 500 (%)	Lehman Gov/ Corp Bond (%)
Annualised return (USD)	12.8	9.3	10.8
Annualised StDev	17.5	16.8	8.6
Sharpe Ratio	45	26	68
Annualised return (EUR)	13.3	7.9	7.2
Annualised StDev	14.6	18.9	3.1
Sharpe Ratio	53	12	50

Source: DB Global Markets Research, Bloomberg

Table 5 Average historic volatility (1992–2002)

Crude oil (%)	Nickel (%)	10Y UST (%)	S&P 500 (%)	EURUSD* (%)
33.4	28.1	16.7	15.7	10.0

*Before 1999, USDDEM
Source: DB Global Markets Research

THE VALUE OF COMMODITIES IN A DIVERSIFIED PORTFOLIO

One of the main concerns expressed by investors in terms of commodity exposure is the high level of volatility compared with other asset classes. Indeed, examining crude oil and nickel historic volatility over the 1992–2002 period shows that these have been significantly higher than historic volatility in the US fixed-income, equity and currency markets (see Table 5).

However, where commodities as an asset class differentiate themselves is in the value they create when added to a fixed-income portfolio. This is the result of the unique properties that commodities possess.

Commodities are not correlated with other assets

This reflects the declining role of commodities in the industrialised world. Only 30% of the value of world equities depend on and are affected by commodities, for example in the energy and utility sectors. However, global economies, and especially developed

Table 6 Correlation of daily returns (1990–2003)

	S&P 500 (%)	Lehman Gov/ Corp Bond (%)
WTI	−7.9	−9.8
Heating oil	−7.0	−7.8
Aluminium	2.5	−6.2
Gold	−13.2	−9.3
Wheat	1.3	−3.2
Corn	1.7	−3.8

Source: DB Global Markets Research

economies, are dominated by services. As a consequence, the returns from commodities have a low, or negative, correlation with equities and bonds (see Table 6). In addition, the commodity sectors, such as agriculture, energy and metals, show a low correlation with each other, which means that portfolios with a mixture of commodities are further diversified.

Another way of examining the properties of commodities' low or negative returns with other asset classes is by examining the cumulative returns for bonds, equities and commodities during periods of either fixed-income or equity market distress, which Deutsche Bank define as a month where returns were negative. Figure 10 considers the period from January 1992 to August 2003 (140 months in total) for bond versus commodity returns. It tracks the performance of commodities during the months when bond returns were negative. What is clear is that, of the 43 months of negative bond returns during the period, commodity returns, as measured by the DBLCI-MR, are positive in 26 of those months, or 60% of the time.

Commodities deliver naturally occurring returns

Many investors consider returns solely on a spot basis. But, as Deutsche Bank have shown earlier, the majority of returns tend to come in the form of the roll yield. This roll yield is often positive where it is difficult to store the commodity or where running out of the commodity would be very inconvenient. For example, for crude oil, this roll yield has been approximately 0.70% per month on average for the last 16 years.

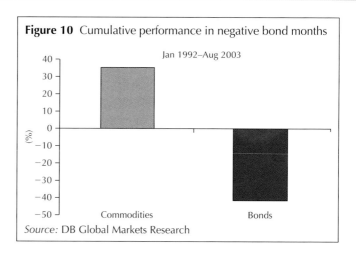

Figure 10 Cumulative performance in negative bond months

Jan 1992–Aug 2003

Source: DB Global Markets Research

Commodities provide protection from economic shocks

Two of the biggest economic shocks in living memory occurred during the 1973 and 1979 oil crises. During both of these crises, financial assets sold off but commodity prices appreciated. In recent years, the dramatic decline in equity prices has occurred at the same time as commodity prices have rallied.

Over the past 16 years, although commodity prices have shown little relation to inflation, they have been positively correlated to inflation shocks – unexpected moves up in inflation that are generally very damaging for equities and bonds. Today, given the high degree of monetary liquidity provided for by global central banks over the past few years, there is a non-negligible risk that inflation shocks could be a recurring feature of global financial markets over the medium term.

Commodities' price behaviour is cyclical and mean-reverting

Commodity prices have tended to remain within wide but well-defined ranges over time. There are sound economic reasons for this: as commodity prices rise, producers will supply more; consumers will reduce demand or seek substitutes; supply cartels will break down; and, in the long term, more production capacity will be brought online. The opposite effects occur as prices fall. Academic studies have also proved that commodities mean-revert by examining the mathematical properties of commodity price series.

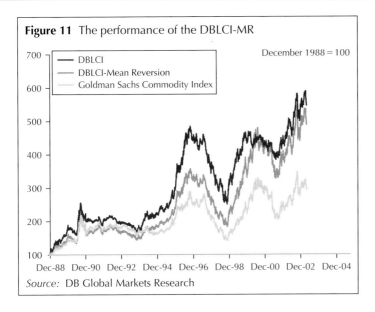

Figure 11 The performance of the DBLCI-MR

December 1988 = 100

- DBLCI
- DBLCI-Mean Reversion
- Goldman Sachs Commodity Index

Source: DB Global Markets Research

By taking advantage of this mean reversion, an investment in commodities can generate extra returns while reducing risks.

THE DBLCI-MR IN MIXED PORTFOLIOS

The high returns of the DBLCI-MR and its low correlation to other assets make it a useful addition to an investment portfolio. An example of a typical commodity linked structured note is outline in Panel 1. The performance of the DBLCI-MR versus the Goldman Sachs Commodity Index (GSCI) is shown in Figure 11.

Table 7 shows the effect of adding the DBLCI-MR index to three benchmark portfolios: the Deutsche Bank Conservative, Balanced and Growth portfolios, over the period 1992–2002. The three model portfolios vary according to their equity allocation with the growth portfolio allocating the highest exposure to the S&P.

Deutsche Bank examined three scenarios:

❑ a base case with no addition of commodities;
❑ the returns with a 10% addition of DBLCI-MR; and
❑ the returns with the optimal amount of DBLCI-MR (the proportion of DBLCI-MR that gives the best risk/return for the portfolio).

PANEL 1 TYPICAL COMMODITY LINKED STRUCTURED NOTE

DB principal protected DBLCI-MR™ LINKED EMTN

Trade rationale

❑ Investor is seeking a USD principal-protected strategy, which gives exposure to the DBLCI-MR™ Excess Return Index.

❑ The note structure below offers a potentially unlimited capital gain paid at maturity. The capital gain is paid according to the cumulative performance of the Deutsche Bank Liquid Commodity Index – Mean Reversion Excess Return Index.

Terms and conditions

Issuer	Deutsche Bank AG, London
Rating	AA−/Aa3
Listing	None
Notional amount	USD 21,500,000
Issue price	100%
Trade date	5 August 2003
Issue date	4 September 2003
Maturity date	7 September 2010
Valuation date	2 business days prior to maturity date
Coupon	Zero
Business days	London and New York. Following business day convention
Redemption	100% plus capital appreciation
Capital appreciation	$100\% \times \max\{0\%, [(\text{DBLCI-MR}^{TM}_{Final} - \text{DBLCI-MR}^{TM}_{Initial})/\text{DBLCI-MR}^{TM}_{Initial}]\}$
DBLCI-MR™$_{Initial}$	The closing value of the Deutsche Bank Liquid Commodities Index – Mean Reversion™ Excess Return Index quoted in USD on the issue date
DBLCI-MR™$_{Final}$	The closing value of the Deutsche Bank Liquid Commodities Index – Mean Reversion™ Excess Return Index quoted in USD on the valuation date
Calculation agent	Deutsche Bank AG, London
ISIN	TBA
Denominations	USD 10,000
Settlement	Euroclear 91255
Governing law	English

Table 7 Performance of various mixed portfolios (1992–2002)

EUR terms	Conservative (%)	Balanced (%)	Growth (%)
No commodities			
Annual returns	7.92	9.04	9.73
Annual StDev	4.22	9.01	14.27
Sharpe Ratio	69	45	33
10% DBLCI-MR			
Annual returns	8.20	9.21	9.83
Annual StDev	4.09	8.24	12.91
Sharpe Ratio	78	51	37
Optimal DBLCI-MR			
Optimal weight	11	25	44
Annual returns	8.23	9.47	10.18
Annual StDev	4.12	7.90	10.84
Sharpe Ratio	78	57	48

Source: DB Global Markets Research

In every case, adding even a modest amount of commodity exposure via the DBLCI-Mean Reversion improved the portfolio performance markedly. Moreover, it was found that the more volatile the portfolio, the greater the proportion of commodities that should be added.

CONCLUSIONS

Commodities provide returns as an asset in their own right. Their unique characteristics, namely different properties across commodity classes, cyclical and mean-reverting behaviour, their low correlation to other asset classes, protection from economic shocks and naturally occurring returns mean that they add significantly to the performance of a portfolio if included alongside other assets.

REFERENCES

Brennan and Schwartz, 1985, "Two Factor Model of the Term Structure of Interest", Working Paper no. 155 (Berkeley: University of California).

Kaldor, N., 1939, "Speculation and Economic Stability", *Review of Economic Studies*.

Working, H., 1949, "The Theory of the Price of Storage", *American Economic Review*.

11

The Uses of Credit Derivative Products for Wealth Management*

Anthony Morris

UBS

Why bother with credit derivatives? By now wealth management professionals have probably received hundreds of brochures from dealers about various credit derivative products, from the credit default swap (CDS) and credit-linked note (CLN) to the collateralised debt obligation (CDO). Yet many advisers, not to mention clients, remain unconvinced that they need to get involved with these products. They believe that they already know everything they need to know about credit as an asset class. They may hold a number of credit bonds directly, or hold shares in a fund that invests in credit bonds. Some may have little interest in credit *per se*, and, only because they bought structured notes linked to a non-credit derivative product (eg, equity, foreign exchange or interest rate derivative), they end up holding credit exposure to the issuer of each Medium-Term Note (MTN). What do they really have to gain from using credit derivatives?

Plenty. This chapter will argue that there are several fundamental problems with the way private investors have traditionally approached credit assets. These include:

❑ undiversified credit bond portfolios;
❑ credit bond funds that deliver little diversification from government bonds;
❑ credit bond funds that underperform benchmark "riskless" indices;

---

*The opinions of Anthony Morris are not necessarily the opinions of UBS.

❏ a bias towards being long both interest rate risk and credit spread risk; and
❏ individual credit assets, from traditional bonds to structured MTNs, that deliver relatively low yield for a given credit rating.

Just as interest rate derivative products have allowed investors to access a broader range of strategies than simple bonds would allow, credit derivatives open a new world of possibilities to private investors. Among other things, credit derivative products allow investors to:

❏ achieve higher issuer diversification than would be possible from bonds alone;
❏ take exposure to credit spreads without taking exposure to interest rates, achieving significant diversification from traditional bond holdings;
❏ capture long-term risk premia documented in credit spreads, achieving outperformance relative to benchmarks;
❏ take long, short, or neutral exposure to credit spreads and interest rates; and
❏ capture competitive pricing on all products with elements of credit exposure, from traditional fixed-coupon credit products to structured notes using common MTN issuers.

This chapter will examine each of these points in turn. While these problems have existed for some time, the tools to solve them have become available only recently, as the credit derivative market has reached greater maturity.

MARKET GROWTH: CREDIT DERIVATIVES COME OF AGE

Over the past several years, credit derivatives have established themselves in the institutional market, following in the footsteps of equity and interest rate derivatives. According to ISDA, the credit derivatives market size reached US$3.58 trillion by the end of 2003, whereas the equity derivatives market reached a smaller US$3.44 trillion at the same time.

Look for a similar pattern in the wealth management market. For many years, clients of wealth management institutions have used equity derivative products, such as capital-protected notes offering partial participation in the upside of common equity index

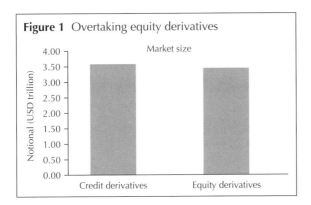

Figure 1 Overtaking equity derivatives

products. Next came interest rate derivative products. In the last several years, high-net-worth investors (HNWI) have started to make sizable use of interest rate derivative products, such as callable daily range accrual notes (CDRAN). In 2003, HNWI began to use a wide variety of credit derivative products. These include such products as the CDS, the CDO, the CLN, the first-to-default (FTD), and credit-linked LIBOR or equity products, where an equity or interest rate derivative product is attached to a CLN.

The future growth potential of credit derivatives in this sector will probably be driven by both tactical and strategic factors. On a tactical level, credit derivative products can deliver more efficient exposure to credit risk than traditional credit bonds, generating higher yields for comparable risks while also offering substantial diversification gains. On a strategic level, the potential of credit derivatives in the wealth management market is transformational – improving the economics of all structured notes sold to wealth management clients without fundamentally altering their risk profile. This is because almost all structured notes already have credit risk, often overpriced, even if these notes are primarily intended as exposures to equity, interest rate, or foreign exchange markets.

Problem 1: Low diversification in private clients relative to credit bond holdings

To the extent that they hold individual credit bonds, many private banking clients hold portfolios that are concentrated. A typical investor might have 5–10 bonds, each from a different issuer. Often these bonds reflect the investor's "home country bias" with Swiss preferring Swiss names, Italians preferring Italian names and so on. But "buying what you know" is not the same as buying what is best for you.

While name recognition seems to be the decisive factor in many private client portfolios, name recognition is not the same thing as high quality and diversification. For example, Swiss investors discovered too late that Swissair could in fact go bankrupt and that ABB was less stable than it seemed. Italians lost out heavily in the demises of Cirio and Parmalat.

Let's run through the problems with these assumptions:

❑ *The knowledge problem*: To be familiar with a company is not the same thing as to "know" a company. There are potential catastrophes, such as accounting fraud, which simply cannot be detected easily, even by experts. Hence, diversification among a relatively large number of issuers is a sensible strategy.

❑ *The numbers problem*: In most countries outside the US, there are relatively few active debt issuers per country. Even if an investor was familiar with all of them (which they typically are not), limiting themselves to only those that they are familiar with is guaranteed to result in high concentration of credit risk.

❑ *The selectivity problem*: If there are few issuers available, it's impossible to exercise much selectivity. Just as you would not want to buy a suit in a store that had only one brand, why limit your choices with respect to credit issuers?

But the bond market does not provide much help in this regard, especially in Europe. Let's return to the unfortunate Swiss and Italian investors we mentioned earlier. Suppose they agreed to expand their holdings outside Swiss and Italian names to the whole European continent, in the belief that they would rather stay within Europe than include American issuers. Consider a Bloomberg search through the EUR-denominated bond market for issuers given the following criteria:

❑ maturity: between 4.5 and 5.5 years;
❑ size: €1,000 (as a proxy for liquidity);
❑ rating: investment grade only; and
❑ issuer origin: European only.

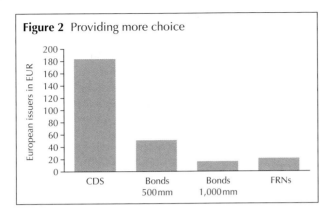

Figure 2 Providing more choice

In the bond market, only 16 issuers are available who meet these criteria. Relaxing the size requirement from €1 bn to €.5 bn (though even some issues with €1 bn outstanding are not easy for private investors to actually buy), the number of available issuers only goes up to 51. Examining the floating-rate note (FRN) market, only 21 issuers are available.

How can credit derivative products help this situation? Adopting the same criteria as above, approximately 180 issuers would be available via CDS, the most common credit derivative product, on which most others are based.

Why can credit derivative products provide exposure to a much wider range of issuers than the bond market alone? This is because credit derivatives can reference both bonds and loans, and many European issuers may be represented in the loan market, even if they are not represented in the bond market. As a result, investors can have more choices using credit derivative markets. Having more choices means that more selectivity and more diversification is possible.

If the diversification problem is bad in the EUR-denominated bond market, it is even worse in the bond markets of other currencies, eg, CHF, GBP, DKK, SGD, SEK, NOK, KRW. But using credit derivative products, even investors based in these currencies can obtain assets according to their choice. Dealers can combine credit swaps with interest rate basis swap packages (which swap floating rate payments in one currency for floating rate payments in another), resulting in a CDN in the investor's base currency.

Credit derivative products, such as CDNs and CDOs, make it straightforward to access a much wider number of issuers than would be available from the standard bond and FRN markets. Doing this enables investors to reduce concentration risk.

Problem 2: Traditional credit bond funds deliver little diversification from government bond funds

Many private investors hold traditional credit bond funds, believing that such products should give them added diversification and higher returns relative to government bonds. We will examine the return dimension of credit bond funds in a later section. For now, let's focus on how much diversification traditional credit bond funds actually provide.

We define "traditional credit bond funds" as funds that have the following characteristics:

❑ investment grade only;
❑ fixed coupon;
❑ minimum size (varies, but typically €500 mm or US$500 mm); and
❑ benchmarked to a standard fixed-coupon, investment-grade bond index, such as iBoxx, Lehman or Merrill Lynch bond indices.

This definition captures most investment-grade credit bond funds. The biggest problem with these funds is that their returns are highly correlated with the returns of government bond funds. Using almost any index series, measurements of this return correlation are around 90%. For example, in their research note, Fabrizio Basile and Frederik von Ameln (2004) measure a 90% correlation between the total returns of corporate bonds and government bonds.

Why is this correlation so high? Because interest rate risk is the main factor driving the total returns of investment grade credit bonds. The volatility of a diversified investment-grade portfolio's credit spread changes is small in comparison with the volatility of interest rates. Hence, for an investment-grade bond fund, the credit component is dominated by the interest rate component. Such funds became pale copies of the government bond funds they are supposed to diversify.

There is a story of a large institutional fund manager who performed rigorous performance attribution analysis on the returns of their credit funds. Somewhat to their surprise, they discovered that the most important factor driving the returns of their credit funds was duration decisions, rather than credit decisions. "It made us wonder what the point was of employing so many credit analysts", one fund manager commented. It also made them explore new ways to take real advantage of their credit expertise through credit derivative products.

How can credit derivative products help? *Most fundamentally, credit derivative products allow investors to isolate the interest rate (duration) decision from the credit decision.* Unlike traditional credit bonds, credit derivative products do not have to be in fixed-rate form. Floating-rate coupons are just as easy to provide. While traditional FRNs also provide credit exposure without exposure to interest rates, the FRN market is difficult to use in practice, with relatively few issuers available at all, as noted previously and shown in Figure 2.

Isolating the credit spread from interest rate risk is not just theoretically interesting. It has material benefits in practice. Compare the correlations presented in Figure 3. These show that isolating the credit spread from interest rate risk can yield an asset whose returns have low (and on average negative) correlation with government bond returns and low correlation with equity returns. In other words, isolating the credit spread can result in dramatic improvements in diversification, especially within a fixed-income portfolio.

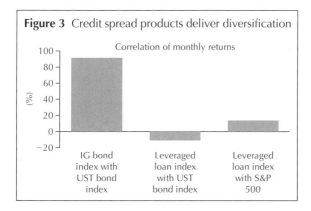

Figure 3 Credit spread products deliver diversification

Looking at the chart in more detail, we see that the left column shows the high correlation (approximately 90%) that exists between the returns of an investment-grade (IG) bond index and a US Treasury (UST) bond index. The data used here are from the classic "Salomon" bond indices, now under the Citigroup brand name.

The middle column shows the correlation between a leveraged loan (source: CSFB) index and the government bond index. This leveraged loan index tracks the performance of speculative-grade bank loans. The important point here is that this index has almost no interest rate risk since it tracks floating-rate instruments. The primary factor driving the returns of this index is credit spread changes, up to and including defaults. Notice this correlation is not just close to zero, but even slightly negative, a dream come true for diversification.

The right-hand column shows the correlation between the returns of the leveraged loan "spread" index and the S&P 500 index returns, a proxy for equity fund returns. As can be seen, this correlation is also low but positive, demonstrating that eliminating interest rate risk to create pure credit spread risk does not simply create a proxy of equity market returns.

While the credit spread index used here refers to speculative-grade loan assets, similar correlation properties can be shown using investment-grade credit spreads, although no natural index for such a return is easily available and a proxy must be implied from other datasets (see Basile and Van Armeln, 2004).

Credit derivative products, such as CDNs and CDOs, make it straightforward to take pure credit spread exposure, ie, without being bundled together with interest rate risk. Doing this enables investors to achieve substantial diversification gains.

Problem 3: Traditional credit bond funds underperform riskless benchmark indices

While the previous section focused on risk, and in particular how isolating the credit spread results in better diversification, this section focuses on return. Investors often hold credit bond funds with the belief that credit assets should outperform bonds without credit exposure, such as government bonds or "AAA" bonds. This belief that credit bonds should outperform is probably driven by the observation that credit bonds are priced with a higher yield than

AAA assets, known as the "credit spread". Unfortunately, there is often a big difference between the credit spread or "yield pick-up" indicated at time of purchase and the realised yield over time. In other words, *ex ante* "yield" can be very different from *ex post* returns. When all is said and done, investors often earn *less* from credit bonds than they would from AAA bonds, despite the higher yield shown at the start. And given the depressing evidence that the average fund fails to outperform benchmark indices net of costs, if the corporate bond indices are underperforming AAA benchmark indices, it follows that the average fund is doing even worse.

Consider an example from the EUR markets (though the same phenomenon is observable in USD and other markets). Figure 4 shows the credit spreads of iBoxx corporate bond indices of various credit qualities (from AAA to BBB) relative to the iBoxx collateralised index. The iBoxx collateralised index is essentially a AAA index, containing bonds that trade close to the swap curve in yield terms. Another way to see the high quality of the collateralised index is to notice that the spread between the AAA corporate bond index and the collateralised index is consistently close to zero. All of the indices have the same 3–5 year maturity range.

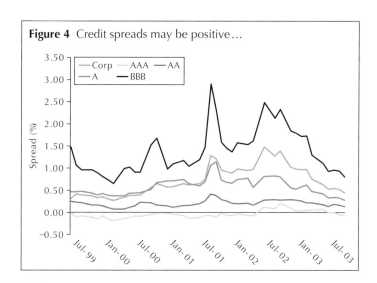

Figure 4 Credit spreads may be positive…

Notice two things in particular about Figure 4:

❑ the credit spread of the BBB index was positive and high at the start of the period, yielding approximately 1.50% more than the collateralised index; and

❑ the credit spread of the BBB index over the collateralised index tightened over the period, finishing at around 0.75%.

The fact that the yield spread was positive at the beginning of the period suggests the BBB index should have delivered a positive excess return relative to the collateralised index. The fact that this credit spread tightened over the period reinforces such a view. But the reality is that the BBB index *underperformed* the collateralised index, as can be seen in Figure 5. In total return terms, the BBB index delivered a *negative* excess return of −0.50%, ie, underperforming the AAA index by 0.50% per year.

This underperformance has a relatively simple explanation, which can be called "return bleed". Return bleed refers to the practice whereby investment-grade indices, and by extension the fund managers who are benchmarked against them, are forced to sell bonds that get downgraded below investment grade at their then-current market value. For many bonds, this means selling at a loss of around 30% of face amount.

Consider the example in Figure 6, which displays the credit spread history of the Ahold 5.875% 2008 bond. The bond was issued in the first half of 2001. At this time, Ahold was still investment-grade, and so this bond joined standard corporate bond indices,

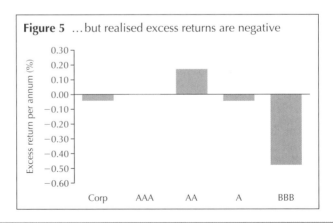

Figure 5 …but realised excess returns are negative

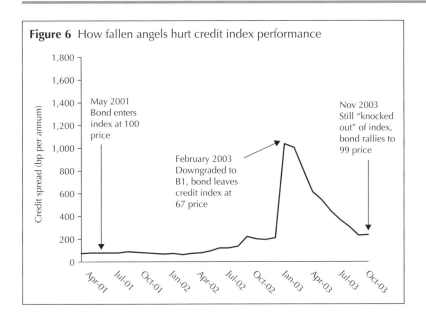

Figure 6 How fallen angels hurt credit index performance

including the iBoxx indices, at a price close to par. However, disaster struck in February 2003, when an accounting scandal surfaced at Ahold. This bond, like other Ahold bonds, fell dramatically in price, trading more than 30% below par. Since Ahold was downgraded below investment grade at this time, the bond had to leave the index, at approximately 67% of face. Though the fortunes of Ahold later improved, and this bond rallied, Ahold was still sub-investment-grade at the time. Hence, the bond rallied while *outside* the investment-grade indices. In other words, the BBB index performance suffered from the downgrade of the bond, but did not benefit from its subsequent rally.

How can credit derivatives help? Credit derivative products that reference portfolios are not required to follow the index rebalancing rules (eg, selling bonds upon downgrade below investment grade) that lead to return bleed. For example, many CDO products use completely fixed portfolios, where the assets are held until maturity or default, similar to how a bank traditionally holds loans in its portfolio. This kind of buy-and-hold approach to investment-grade credit may seem primitive, but appearances are deceptive, as we have seen before, especially with respect to realised excess returns of credit assets.

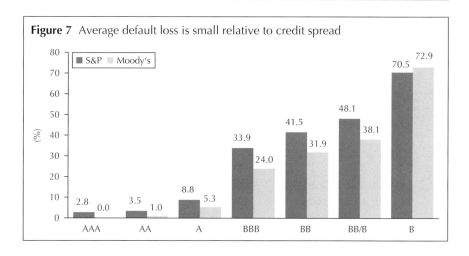

Figure 7 Average default loss is small relative to credit spread

Why is buy-and-hold a good strategy for investment-grade credit? Simply put, historical data provide clear evidence that buy-and-hold allows investors to capture excess returns over the long term. This is in abundant contrast to the case of corporate bond index returns. Consider Figure 7, which is taken from the research of Douglas Lucas, author of the UBS research publication *CDO Insight*.

This chart displays the proportion of credit spread (ie, the yield difference between corporate bonds and non-credit-risky bonds) that can be explained by expected default losses across different rating classes. Expected default losses are estimated for a given credit rating class by taking the product of:

❑ average default rate for a given credit rating class; and
❑ average loss given default.

For example, the expected default loss for A-rated bonds accounts for less that 10% of the total credit spread of A-rated bonds. What explains the other 90% of the credit spread is a hot topic of debate. Some argue the extra premium is compensation for reduced liquidity of corporate credit assets. Others argue the extra premium is compensation for non-default volatility and correlation risk. For our purposes, what matters is simply that this 90% is *not* credit default risk. Furthermore, only long-term buy-and-hold investors can capture this premium. Investors who sell given a downgrade cannot.

That corporate bond indices underperform AAA indices is a fundamental problem. Arguably, it is more fundamental than the often-discussed question of whether actively managed funds can actually deliver any alpha relative to index funds. This is because if even corporate bond indices cannot outperform riskless indices, what is the point of even talking about whether active fund managers add alpha over the indices themselves? In other words, it is not clear that even corporate bond indices themselves add alpha relative to AAA bond indices. Whether managers of corporate bond funds add alpha relative to corporate bond indices seems a moot point in comparison.

Nevertheless, investors do not have to take this return bleed problem on their shoulders. With the advent of credit derivative products, investors can hold credit assets without being forced to adhere to index rules. In other words, investors can follow a truly buy-and-hold approach to credit, as a bank traditionally does with its loan portfolio. After all, the historical data do not support the traditional "index" approach to investment-grade credit. But the historical data do support the buy-and-hold approach to investment-grade credit. And credit derivatives allow investors to take advantage of this.

Problem 4: The bias towards being long credit spreads

It is a fact that most private investors who hold credit assets are typically long credit risk, ie, exposed to defaults by one or many issuers. Before the advent of the credit derivatives market, it was difficult to be positioned any other way. In a similar fashion, before the equity derivatives market developed, most private investors who held equity exposure were long. As that market has matured, investors have come to realise they can go long or short equity risk. In fact, they can even be neutral to the direction of the equity market, and take exposure, long or short, to the volatility of the equity market.

Mechanically, going short a security requires borrowing the asset, selling it, buying it back later, and returning the asset to the lender. Getting short credit bonds requires use of the corporate repo market, where dealers are prepared to lend bonds to investors wanting to short-sell them.

While some institutions make frequent use of the corporate repo market, other institutions find it operationally complicated.

Private investors would probably find it infeasible. However, both institutional investors and private investors can get short more simply using CDS markets.

More generally, new credit derivative products enable investors to avoid the traditional bias towards being long only. Short exposure is available in convenient warrant form, enabling investors to profit from credit defaults or credit spread widening. More sophisticated products enable investors to be neutral to the directional changes in credit spreads, but express a view on credit spread volatility.

Problem 5: Credit bonds are often overpriced relative to credit rating

Bonds are often more expensive than they deserve to be on credit risk grounds alone. This mispricing can be driven by a number of technical factors, such as:

❑ *Rarity premium*: The bonds of a given issuer can trade with a credit spread much tighter than identically rated issuers if that issuer is relatively rare in a given bond market, or bond market segment.

❑ *Implicit repo costs/benefits*: If a given bond is "special" in the repo market, it is often because many traders are looking to short that particular bond, believing the outlook for the bond's issuer is negative. If a bond is "special" in this way, a holder of the bond can borrow money below market rates by using the bond as collateral, earning an extra yield in the process. As such, the true yield from owning the bond is much higher that the yield quoted by bond traders, but many private investors are not in a position to capture this value. The bottom line for such private investors is that they are getting paid less than they should be for owning the bonds.

❑ *Tax effects*: Many bonds trade above/below par, as they were issued in higher/lower-rate environments and thus have coupons that are off-market. Since coupons (ie, interest income) are taxed differently than capital gains in many jurisdictions, such bonds may be priced differently in spread terms relative to bonds priced closer to par.

The CDS market is not affected to the same extent as the bond market by such factors. In general, institutions drive the CDS market.

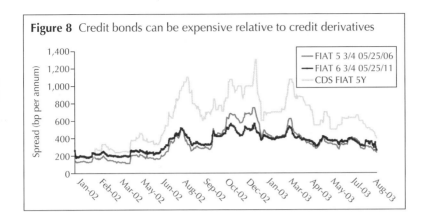

Figure 8 Credit bonds can be expensive relative to credit derivatives

Retail is much less prominent than in the bond market. For this reason, among others, pricing is likely to be more efficient. In addition, because CDS are swaps rather than physical securities, they are not hostage to rarity premium and other supply/demand imbalances to the same extent as bonds. After all, bonds are like real estate: limited supply can lead to expensive pricing.

With respect to repo effects in particular, the CDS spread levels usually trade well above bond spread levels when that bond is special. In other words, CDS represent a way for private investors to capture the specialness premium without directly participating in the repo markets. Figure 8 shows an example of this.

Fiat was perceived to be in crisis during much of 2002–3, and the credit spreads of their bonds and CDS widened as a result. But the degree to which Fiat bond spreads widened was much less than the degree to which Fiat CDS widened. Again, Fiat bonds were special in repo. Because of this, those brave private investors who believed that Fiat was going to avoid default would have been better off expressing that view with CDS (or equivalently using a CLN) than with a bond.

Lastly, consider the case of MTN issuance levels. Even those clients that do not wish to be involved in credit assets are forced to take credit exposure every time they buy a structured note that embeds another kind of derivative exposure, for example a CDRAN – the popular interest rate derivative. The MTN has to be issued by some entity, and some entities are especially popular issuers. Alas, the usual suspects are perfectly well aware of their popularity as issuers, and tend to charge a premium for taking investor capital. It is not uncommon for popular to AA-rated issuers to offer MTNs at LIBOR minus 15 bppa, much tighter than their level in institutional secondary credit markets. For example, in the CDS markets, the same AA issuer issuing MTNs at LIBOR minus 15 bppa might be trading at a spread of 15 bppa above LIBOR, an absolute spread difference of 30 bppa.

Using credit derivative products, investors can create "synthetic" MTN issuers, and capture this difference between MTN issuance levels and secondary market levels.

This is a truly transformational opportunity. Imagine the volume of structured notes issued to service the investment needs of private clients. Now imagine that all that volume could be done at levels 15 to 30 bppa cheaper than current practice. You don't have to be a genius to recognise yet another opportunity for credit derivative products to enrich both the product scope and efficiency of the wealth management industry.

REFERENCES

Basile, F., and F. von Ameln, 2004, "Beyond Bonds – Credit as an Asset Class", UBS Wealth Management Research, March.

Lucas, D., 2003, "After-Default Collateral Spreads: Driving CDO Equity Performance", UBS Investment Bank Research, CDO Insight, 31 July 2003.

12

Funds of Hedge Funds – A Safer Way to Gain Hedge Fund Exposure

Urs Alder

Man Glenwood

Hedge funds have become increasingly popular with institutional and retail investors in recent years. However, direct hedge fund investing requires highly specialised knowledge to pick and monitor funds and is often best left to a specialist provider of fund-of-hedge-funds products.

INTRODUCTION

The hedge fund universe is opaque, even for investment professionals not specialising in alternative investments. Aside from limited transparency, hedge funds face little regulation and are typically domiciled in offshore centres. They deal in liquid and illiquid listed and non-listed securities to execute complex investment strategies that are difficult for any third party to understand. And they employ long and short selling of securities and derivatives and often leverage.

These generic commonalities show that the term *hedge fund* refers to a broad universe of distinct but different smaller and larger trading companies. They differ in the strategies they employ, in the targeted level of risk and return, the level of leverage employed and the markets that they trade. Some employ highly levered strategies to exploit small market inefficiencies or achieve higher returns while others employ no leverage at all and target steady returns at small risk. Some employ fully automated high-frequency trading systems while others engage only in a couple of large transactions over the year. Every hedge fund is unique.

Providers of funds of hedge funds usually focus exclusively on hedge funds, have been in the industry for years and have acquired the skills and operational infrastructure to deal with the peculiarities of the industry. This is why many institutional and private investors decide to gain hedge fund exposure via funds of hedge funds. Funds of funds domiciled in financial centres help develop the industry and enable investors to gain hedge fund exposure with little manager-specific risk.

PRODUCT OFFERINGS

Funds of hedge funds are investment portfolios that comprise multiple hedge funds. By combining several hedge funds, providers seek to produce diversified portfolios that are both efficient and pay tribute to the peculiarities of hedge fund returns, which will be discussed later. There is a wide range of products built from single hedge funds that can be classified into two broad categories:

❑ *Multi-manager funds of funds:* Multi-manager funds of funds are products that combine several hedge funds generally applying a similar investment strategy, eg, equity hedge or relative value. Style funds offer specific exposure to the style chosen. The manager-idiosyncratic risk is mitigated by combining several managers within the same style.
❑ *Multi-manager, multi-style funds of funds:* Multi-manager, multi-style funds of funds are diversified across managers and hedge fund styles. Exposure to single styles is limited and the portfolio overall benefits from diversification across styles.

Style funds of funds give the investor the option to compose their own asset allocation, ie, determine the optimal asset allocation in the hedge fund portfolio by combining several style portfolios. However, this is worthwhile only if the investor has a good view on how hedge fund styles will perform in the future. Style funds can also be added as "satellites" to the existing core investment portfolio.

Whether an investor should choose multi-manager funds of funds or multi-manager, multi-style funds of funds also depends on the goals to be achieved with hedge fund investing. The two main reasons for investing in hedge funds are:

❏ adding spice to an existing portfolio (return driver) and
❏ protecting the existing portfolio from the downside in rough market environments (portfolio stabiliser).

Well-diversified multi-style, multi-manager funds typically feature low single-digit volatility of around 4–7% and returns in the high single digits/low double digits of around 8–12%.[1] The potential for driving up returns of a portfolio in bullish equity markets is low. However, the potential for stabilising the portfolio and protecting it in down markets is high.

Style funds are usually more aggressive than multi-style, multi-manager funds and typically target returns of around 10–20% (see Schneeweiss, 2002) and volatility of 3–15%. In particular, directional styles such as equity long/short or global macro can add additional return potential to a traditional portfolio.

COMPARING DIFFERENT PRODUCTS

Comparing products from several providers can be extremely difficult. The hedge fund industry is very diverse and, as it is not yet as mature as the traditional investment industry, terms of reference can vary dramatically across product providers.

One distinguishing feature is certainly fees. However, there is no widely accepted definition of fees and every provider uses its own terminology. This makes it difficult to compare on a like-for-like basis. The total fee load of products can be compared by adding up all fees a provider charges but total expense ratios (TER), which are becoming standard in the traditional world, are not available in the alternative world yet. Further market penetration will certainly direct providers in this direction as well.

It is important to analyse why fee loads vary since a higher fee load does not necessarily mean that one product is more expensive than another. The bottom line is the net return to the investor and higher fees could be justified by the product set-up. Reputed funds of hedge funds often include highly successful hedge funds in their portfolios, which are closed to other investors, including other funds of funds. Reputed funds of hedge funds can also gain access through their relationship network to young but promising hedge fund managers. The quality of hedge funds included in the portfolio is a make-or-break criterion for performance. The best single hedge funds choose their investors and they often do not report their return data to commercial hedge fund databases since they do not want to attract additional attention. Hence premium portfolios can sell at a premium and the fee load may be justified.

Going up one level, it is important to check which hedge fund styles are included in the portfolio. Some providers include styles that others might avoid, eg, global macro or managed futures. It is important to check the rationale for style selection. Styles can be avoided/included due to risk and return considerations or for liquidity reasons, since hedge fund styles differ strongly in their liquidity. Some styles, such as managed futures, may feature daily liquidity – ie, the investor can subscribe or redeem daily – while other styles, such as distressed securities or global macro, may feature semiannual or even just annual liquidity. These styles tend to generate their returns over the longer run and investors usually benefit from an illiquidity premium for accepting low liquidity. In return, the hedge fund manager does not have to fear that investors will withdraw their money in the midst of a transaction, which would hurt the whole fund.

Obviously, investors like liquidity and generally prefer daily liquidity just as for traditional securities. Some funds of funds offer daily liquidity, which is a popular selling point. However, this quite often means that styles with little liquidity are excluded, since the fund of funds typically cannot offer better liquidity terms than the underlying hedge fund portfolio. Excluding illiquid styles often compromises return expectations. Liquidity means limitations on the portfolio side and comes at a price. Investors seeking hedge fund exposure should have a fairly long time horizon and hence quarterly liquidity should not deter them from investing.

Product reporting is another point that should be compared. Product reports differ widely in the level of information and the level of transparency they provide. Some investors appreciate a high level of transparency and information while others care only about performance. Good reporting is not yet a standard feature of the industry.

Further points that should be scrutinised are the market (beta) exposure of the fund of funds and the maximum drawdown that it could potentially incur. These points will be discussed in depth later.

FINDING THE RIGHT FUND-OF-FUNDS PROVIDER

There are a large number of products and providers competing for clients. Just as important as finding the right product is finding the right provider. Currently there are about 1,400 funds of funds worldwide, of which around 80 manage more than USD 1 billion. The number of providers is growing steadily, making it harder to separate the wheat from the chaff. In-depth due diligence for each provider is indispensable and should cover both *qualitative* and *quantitative* aspects, the key points of which are summarised in Table 1.

Qualitative points in due diligence

Qualitative criteria should show whether the fund-of-funds provider has the ethics, integrity and infrastructure to successfully manage funds of funds. Qualitative points involve gauging the provider's size and reputation and the regulation it is subject to. Managing hedge fund portfolios is a complex task that requires an appropriately large and specialised team supported by an efficient infrastructure, and this can be ensured only if the provider is large enough (in terms of assets under management [AUM]). Currently the threshold capital to afford a fully fledged infrastructure is estimated to be roughly US$1 billion.

The provider must have a good reputation and be subject to strict regulation in order to limit the risk of investing in unregulated hedge funds. Size, reputation and regulation need to be paired with the skills required to manage the whole investment process, which is displayed in Table 2.

Quantitative points in due diligence

The main quantitative points are track record, fee structure and investment objectives. A provider should have a relatively long track record (at least 3–5 years) and focus on capital preservation during market downturns rather than maximising return. The longer the track record, obviously, the better, since it shows the portfolio performance in different market environments. The fee structure should be balanced, which means that the performance fee should make up a sizable part of total income in "normal" years. To some extent, management fees should finance people and infrastructure while performance fees should be bottom-line profits.

Table 1 Key points in fund-of-funds manager due diligence

	Qualitative factors		Quantitative factors
Skills	*Sufficient skills to perform* – Manager due diligence, selection and monitoring – Portfolio-construction, asset allocation risk management – Product management and reporting	**Track record**	*What is the track record regarding* – Annual risk & return, downside deviation, drawdown – Performance during worst equity and bond markets – Length of track record – Did he go through a full investment cycle?
Size/ Operations	*AuM sufficient to* – Afford comprehensive and efficient infrastructure – Benefit from economies of scale	**Fees**	*What is the fee structure?* – Management fee vs performance fee – "All-in Fee" incl. admin. fee, director's fees …
Reputation/ Regulation	*Reputation of FoHF manager in the industry enabling* – Access to outstanding hedge fund managers – Is the manager tightly regulated and has he always complied with all regulations?	**Capital protection**	*Sufficient emphasis put on capital preservation?* – Strong focus on downside deviation? – Performance in glooming and booming markets?

Source: Glenwood Capital Investments

Table 2 Hedge fund investment process

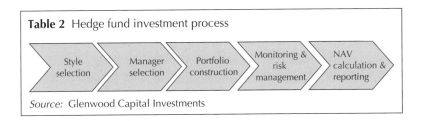

Source: Glenwood Capital Investments

Often, investors pay too much attention to quantitative points versus qualitative points. It cannot be emphasised enough how important the integrity and ethics of a company are. However, due to the importance investors assign to historic performance it is worth explaining how to properly analyse a track record.

ANALYSING A TRACK RECORD

Funds of funds, just like hedge funds, are in the absolute return business. That is, they look to deliver positive returns regardless of market circumstances. The "hard" performance of a fund of funds is its track record and serves as the calling card of the company. Without in-depth analysis its quality cannot be assessed and it might even be deceptive.

Non-normal distribution of hedge fund returns

Quantitative analysis of hedge fund returns usually assumes that hedge fund returns over time follow a normal distribution. That is, that mean return and volatility completely describe the distribution of past and future returns. This assumption is used when analysing equity returns and works well. However, returns of most hedge fund styles do not follow a normal distribution. This should not lead to the conclusion that the mean return and volatility of a portfolio may not be used as proxy for the distribution of future returns. But additional risk measures such as downside deviation, Omega and the Stutzer Index should be used as well. The most disturbing shortfall is the occurrence of a positive excess kurtosis or fat tail in combination with negative skewness, ie, the occurrence of very negative returns in certain market environments that do not exist in normal distributions.[2] Some strategies, eg, managed futures, are close to normal distribution of returns while others, eg, relative value, are less close to normal distribution.[3] The excess kurtosis of the HFRI Fund of Funds Composite Index is roughly 4.58.[4] Liquid listed equities have an excess kurtosis of close to 0, indicating that returns are normally distributed.

The real track record obviously shows whether large negative returns have occurred in the past. To assess the future likelihood of fat tails the portfolio needs to be divided into the styles making up the portfolio. Public data, such as HFRI style return data, can serve as a proxy for the likelihood of fat tails. This public return data often goes back a longer time than the track record of the portfolio.

Adjust track record for market exposure (beta)

Hedge funds and funds of funds are paid for by producing alpha, ie, returns generated by skills rather than market exposure (beta).[5] However, most single hedge funds as well as most hedge fund portfolios feature some positive beta, ie, some of the total return generated by the fund of funds can be attributed to the returns generated by a (passive) market index. A fund-of-funds manager, just like a hedge fund manager, should not be rewarded for providing market exposure and market returns. Quite the opposite! Market excess returns (over the risk-free rate) should be subtracted from the returns achieved over any given time period and compensation should be adjusted accordingly.

If a fund of funds has a beta of 0.4 over its five-year track record and the excess return of equities over (risk free) government bonds was 7% for that time period, the mean return of the hedge fund portfolio should be reduced by 2.8% a year. If the investor worries about market exposure and hedges it out completely, the track record should be corrected to the downside additionally by the cost of hedging, ie, the cost of implementing a rolling six-month market hedge (via shorting of market futures contracts). If hedging cost (including internal and external cost) come to 20 basis points (bps) per annum, that would increase the total adjustment to 3% a year. A manager who did not account for these factors would, to some extent, be charging alpha fees for beta returns and thus be overcharging the investor. If the manager's performance fee is 10% he would thus be earning 30 bps,

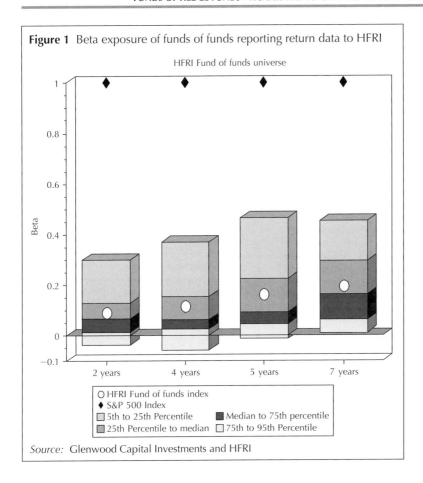

Figure 1 Beta exposure of funds of funds reporting return data to HFRI

Source: Glenwood Capital Investments and HFRI

which are not due to his skill but rather due to mere market exposure.

In day-to-day risk management, the problem of market exposure in the portfolio is compounded by two factors. Usually, a fund of hedge funds is added to an existing portfolio comprising, to a smaller or larger degree, equities, and usually intermediate losses matter to the investor. The worst-case scenario is that the investor is not aware of the market exposure "gained" through his fund of hedge funds and equity markets drop in value. In that scenario, he will not only incur losses from his equity portfolio, but returns from the hedge funds portfolio will also be lower during that period. As a matter of fact, portfolio protection will not work as well as expected when it is needed most.

Most multi-manager, multi-style funds of funds in the HFRI universe feature at least some beta exposure and 25% of them feature beta exposure between 0.3 and 0.5 over a five-year period.

The problem of charging (expensive) alpha fees for providing (cheap) beta exposure is obviously widespread.

While beta exposure is material for diversified funds of funds, it is even more of an issue in portfolios relying more heavily on directional styles such as equity long/short or global macro. As can be seen in Figure 2, over a five-year period betas of the HFRI equity hedge manager universe ranged from −0.2 to +1.2.

Beta exposure of funds of funds is measured assuming daily liquidity. Hence the portfolio beta should be adjusted for the

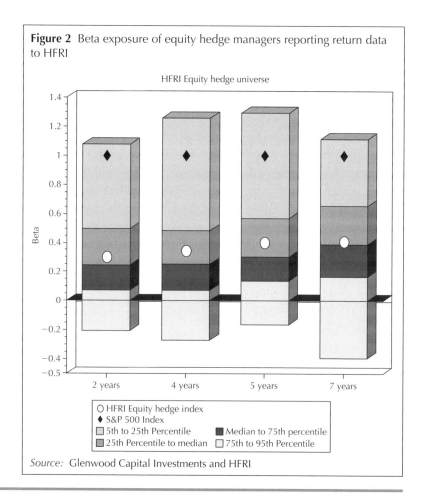

Figure 2 Beta exposure of equity hedge managers reporting return data to HFRI

Source: Glenwood Capital Investments and HFRI

illiquidity of most hedge fund strategies. Adjusted betas can be substantially higher than the apparent beta. For some strategies, such as equity long/short, the adjusted beta is roughly two times the apparent beta. For other strategies, for example global macro, the increase in beta is even larger (Asness, Clifford *et al*, 2001).

A fair and objective comparison of returns between several funds of funds can be done only if returns are compared net of market exposure. This net return shows the alpha generation over time.

Track record during difficult market conditions and implied factor bets

Hedge funds and funds of hedge funds should deliver alpha in all market conditions, eg, during significant equity market drawdown, credit crunches, currency devaluations and macro shocks such as war and terror.

Other implications aside, all these events generally have led in the past to sudden increases in volatility for equity markets. Higher volatility means higher uncertainty about the future and should translate economically into higher expected risk premiums (over risk-free assets, ie, government bonds).

For the equity markets, higher return expectations can be witnessed only over time and in hindsight. However, corporate bond markets immediately reflect higher return expectations via increasing credit spreads, ie, the spread between the yield of (risk-free) government bonds and the yield of (risky) corporate bonds of different issuers.

Why does this matter to hedge fund investors? Hedge fund strategies react differently to such macro changes: some will be affected negatively (eg, distressed securities or credit-exposed convertible bond managers usually suffer from credit spread widening); others may benefit (eg, managed futures or dedicated short sellers). The vulnerability of a hedge fund portfolio to such shocks is thus determined by the number of hedge fund strategies included and their value drivers: only a portfolio diversified across strategies *and* value drivers is capable of weathering difficult situations without incurring large drawdowns. Hence a portfolio that at first glance seems well diversified may in reality be poorly diversified because the strategies included rely on the same value drivers.

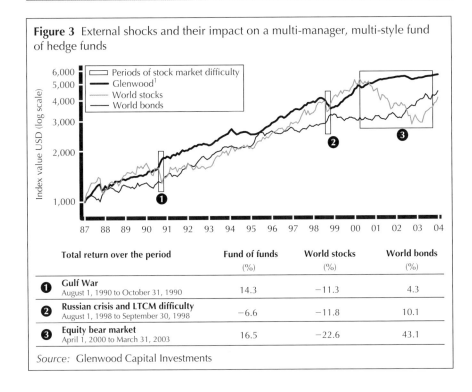

Figure 3 External shocks and their impact on a multi-manager, multi-style fund of hedge funds

Total return over the period	Fund of funds (%)	World stocks (%)	World bonds (%)
❶ **Gulf War** August 1, 1990 to October 31, 1990	14.3	−11.3	4.3
❷ **Russian crisis and LTCM difficulty** August 1, 1998 to September 30, 1998	−6.6	−11.8	10.1
❸ **Equity bear market** April 1, 2000 to March 31, 2003	16.5	−22.6	43.1

Source: Glenwood Capital Investments

While it is uncertain what the future will bring, a "real" track record (not a pro-forma, simulated performance) can demonstrate the stability of a hedge fund portfolio during such times in the past and what factor bets may be implied in the portfolio. Figure 3 shows the track record of a sample fund of funds for illustration purposes between 1987 and 2003.[6]

The table following the graph shows performance during the run-up in 1990 to the first Gulf War, the Russian crisis/default and the LTCM blow-up in 1998 and the equity bear market from April 2000 to March 2003. Since the holding period for every investor is different, intermediate losses matter and funds of funds should show stability.

Focus on the maximum drawdown of the portfolio

A good indicator for stability is the maximum loss a fund of funds incurred in the past, which is the difference between the peak and bottom value of a fund looking backwards. Maximum drawdown

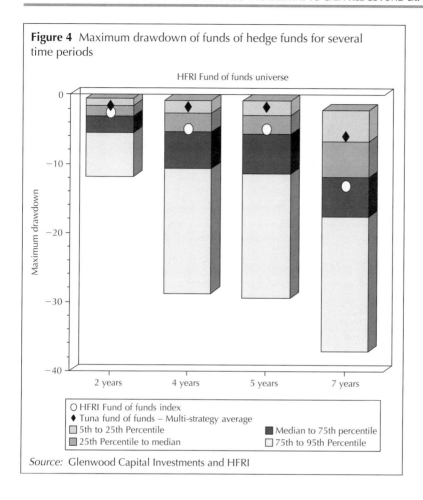

Figure 4 Maximum drawdown of funds of hedge funds for several time periods

Source: Glenwood Capital Investments and HFRI

of the funds of funds in the HFRI universe can be seen in Figure 4 for several time periods. The range is huge. Over a time period of five years the safest funds had a maximum drawdown of around 4%, while the riskiest funds had a maximum drawdown of around 30%. Higher short-term returns can be achieved at the price of higher maximum drawdown. Investors need to think about their priorities and get them right to avoid unpleasant surprises.

STRUCTURED PRODUCTS
Structured products have become popular in the hedge funds area. Many products featuring exotic payoff options have been constructed. To some extent the development of structured products

was driven by institutional and private investors facing legal and regulatory restrictions when attempting to gain direct hedge fund exposure. In some instances, structured products were and still are the only way to gain access to hedge funds. Unfavourable tax implications of direct hedge fund investments in some jurisdictions were another major force driving the creation of structured products. But the main driving force for structured products has been investors seeking alternative payoff patterns not achievable from direct hedge fund exposure.

Some of the most popular structured products are principal protected and leveraged funds of funds. We will look at these products in more detail.

Principal protected products

Hedge funds are still a fairly new asset class to many investors. Interest in the asset class has increased over the last couple of years, in part "thanks" to the bearish equity markets between April 2000 and March 2003. During that time, many private and institutional investors posted significant losses in their portfolios and have begun looking actively for investment opportunities that preserved capital. Funds of hedge funds have proved that they can protect capital in rough times. However, investors have little experience with the asset class and wish to limit their downside risk to the absolute minimum. Capital guaranteed products do so by guaranteeing repayment of principal at maturity. While the investor maintains the upside, he effectively limits his downside risk to almost 0.[7] Every principal protected product is different. However, most of them combine some of the following features:

- ❏ *Principal protection:* Usually repayment of 90–100% of the capital invested at maturity.
- ❏ *Minimum guaranteed return/coupon:* Some products feature a coupon paid over the lifetime of the product or a minimum return paid at maturity.
- ❏ *Formal capital guarantee:* A reputed financial institution guarantees repayment of principal at maturity.
- ❏ *Defined lifetime of product:* Products are closed-ended with time to maturity depending highly on prevailing interest rates. General

rule: the lower current interest rates are, the longer the time to maturity of the product will be.

❑ *Exposure to hedge funds:* Products feature exposure to a hedge fund portfolio of between 0% and 100%. Some products on the upside offer leverage, hence offering hedge fund exposure in excess of 100%. Some products on the downside offer a minimum hedge fund exposure regardless of performance, eg, minimum exposure of 20%.

❑ *Profit lock-in:* In predefined time intervals, a part of or all the profits generated over that period will be locked in. At maturity the principal and accumulated profits will be returned.

❑ *Secondary market:* Usually the issuer supplies a secondary market to enable investors to exit the product before maturity.

Techniques for providing capital protection

To describe issues to be considered when investing in capital-guaranteed products it is important to look at the mechanics of a capital guarantee. There are several techniques used for providing capital protection. The most commonly used (see Giraud, 2004) are:

❑ dynamic hedge or CPPI (Constant Proportion Portfolio Insurance) is the most interesting structure, as the issuer can easily construct the hedge by monitoring a dynamic reference curve constituted by the nominal value of a zero-coupon bond that would pay back the required capital at maturity, and includes a buffer based on the market risk of the underlying fund in order to allow for its orderly liquidation in case the value of the underlying fund happens to drop below the reference value. As long as the underlying fund net asset value (NAV) remains above the dynamic threshold, 100% of the capital is invested in the hedge fund, but, when this NAV decreases below the reference, the structure will divest from the fund and allocate capital to a bond.

❑ in zero-coupon bonds with an embedded call option structure, the capital guarantee is provided through a zero-bond deposit. The exposure to the hedge fund portfolio is achieved through the purchase of a call option.

❑ with a total return swap, the capital guarantee is provided through a zero-bond deposit. The indexation to the hedge fund portfolio is achieved via a financing facility provided through a bank, which, for a spread, offers the client leverage against the portfolio of hedge funds.

Issues to consider in capital-guaranteed products

Regardless of the technology employed, capital-guaranteed products are useful for investors seeking additional security. But it is important to be aware of the implications and the conditions of the capital guarantee.

Principal protection adds another fee layer to the fund of hedge funds – sometimes in excess of 100 bps per annum. This problem is mitigated when leverage is used to increase exposure above 100% of invested capital (as can be done when using CPPI or total-return swap technology). In fact in these cases the payoff of the guaranteed product can be even better than for the underlying fund of hedge funds. The cost of leverage, however, needs to be monitored (due to the higher amount of leverage required in particular when using the swap technology).

Investors should be aware that the capital guarantee applies only if the product is held until maturity, which is usually measured in years. If the product is redeemed before maturity, the investor receives the NAV of the product at that time. Depending on the structure of the guarantee, the NAV is composed of the net asset value of the hedge fund basket and the value of a zero bond at that time (this is not the case when CPPI-technology is used). In these cases the investor will bear the interest rate risk on the zero-bond. He will also bear the market risk to the downside of the hedge fund portfolio. Furthermore, depending on the provider, there might be a discount subtracted from the NAV of the product for providing liquidity. Time to maturity of products needs to be watched carefully.

In the current low-interest-rate environment of major currencies, successful products usually require time to maturity in excess of 8–10 years to offer investment exposure of 100% or more. Shorter-dated products may claim that they offer 100% exposure. While this might be true at inception, there is a high probability that exposure will decrease quickly if the product does not perform well in the first six months. If exposure falls below 100% at any time, it is very difficult to get back to 100%. In fact a de-gearing (reduction of exposure) is likely to trigger further de-gearing. Hence the safety margin, ie, the amount the product can lose before exposure is adjusted to the downside, is crucial and should be checked before buying a principal protected product. Shorter-dated products usually feature a lower safety margin than longer-dated products.

Investors in capital-guaranteed products rely on the financial strength of the guarantor and usually a minimum rating of A+ should be requested. However, in most cases the investor is not protected against deteriorating credit quality of the guarantor – the longer the time to maturity of a product, the greater the risk of a downgrade during the lifetime of the product.

Capital-guaranteed products may also face limitations on the investment side. Portfolios used for principal protected structures need to be agreed between the guarantor and the fund-of-funds manager. The fund-of-funds manager may lose some of his discretion over the management of the hedge fund portfolio. The guarantor has a legitimate interest in shaping to some extent the risk and liquidity of the portfolio since it will have to provide principal repayment if the portfolio value at maturity is below the guaranteed repayment amount. To minimise the risk that the portfolio value will fall below the guaranteed repayment amount, the guarantor wants a low-risk and highly liquid portfolio. Liquidity is important for quickly reducing exposure to the hedge fund portfolio when its value falls. As has been discussed earlier, focus on liquidity may reduce the number of strategies that can be included in the portfolio and potentially compromise expected return. Investors, however, seek higher volatility, as there is no downside risk and they want to maximise their upside.

It is important that the conflicting interests of the guarantor and the investor be well balanced. The guarantor receives a fee for taking on risk and proper risk management allows for some volatility in the product. Low-volatility hedge fund portfolios do not need capital protection since the portfolio is already well protected against losses.

Leveraged products

Leveraged products are another popular structured-product family. Products featuring risk of 4–6% annual volatility and returns around LIBOR plus 6–8% can be leveraged at relatively little risk. Credit lines for these products are generally cheap due to the stable nature of the hedge fund assets serving as collateral.

This is perfect for investors who want to modify the risk-and-return characteristics of a portfolio without changing the underlying investment strategy. They can use borrowed capital to increase their exposure to a proven investment strategy by investing in leveraged share classes of existing funds of funds.

The concept of offering an unlevered fund of funds as well as two-times-, three-times- or even four-times-levered share classes on the same fund portfolio is particularly appealing to investors. Based on their risk appetite, they can choose the right product for them. A four-times-levered product offers US$4 exposure for every US$1 invested in a hedge fund portfolio with a bank providing the additional US$3 of exposure.

Obviously, leverage works both ways: if the return on the underlying hedge fund portfolio is below the cost of leverage, the investor faces substantial losses; in case of negative returns the losses can be severe. If a fund loses 5% in a year and the cost of leverage is 5%, the total loss of the investor on a four-times-levered product in that year would be 35%.

Leverage is employed at single-manager level and at portfolio level
Leverage is usually employed at two levels – single hedge funds in the hedge fund portfolio often employ leverage and leverage can be added at the portfolio level.

This is sometimes not effective as single hedge fund managers do not always find ample opportunities to invest their capital. Sometimes they run their portfolio below 100% investment exposure, which means that a proportion of the available capital is held in cash. In this case leverage on top of the product will not add to performance, as the manager cannot put the additional capital to work and may rather reject any additional money inflow.

Trading opportunities in some hedge fund strategies, such as distressed securities, risk arbitrage or convertible bonds, are fairly cyclical; sometimes opportunities are ample and sometimes they are scarce. For leverage to be sensible a portfolio should consist of several hedge fund strategies together offsetting cyclicality. When managers in one strategy cannot put all capital to work, others should find ample opportunities to put more capital to work. Hence multi-manager, multi-style portfolios are better suited for long-term leverage than pure multi-manager-style funds.

Leverage is neither good nor bad. Depending on the hedge fund portfolio, it can increase returns in a portfolio. The risk appetite and risk tolerance of the investor should guide the decision on what leverage is appropriate. However, the ratio between return generated per unit of risk (Sharpe Ratio) will decrease with increasing leverage since the product risk is increasing linearly while return is increased by the factor of leverage minus financing cost. Additionally, with higher leverage, financing cost will increase, since the provider of leverage faces a higher risk.

CONCLUSION

Hedge funds are generally loosely regulated investment companies. This lack of regulation gives hedge fund managers the necessary freedom to generate steady and uncorrelated returns *if* they have the level of skill required. Strategies employed are often complex and difficult for any third party to understand. Many investors do not have the specialised knowledge and infrastructure required to handle these risks and as a result outsource the hedge fund investment process to a fund of funds. Funds of funds focusing exclusively on hedge fund investing act as agent of investors and can mitigate operational and investment risks.

The selection of the right fund of funds is of paramount importance. Qualitative and quantitative in-depth due diligence is required to find the right provider. The key qualitative criterion for choosing a fund of funds provider is its ethics since the investor needs to be able to fully trust the provider. Investors often focus on quantitative criteria, ie the trackrecord of a fund of funds provider. A good track record is certainly necessary but not sufficient grounds for selection.

Analyzing the track record properly is indispensable to drawing the right conclusions. If not analysed properly the trackrecord may be deceptive. It is important to keep in mind that hedge fund returns usually do not follow a normal distribution and feature fat tails, ie occasionally large negative returns occur. To mitigate this problem the hedge fund portfolio needs to be analysed qualitatively. It is equally important to understand the value drivers of all strategies included in the portfolio. Only a portfolio that is diversified across strategies *and* value drivers is well diversified.

Investors new to the asset class may like the concept of absolute returns but still feel uncomfortable investing in a fund of funds without an additional layer of protection.

Capital guarantee or principal protection adds another strong layer of protection by usually fully mitigating the downside risk, ie the investor gains hedge fund exposure while his capital is protected. There are many types of capital guaranteed products but most of them feature similar characteristics. The main differences lie in the level of fees and the underlying portfolio, both of which need to be scrutinized before conducting any investment. The portfolio should be able to generate returns high enough to bear the additional fee layer.

Investors who have experience with the asset class, on the other hand, may look for more aggressive products. Leveraged products satisfy this desire by offering more than US$1 exposure for every US$1 invested, eg exposure of US$2 or more. These products certainly have their merits and may perfectly match some clients' requirements. However leverage obviously works both ways. If the return on the hedge fund portfolio is below the cost of financing, the investor might face substantial losses. Even when an investor has been satisfied with the performance of their hedge fund investments over a period of years, they should always maintain diligent risk management.

1   In the HFRI universe of multi-manager, multi-style funds of funds the average risk and return for the period from January 1990 to February 2004 was 5.18% and 9.32% respectively.
2   Kurtosis and skewness are a further characterization of data. Skewness is a measure of symmetry, or more precisely a measure of asymmetry of the distribution. For a normal distribution the skewness is 0. Negative values for the skewness indicate data that are skewed left. Kurtosis is a measure indicating whether the data are peaked or flat relative to normal distribution. Data sets with high kurtosis have heavy (fat) tails.Highly unliked by investors hence is high kurtosis combined with negative skewness, i.e. the occurrence of very negative returns.
3   Based on HFRI style data from Jan 1995 to Mar 2004 kurtosis and skewness for the HFRI Relative Value Arbitrage Index is 22.4 and −3.2 respectively indicating highly fat tails.
4   Based on HFRI style data from Jan 1995 to Mar 2004.
5   Sometimes the value added generated by the manager which cannot be explained by Markowitz is referred to as Jensen's Alpha.
6   The fund of funds' name is not provided since the trackrecord serves for illustration purposes only.
    World stocks: MSCI World Stock Index (total return).
    World bonds: Citigroup World Government Bond Index (total return).

7 In case the guarantor does not default over the lifetime of the product. Downside risk is hence equal to the credit risk of the guarantor apart from opportunity cost of foregone returns.

REFERENCES

Asness, C. et al, fall 2001, "Do Hedge Funds Hedge?", *Journal of Portfolio Management*.

Giraud, J-R., 2004, "Market Risk – Technicalities of Structured Products on Funds of Hedge Funds", Edhec-Risk Advisory.

Schneeweiss, T., 2002, "Hedge Funds: Magic or Science?".

Index

R
Reverse Cliquet option 37, 46
Rogers and Satchell (1999) 52

S
S&P 500 7–8, 210–11, 224
Schneeweiss (2002) 235
Self-Investment Pension Plans
 (SIPPs) 84
Sharpe Ratio 197, 210, 215, 251
Small Self-Administered Pension
 Schemes (SSASs) 84
Société d'investissement à capital
 variable (SICAV) 80
Solnik (1974) 95
special-purpose vehicle (SPV)
 79, 190
Stein and Stein (1991) 43
"strike price" 15–16, 23–4,
 48, 121, 134–5, 141, 143,
 154–5, 167
Swap Market Model (SMM)
 171

T
Tactical asset allocation (TAA) 2
Taleb (1997) 45

Tax-Exempt Special Savings
 Accounts (TESSAs) 84
total expense ratios (TER) 235

U
Undertakings in Collective
 Investments in Transferable
 Securities (UCITS) 81
US Treasury (UST) bond index
 224

V
Variable-proportion portfolio
 insurance (VPPI) 59

W
Walmsley (2000) 144
Wilmott (2002) 51
Windcliff, Forsyth and Vetzal
 (2003) 51
Working (1949) 199
World Bank *see also* Bank for
 Reconstruction and
 Development

X
Xin (2003) 108

Other titles by Risk Books

Credit
Credit Ratings – Methodologies, Rationale and Default Risk
Edited by Michael K. Ong
ISBN: 1 899332 69 3

Credit Risk: Models and Management – 2nd Edition
Consultant Editor – David Shimko
ISBN: 1 904339 21 2

Credit Derivatives – The Definitive Guide
Edited by Jon Gregory
ISBN: 1 904339 12 3

Operational Risk
The Basel Handbook – A Guide for Financial Practitioners
Edited by Michael K. Ong
ISBN: 1 904339 16 6

**Advances in Operational Risk 2nd Edition –
Firm-wide Issues for Financial Institutions**
Published in association with SAS
ISBN: 1 904339 16 6

**Internal Credit Risk Models –
Capital Allocation and Performance Measurement**
By Michael K. Ong
ISBN: 1 899332 03 0

Investor
Portfolio Construction and Risk Budgeting
By Bernd Scherer
ISBN: 1 899332 44 8

**Hedge Fund Risk Transparency –
Unravelling the Complex and Controversial Debate**
By Leslie Rahl
ISBN: 1 904339 04 2

Intelligent Hedge Fund Investing
Edited by Barry Schachter
ISBN: 1 904339 22 0

Derivatives
Modern Risk Management – A History
Introduced by Peter Field
ISBN: 1 904339 05 0

Derivatives – The Tools that Changed Finance
By Phelim and Feidhlim Boyle
ISBN: 1 899332 88 X

Rubinstein on Derivatives
Mark Rubinstein
ISBN: 1 899332 53 7

For more information of these titles, as well as the full range of titles published by Risk Books,
please visit the online bookstore **www.riskbooks.com**. Alternatively
phone +44 (0) 870 240 8859 and request a current catalogue.